HIGH FIVES, PENNANT DRIVES, AND FERNANDOMANIA

A Fan's History of the
Los Angeles Dodgers' Glory Years
1977–1981

PAUL HADDAD

SANTA
MONICA
PRESS

Published by:

Santa Monica Press LLC
P.O. Box 850
Solana Beach, CA 92075
1-800-784-9553

www.santamonicapress.com
books@santamonicapress.com

Printed in the United States

Santa Monica Press books are available at special quantity discounts when purchased in bulk by corporations, organizations, or groups. Please call our Special Sales department at 1-800-784-9553.

ISBN-13 978-1-59580-067-1

Library of Congress Cataloging-in-Publication Data

Haddad, Paul.
High fives, pennant drives, and fernandomania : a fan's history of the Los Angeles Dodgers' glory years (1977-1981) / Paul Haddad.
    p. cm.
ISBN 978-1-59580-067-1 (pbk.)
1. Los Angeles Dodgers (Baseball team)—History—20th century.
2. Los Angeles Dodgers (Baseball team)—History—20th century—
Miscellanea. I. Title.
GV875.L6H33 2012
796.357'640979494–dc23
                              2011049063

Cover and interior design and production by Future Studio
Cover and interior photos courtesy of the Los Angeles Dodgers

CONTENTS

FOREWORD

The power of Vin Scully could be seen in the thousands of kids who grew up in Southern California dreaming not of being the next Sandy Koufax or Steve Garvey, but the next Vinny.

I was one of those kids. Like many young Dodger fans un-big of stature and un-strong of skill who realized early on that being a professional athlete was not a viable aspiration, following in Scully's footsteps seemed to be not only a logical alternative, but quite possibly a superior one. Koufax retired the year I was born, but Vinny was still the best. Garvey was leaving his prime in his thirties, but Vinny was still the best. You could be a member of the orchestra—but perhaps even better, you could be the conductor. And so I, like those thousands of other kids, gave broadcasting a whirl, queuing up a tape recorder with Dodger games on TV with the sound down and trying to match the master.

Of course, with age and experience came the revelation that becoming the next Vin Scully was every bit as unrealistic as becoming the next Koufax. There is no "next" Vinny; there is and always will be only one. But the passion of his voice has had a lasting effect on so many of us, no matter what we grew up or will grow up to be.

Paul Haddad was inspired to a precocious and fortuitous level, setting out as a child to keep a self-narrated library of home run calls by Scully, his Dodger radio colleagues Jerry Doggett and Ross Porter, and others. This evolved into a primary-source history of the team during some of its most fun years in Los Angeles: 1977–81. The recordings first gained prominence in 2010, when they were used to support the ESPN *30 for 30* documentary "Fernando Nation," about the iconic Dodger lefty Fernando Valenzuela. Now, they are the foundation for this book that is in your hands.

This book will help you forget all the hard times that arrived for the Dodger community in the run-up to Frank McCourt's decision to sell the team, instead transporting you back to an era when the only thing that mattered was the game, and the biggest internal conflict was whether you supported Garvey or Don Sutton in their clubhouse fight. The book takes you through the best memories of those five seasons, which featured three National League titles and one World Series championship for the Big Blue Wrecking Crew, but also digresses nicely into musings on everything from the players to the donations of Union Oil Auto Script for each Dodger home run.

I am nothing if not the jealous type, and the thing that makes me most jealous is how Haddad has taken advantage of this window into his childhood self. To be able to hear himself as a fan, to revisit exactly what it was like when he was first being inspired, is an indescribable gift. The rest of us can live vicariously through his time travel machine, reliving moments long-buried in the back of our overstuffed memory banks. Indeed, it's a reminder that it's never too late to appreciate the good times, whether they took place three decades ago or yesterday.

—JON WEISMAN
Dodger Thoughts blogger and author of
100 Things Dodger Fans Should Know & Do Before They Die

INTRODUCTION
Leading Off

My first introduction to the Dodgers was one of heart-break. The perpetrator was Reggie Jackson. His crime, by now legendary, was three successive home runs in the deciding game of the 1977 World Series. I had followed the Dodgers from afar for most of my first 11 years, even attending a couple games at Dodger Stadium with my summer camp. But I never understood what it meant to be a *fan* until that moment.

Outside of my dad betting on football and playing the horses, I grew up in a household that was largely indifferent to professional sports teams. I never even played Little League. As a result, baseball and I were relative strangers. I didn't understand the nuances and rhythms of the game, and I lacked that mentor who might explain the strategy behind a hit-and-run, how to keep a scorecard, or what a sacrifice fly was. ERA? I didn't know an Earned Run Average from an Equal Rights Amendment. And if you were talking about the Penguin, my mind flashed, "*Batman*," not "Ron Cey."

But the seeds of my Dodger fandom began to bear fruit in that '77 Fall Classic. It's hard to say what triggered my obsession with the team sporting crisp white uniforms with red numbers and blue trim. It was probably an accumulation of things leading up to the Series. With the Dodgers making the playoffs, Mom had started following the games on the radio. I remember one day she picked me up from school, and she was listening to the third game of the NLCS against the Phillies. Burt Hooton had just gotten pulled in the second inning after walking three batters in a row with the bases loaded. Mom's first words to me when I got into the car were: "Burt Hooton just lost his cool." I had never heard that phrase before, and I was intrigued. How does one lose his "cool," and if he does, can he ever get it back? I thought of the Fonz on *Happy Days* and could never imagine that happening to him.

There was also a palpable buzz in Los Angeles surrounding the Dodgers getting into the postseason, an excitement that trickled down to the schoolyard and classrooms at West Hollywood Elementary. On the eve of the World Series, a fellow sixth grader named Trevor asked me if I wanted to make a bet on Game 1. After careful consideration, I passed on his fifty-cent wager. I couldn't rationalize risking money earmarked for cherry Now-N-Laters on a sport I was only now beginning to understand. By the third game, Trevor dropped his bet to a quarter. Perhaps sensing a sucker, he even let me pick the team. I caved and chose the Dodgers, knowing that Game 3 would be played at home. The Dodgers answered my loyalty by losing 5–3.

All of this set the stage for the deciding Game 6 at Yankee Stadium. New York held a one-game edge, three games to two. For the first time in my life, I sat down in front of the TV to watch a game from start to finish. By this point, my mom, dad, and older brother, Michael, were invested in the series. The Dodgers had just shellacked the Yankees in Game 5, once leading 10–0 to seemingly recapture the momentum, and there was every reason to believe they would win Game 6 and force a deciding Game 7. I remember we were allowed to eat dinner on TV trays in the den so we could take in the broadcast on our giant Zenith set. Even though I didn't have any money riding on the game, I was inexplicably nervous and fidgety, pacing the room like a recovering smoker. Suddenly, the Dodgers' battle had become my battle—this was *personal.*

At this point I should probably mention that I have always had a notorious competitive streak. It pains me to admit it, but my parents have Super 8 footage of me throwing an epic tantrum while playing miniature golf with three friends on my eighth birthday. By the final hole, I am bringing up the rear, at which point I raise my pee-wee club and pummel an unsuspecting windmill as if it were a piñata. This would also explain why I detested tennis player John McEnroe when he came on the scene. His antics reminded me too much of myself.

The Dodgers got out to an early 2–0 lead in that sixth game, thanks to a two-run triple by my future idol, Steve Garvey. Things were looking good. L.A. held a 3–2 lead going into the bottom of the fourth, when suddenly any hope of forcing a Game 7 began to dissipate. Mr. October saw to that himself, crushing the first of three home runs. The pitcher? Burt Hooton, looking about as cool as Dustin Hoffman in that dental chair in *Marathon Man.* By the time Reggie stepped up in the eighth inning, the crowd's chants of "Reg-GIE, Reg-GIE, Reg-GIE" were like ice picks in my ears. His third home run—an estimated 475-foot blast on the first pitch—cut into my skull.

"Oh, what a blow!" gushed Howard Cosell on TV. "What a way to top it off!"

Clutching my ears, I tore out of the den and collapsed in a heap of rage in my bedroom, thrashing my elbows against the floor. I hated Reggie Jackson, with his cocksure grin and streetwise swagger. I wanted to *throttle* him. He had made the Dodgers look like a Wiffle ball team, swatting three homers with a flick of his wrist, hop-skipping around the bases before flashing "Hi, Moms" to the camera as he unfurled another digit for each homer. Who did he think he was, anyway? At some point my mother came in and tried to calm me down, but I would have none of it. I was inconsolable. I had lost my cool.

And I was hooked.

Because you're reading this book, you too probably remember what it felt like to fall for the Los Angeles Dodgers. If you're like most, your devotion was fashioned around happy, random moments, like jostling along Dodger Stadium at field level for an autograph from your favorite player, or witnessing a momentous home run as you ripped into your double-bag of salted-in-the-shell peanuts. Or perhaps it was Vin Scully lulling you to sleep on your transistor radio, or the ritual of you and Dad pulling up a chair in front of KTTV Channel 11 to catch a game. Before you knew it, they had you hooked, too. Not just on the Dodgers, but on baseball. For me, the Dodgers and baseball struck like a double lightning bolt, not unlike falling in love at first sight. Even Reggie Jackson couldn't squelch their power—in fact, he only amplified it. For just like your first love, who may rip your heart into a thousand pieces before liquefying it in a blender for good measure, you never get over that feeling. And yet all of us keep coming back for more, enduring years of torment for those rare, fleeting moments of pure bliss. Baseball proves the old axiom: It's better to have loved and lost, than to not have loved at all.

With my "hazing" behind me, I couldn't wait for the 1978 season to roll around. Next year was going to be *different*. For starters, I began to educate myself in the ways of the game. I was what you might call a self-made fan. During spring training games, I studied box scores and paid attention to the words of the Dodgers' announcers, gradually figuring out what things like AB, RBI, AVG, BB, and, yes, even ERA stood for. I began to grade the players on a primitive, grid-based rating system that no one today would ever confuse with sabermetrics.

But the pièce de résistance was yet to come. The previous winter, my father had bought Michael and me a big, boxy cassette recorder with a built-in radio and microphone (the first of his many impulse buys, which pissed Mom off to no end). We quickly realized we could record songs off our favorite stations. More importantly, I could now record Dodger games off KABC 790, the team's flagship station. Unlike today, when virtually every Dodger game can be seen on television, radio was *everything* in those days. Televised home games were nonexistent, and road games were hit-or-miss; sometimes entire road series were not even televised, especially if they fell on workdays. As a result, the words and descriptions of Vin Scully, Ross Porter, and Jerry Doggett held sway over captive Dodger fans like me.

On the cusp of the '78 season, I was so pumped for Dodger baseball, I resolved to record every inning of every game (minus weekday games when I was in school or other special circumstances). Michael reminded me that an average game took two and a half hours to play. At that rate, I'd run out of our stock of Scotch brand tapes sometime in mid-April. This shortcoming led to an even more brilliant idea. Why not do a sort of "greatest hits" tape, much like musical acts do on albums? To do this, I would need to record games in their entirety, then transfer all the best home runs to another tape using a second cassette recorder. Once all the highlights were dubbed to this second tape, I would simply record over the raw tapes for the next day's game, continuing this process throughout the season. By the end of the year, I would have cataloged the best moments of the Dodgers' 1978 season, hopefully culminating in a World Series Championship that had eluded them the year before. I would call the finished tape *Home-run Highlights*. (It wasn't till later in '78 that I realized "Home Run" should be two words, but by that point I had devised a logo in which I had spelled it out as one word.)

On April 7, 1978, I recorded my first Dodger game off the radio. It was the team's opener against the Braves at Atlanta-Fulton County Stadium. The Dodgers crushed them, 13–4. Davey Lopes and Rick Monday hit home runs. My obsession with cataloging the Dodgers' greatest offensive highlights was officially born.

Little did I know it wouldn't end until four seasons—and ten 90-minute tapes—later.

But wow, what a journey! After the 1978 season, I started to become a real student of the game and realized that sticking to home runs was too limiting. My repertoire expanded to include incredible comebacks, shoestring catches, stellar pitching performances, even great moments by opposing players. Which led to another feature called "The Dodgers Blow It Again." As you can guess by the title, these sequences chronicled turns of events in which the Dodgers squandered big leads or lost in some other gut-wrenching fashion. Even with the passing of decades, these moments are still painful to listen to. Fortunately, 1978 to 1981 were mostly fruitful years for the Dodgers. And there is something neat about my audio anthology being bookmarked by two World Series seasons. While the beginning of my collection features the Boys in Blue laying another egg against the Yankees in the World Series, tape ten documents the Dodgers' sweet revenge against the Bronx Bombers before riding off into the sunset, their fabled infield breaking up after that year.

There were other storied moments in between: Jerry Reuss's no-hitter against the Giants; Davey Lopes's amazing 1979 season; the Dodgers' exciting sweep of their last three games against the Astros in 1980 to force a one-game playoff; the odd split-season strike of 1981; that year's improbable postseason run, punctuated by Rick Monday's legendary homer against Montreal; and the final year of the record-setting Garvey/Lopes/Russell/Cey infield, which stayed intact for eight and a half seasons. And, of course, what will ever be greater than Fernandomania? Fernando Valenzuela's storybook rookie season also saw Vin Scully elevate *his* craft to new heights, if such a thing is possible.

"It is incredible," Vin gushed after Fernando threw his fourth shutout in only his fifth big-league start. "It is fantastic. It is Fernando Valenzuela. He has done something I can't believe anyone has ever done, or will ever do. Unbelievable."

These goosebump-inducing moments made me realize that baseball rewards the patience of its truest fans. Stick around long enough and you're bound to witness the occasional miracle. It was times like these that my whole exhaustive, single-minded mission of archiving the Dodgers felt justified. While other kids collected baseball cards, I was collecting history.

And now, oh ye faithful Dodger fan, I invite you to hop into my time capsule and share in the history of what was arguably the last great Dodger nucleus to take the field. Our trip will be mostly chronological, with much of the action lifted directly from my 15 hours of *Homerun Highlights* tapes. On occasion, I will also be shifting into "I" and "we" mode, which is what "we" fans tend to do with our favorite teams.

This should also serve as a reminder: I am not a professional baseball writer. I am a *fan*. As such, much of this book will be told through the perspective of my wide-eyed, early-adolescent self, balanced with the present-day version, who will offer, hopefully, the kind of insight that comes from hindsight. Sifting through the statistical strata of those magical years yielded many gems I had either forgotten with time or didn't know about. Fortunately, we live in an era of unprecedented access to baseball research, so I am forever indebted to websites like www.baseball-reference.com, www.baseball-almanac.com, and www.retrosheet.org. They were invaluable resources for this book, along with my personal stash of old *National League Green Books*, *Los Angeles Times*, and *Los Angeles Herald Examiner* sports pages, and magazines like *Sports Illustrated, The Sporting News, Sport,* and *Inside Sports.* (If it had the word "sport" in the title, it's a safe bet that I had a subscription.)

Of course, no trip to the Land of the Late '70s/Early '80s Dodgers would be complete without hearing from the announcers who brought us the action, and so on occasion I have transcribed, word-for-word, some of the more memorable calls as described by Ross, Jerry, and, of course, Vinny. Yes, *you will be there as they broadcast the action!* If you were lucky enough to have followed the Dodgers from 1978 onward, you will nod your head in recognition at many of the events that unfold in these pages.

If you were not born yet, or are simply curious about catching up with the team's past, you're also in for a treat. You will experience not just what it was like to be a Dodger fan, but also what it sounded like to listen at the knee of a master storyteller at the top of his game—Vin Scully.

Finally, there will be the occasional "Bullpen Session," "Who Knew?" and other sidebars to allow for lists, asides, and other passing thoughts, much in the same spirit of idly chatting with a friend at Chavez Ravine itself.

So sit back, enjoy, and pass the peanuts. I'll bring the Dodger Dogs (grilled, of course).

—PAUL HADDAD
Los Angeles, CA

Me and my pet parakeet, Tweety, at the breakfast table, scouring the *L.A. Times* sports page for preseason baseball stats, February 1979.

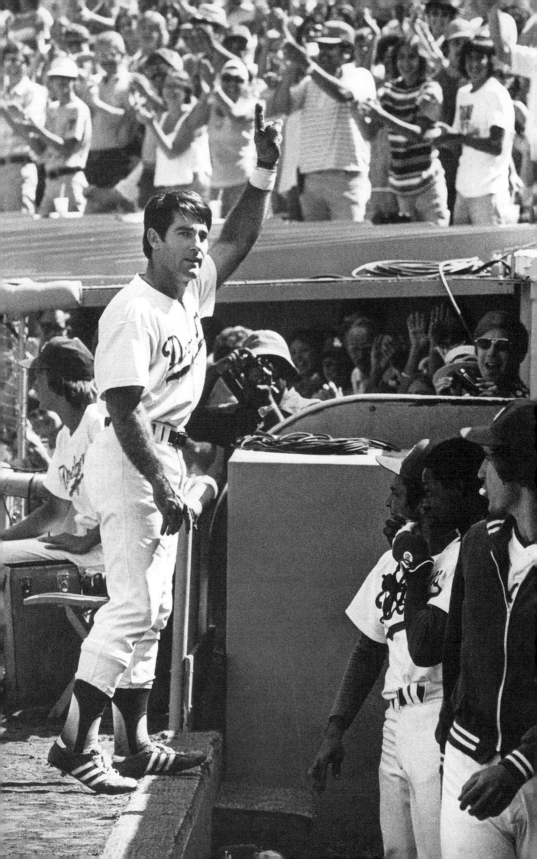

1ST INNING
April - June 1978

Hello, I'm Paul Haddad, and I just took a tape of Dodger games on TV or radio. And, as you know, just about in every game, at least one person hits a home run. Sometimes there aren't any, but usually there are. And I took home runs from various players. And it will give you the feeling of how the announcer announced it when the home run happened. Now, let's hear our first home run . . .

—PAUL HADDAD, April 7, 1978

The year 1978 was a momentous one in Los Angeles. USC football won another national championship. *Three's Company*, a randy sitcom that celebrated the Southern California lifestyle, remained near the top of the TV charts. The deteriorating Hollywood sign got a face-lift (thanks to generous donations from the likes of Hugh Hefner and Alice Cooper), and *Homerun Highlights* made its debut from the Beverly Hills bedroom of an 11-year-old budding Dodger fanatic with a Mickey Mouse voice. In his mind, his audience was vast and riveted to his every word. In reality, his was an audience of one: himself.

Crowd favorite Steve Garvey.

But reaching others' ears was really beside the point. I think the real impetus behind my desire to immortalize Dodger broadcasts was so that I could play those home runs back again, over and over, and feel that same rush of excitement that I experienced when I first heard them. Fortunately, the Dodgers gave me plenty of material to work with. This was a team, after all, that became the first in major league history to have four players (Steve Garvey, Reggie Smith, Ron Cey, Dusty Baker) reach 30 or more home runs the year before. The Reds may have been the Big Red Machine, but the Dodgers' nickname—the Big Blue Wrecking Crew—was well-earned too. The year 1977 saw the first of five years in a row—and six out of seven—in which the Dodgers would lead the NL in home runs.

In the present era of smaller, hitter-friendly ballparks, it's highly unlikely that the team will ever go on that kind of run again as long as they play in Dodger Stadium. Nonetheless, whenever I hear sportscasters today proclaim that the team plays in a pitcher's park and will always be built around pitching, I feel like jumping through the TV and pointing out the team of the late '70s and early '80s. Those teams had it both ways—teams that led the league in ERA *and* home runs. In fact, the Dodgers of my youth played in even more of a pitcher's park than the stadium we know today. Renovations after the 2004 season drastically reduced the amount of foul territory, resulting in pop-ups going out of play that otherwise would've been caught. This makes the Wrecking Crew's power display all the more impressive.

THE PLAYERS

The 1978 opening day starting eight was identical to the 1977 version. The only difference was Dusty Baker and Rick Monday swapping spots in the lineup. Davey Lopes was the only legitimate base-stealer, but that didn't stop the Dodgers from leading the league in runs, thanks to their high on-base percentage, team batting average, and slugging, all of which also led the NL. Calling the shots was Tom Lasorda, beginning his second full year as manager.

From top to bottom, it was a well-balanced lineup:

• **2B Davey Lopes**—The Dodgers' team captain banged out a surprising 17 homers to go with 45 stolen bases. What's interesting about Lopes is how much of a late bloomer he was. There is a school of thought that a majority of ballplayers often peak at 27 years old. Davey didn't even make an *appearance* in his first big-league game until he was 27. He turned an ancient 33 during the '78 campaign, with his best offensive year still ahead of him. Lopes also claimed the title of Best Mustache by a Dodger during his era. They just don't make Brillo-pad 'staches like that anymore.

> ### Who Knew?
>
> Davey Lopes stole 47 out of 51 bases (a 92 percent success rate) in 1985 for the Chicago Cubs in his age 40 season. This shattered the "Most Steals by a 40-Year-Old Dude" single-season record of 27 stolen bases, set by some guy with the unfortunate nickname of William "Dummy" Hoy back in 1901.

• **SS Bill Russell**—The Dodgers' second-leading player in overall appearances (2,181 games) would establish a career high in batting average (.286) in 1978. He had a flair for the dramatic during the postseason, hitting the pennant-clinching single off the Phillies' Tug McGraw in the National League Championship Series. He went on to bat .423 in the '78 World Series. I used to always compare Russell to the Angels shortstop, Dave Chalk, to see who choked up on their bat more (the winner: Dave Chalk).

- **RF Reggie Smith**—Perhaps the most underrated (and underappreciated) player during his era, Reggie was an on-base machine with power from both the left and right sides. He would lead the Dodgers with 29 homers in '78, despite missing 34 games. When healthy, he was the Dodgers' best player, but was somewhat overshadowed on a team of big personalities. Over the years Reggie developed a reputation for being sort of ornery (Giants fans can do that to you—he infamously went into the stands to fight some of them in '81). But I loved his all-business approach to the game.

- **3B Ron Cey**—Cey finished 1978 with 23 homers—his fourth of 10 years in a row (not including the 1981 strike season) of 20 or more dingers. Stats-wise, history has been kind to the Penguin, so-called, of course, because of his large torso and the way he seemed to waddle around the field. (He appeared to not move his ankles when he ran, which made him fun to imitate on the playground.) After trading Cey before the 1983 season, the Dodgers have famously had trouble finding a long-term replacement at third who could match his year-in, year-out durability and consistency.

- **1B Steve Garvey** (mostly batting fourth by mid-season)—My first sports poster was of Steve Garvey. It hung proudly above my bed next to my Farrah Fawcett poster (this was years before I would even understand such irony). The Garvey poster was distributed by *Sports Illustrated*, and it was a classic: an action shot, the Garv caught in his follow-through after lacing a probable line-drive. His massive, hairy right forearm almost appeared to be posed in a karate chop. But what was most striking was his smile. Not a grimace, but a smile. He made it look so easy. I'll have plenty to say about Mr. Clean later.

- **LF Dusty Baker**—Dusty's power dropped appreciably in 1978, going from 30 homers to 11. But next to Garvey, he remained my favorite player—and the favorite of many other fans. Decades before Mannywood, there was Bakersfield, the name given to the stands beyond left field. One of my fondest memories of going to Dodger Stadium involved Bakersfield fans serenading Dusty with cheers after a home run, often tossing packages of gum or even money onto the playing field. (Nowadays if someone threw money on the field, it would be considered an act of sarcasm. This, after you got ejected, too.)

> High fly ball, deep left field . . . waaaaay back . . . this one is in Bakersfield!
> —JERRY DOGGETT, May 19, 1981

- **CF Rick Monday**—Monday was my first infatuation as a newbie Dodger fan in the early part of '78. That's because every time I picked up the *Los Angeles Times* sports page, he seemed to be leading the National League in most offensive categories. Not surprisingly, he was named Player of the Month for April, batting .353 with eight home runs, 22 RBIs, and a 1.202 OPS (On-Base Percentage plus Slugging Percentage). He would hit only 11 more homers the rest of the year while battling back problems.

- **C Steve Yeager**—The perm. The sideburns. The tinted glasses. The trendy throat-protector thingy he invented and wore behind the plate. The fact that he later posed for *Playgirl*. If you had to sum up one player who oozed the 1970s, it was Yeager.

On the bench, Lee Lacy continued to make the case for being the most valuable utility man in baseball, playing five positions, swatting five pinch-hit home runs, and OPS-ing .853. Billy North and Joe Ferguson also saw a lot of duty.

On the mound, the Dodgers' starting five—Don Sutton, Tommy John, Doug Rau, Rick Rhoden, and Burt Hooton (who finished second in Cy Young voting)—all won 10 games or more. Like the offense, this was the same corps as in 1977, though a 21-year-old phenom named Bob Welch did make some key starts in August and September. Knuckleballer Charlie Hough and flash-in-the-pan Lance Rautzhan carried the bulk of the bullpen load, while closer Terry Forster, brought over from Pittsburgh during the off-season, led the staff with a 1.93 ERA and 22 saves. In addition to Welch, the '78 staff also saw the debuts of young farmhands Dave Stewart and Rick Sutcliffe. All three would go on to have their best years in the American League, with two Cy Youngs and six 20-win seasons between them.

To be honest, I didn't really appreciate the Dodgers' pitching staff as much as I should have as a kid. I had longball on the brain!

THE VOICE

> Hi, everybody, and a very pleasant "good evening"
> to you, wherever you may be.
> —Vin Scully

I've already stated how my excitement for the home run—and the Dodgers' tendency to hit a lot of them—propelled my desire to record them for posterity. But without Vin Scully behind the microphone, my obsession would not have reached its fever pitch. For one thing, even though I had only recently discovered the Dodgers at age 11, I came to realize that Vin's voice was *always* a part of my childhood, much as the legendary Chick

Hearn's was as the broadcaster for the Los Angeles Lakers. In those days, both Vin and Chick covered all their teams' games, home and away. Anywhere you traveled in L.A., depending on the season, you would hear their polished tones providing an aural backdrop as you went about your daily life. I can remember Mom pulling into the Union 76 station at Crescent and Little Santa Monica in Beverly Hills and regularly hearing Vinny's voice spilling out of the station's office as the full-service team filled 'er up with leaded and checked under the hood (and for those who remember the old Union 76 commercials during Dodger games, unfortunately, Murph was nowhere to be found).

Other times, our station wagon would pull up to a red light, and there would be that same warm lilt emanating from the radio of the car next to ours. I can also remember Vin's voice wafting over picnic areas in Griffith Park on Sunday afternoons. He was the tie that bound an entire metropolis across all socio-economic lines. By the 1978 season, already in his 28th year of broadcasting for the Dodgers, my familiarity

Bullpen Session

The Magic of 11

There must be something about the age of 11 being significant when it comes to kids recognizing Vin Scully's brilliance. When I set out to write this book, I came across a letter to the editor of the *Los Angeles Times* sports page, dated November 14, 2009. A man from Culver City wrote that *his* 11-year-old son was requesting 100 blank DVDs for the holidays so that the boy could record for posterity every televised game that Vin Scully had called for the 2010 season (in later years, Vin stopped doing television and radio for road games east of Colorado). The boy's father added that when he was 11, he too became enamored with the Dodgers' Hall of Fame broadcaster. Vin is one of those rare voices whose influence regularly spans three generations—grandparents, parents, and kids (at least, those turning 11).

with "that voice" was akin to a baby in his mother's womb hearing the muffled intonations of his parents for nine months. For, as I discovered the Dodgers, there was Vin, waiting to ease my transition into the exciting new world of baseball that awaited me. *Oh yeah*, I thought. *That guy.*

Like anyone new to the game, I initially gravitated to the quick-fix thrill that came with home runs, not yet attuned to baseball's finer points. In those days, Vin Scully split time in the booth with Jerry Doggett and Ross Porter. If the Dodgers hit a home run and Vin Scully was not behind the mic, my elation was always mitigated by my disappointment that Vinny did not make the call. It wasn't that I didn't like to hear Jerry and Ross call home runs. It was just that Vin tended to adhere to predictable, rhythmic phrases that I found exhilarating and reassuring. To me, it was no different than hearing someone other than Ed McMahon—say, bandleader Doc Severinsen—introduce Johnny on *The Tonight Show Starring Johnny Carson.* Without Ed's famous "Heeeeeeeeere's Johnny!" the show just wasn't the same.

Over the years, I've noticed that Vin has added more variety to his home run calls, but in the late '70s and early '80s, he trotted out two phrases more than any other, depending on the type of home run. For high-arching homers that just cleared the wall, the formula usually went something like this:

> *Hiiiigh* drive into deep [left/center/right] field. Back goes [outfielder's name] . . . to the warning track . . . to the wall . . . it's *gooone!*

Vin rarely references the warning track in calls today. I have a theory about this. Back in the day, the Dodgers' primary power hitters were five foot ten and under (Garvey, Cey, sometimes Lopes) or sort of skinny (Baker and Monday). Their drives were often high fly balls with good backspin that stayed in the air longer, not line-drive, tape-measure shots where the outfielder takes two steps and watches it leave, as is so common today. Consequently, Vin had a few more seconds to actually describe the trajectory of the ball.

That's not to say that the Dodgers didn't have their share of bullets either. These "no-doubt-about-it" calls were just as exciting, mostly because of a variance in one word that offered clues on how far the ball went. A ball's distance always seemed directly proportional to how long Vin dragged out the word "way."

> Swung on and *belted* to [left/center/right] field. Back goes [outfielder's name], a-*waaaaaaaaaaay* back . . . it's gone!

What I also like about Vin's calls is that they are, for lack of a better word, organic. That same year, I sampled many California Angel broadcasts down the dial on KMPC 710. The great Dick Enberg was an above-average baseball announcer himself, but I always found his signature home run phrase—" . . . And he will touch 'em all!"—to be marred by an air of calculation. In more contemporary times, New York announcer Michael Kay's insistence of dropping in a "See ya!" for almost every Yankee home run, or Ken Harrelson's "You can put it on the booooard, yes!" catchphrase for White Sox homers, are equally cringe-worthy. Vin doesn't dress his calls up with cute phrases or homerism. He's selling the action, not himself. Thank goodness, too, otherwise we all might've grown up hearing: " . . . To the warning track, to the wall, *holy smokes, Sister Sally, it's a rooooooouuuuund tripper!*"*

After several months of listening to Dodger games, Vin became more than just about great home run calls. Slowly but surely, he was working his magic on my malleable mind, painting words with pictures that took hold of my imagination and didn't let go. Where once I listened only to the bright and shiny colors,

---

* Having said all this, any announcer born before 1930 gets an automatic free pass in my book. So trot out your holy cows, Mr. Harry Carey. And, oh doctor, hang a star on that one, Mr. Jerry Coleman. Ernie Harwell, Jack Buck, Mel Allen—you, too . . . Your old-school color evolved naturally out of folksy upbringings that you simply carried into the booth. It will be dearly missed.

now I heard the brush strokes. It wasn't enough to just record Vin's home run calls. By the 1980 season, I began to include long stretches on *Homerun Highlights* in which Vin called Dodger rallies or great pitching performances. Even crushing defeats went down smoother when Vin called it, as he would invariably work in some Shakespearean phrase or Broadway lyric that would connect what I was feeling to a more universal truth. A tough loss would fall under "the best laid plans of mice and men," or another favorite, "We have met the enemy and they are us." He even ascribed greater meaning to the little things that helped win ballgames. A successful swinging bunt was "a humble thing but thine own," while a role player off the bench always seemed more important when accompanied by "they also serve who only stand and wait." His own phrases were no less clever or memorable.

Soon I noticed my own narration for *Homerun Highlights* starting to improve, thanks to lessons from Vin. Where my early voice-over attempts to set up home runs and rallies were clunky and lacking in context, I began to see the importance in setting the stage for maximum drama. Unfortunately, I didn't stop there. Much of the time I was also trying to emulate Vin's singsong-y pitch—an unfortunate error in judgment even more embarrassing than the pink-trim tuxedo I wore to my 1984 high school prom. As Vin himself might say, "Ah, youth."

Of course, since most Dodger games ended well past my bedtime in my pre-teen years, it became apparent rather quickly that I wouldn't be able to record every inning of every night game, as I had planned. And so I embarked on a ritual that generations of kids devised without any of us even realizing that others were doing the same: sneaking transistor radios under our pillows at night for no other reason than to hear Vin Scully's voice. Vin has often stated that his preference to work alone in the broadcast booth has nothing to do with ego, but with a desire to directly connect with the listener. In this, he succeeded. Adolescence can be a trying, scary time for kids. We're not children, but we're not adults, either. We're not even teens. We're in-betweeners (or, as they say now, 'tweeners), searching for who we are amidst growing peer pressure and increasing responsibilities. At age 11 and 12, I wanted to be older, but was still terrified of girls and bullies and confused by adult behavior. What I really sought was to feel safe. Vin's voice, muffled through my pillow, wrapped me in a cocoon of assurances, seemingly speaking only to me. *Homerun Highlights* didn't matter in those moments. Nothing mattered as I dozed off to his warm timbre.

As an adult, I treasure Vin now even more than I did as a child. I may not have to hide a radio under my pillow to hear him, but even in my most insecure moments as a husband and father of two, I can still turn to some old standbys that put me in my own personal comfort zone: grilled cheese on wheat; Campbell's Tomato Rice soup; a favorite old plaid shirt; and Vin, preferably on a transistor radio.

5-FOR-5
FIVE GAMES THAT DEFINED THE 1978 DODGERS

In a tidy attempt to distill the Dodgers' 1978–81 campaigns down to their bare essentials, I have isolated five games from each season that, in my view, offer snapshots of that particular year. Since postseason play is another matter entirely (one which I will delve into separately), these "5 Game" recaps only include games from the regular season. I will present the games in chronological order, broken up over the course of these chapters. On that note, let's take a closer look at this fiery 1978 squad, starting with an eventful game on May 14 that is more well-known for what transpired *after* the game than during it.

#1—MOTHER'S DAY MASSACRE
Dodger Stadium, May 14, 1978

If I had to choose one word to describe the 1978 Dodgers, it would be "cranky." Who could blame them? This was no longer a team that was just happy to get into the postseason. They had already overachieved in 1974 and managed to face off against the A's, then outclassed the rest of the NL in 1977 to face the Yankees. They lost in the World Series both years. The sting of losing to their longtime rivals in a humiliating Game 6 the year before was, I'm sure, just as fresh in their minds as it was in mine. On the eve of the '78 season, they were no longer a team with nothing to lose, but rather one burdened with high expectations of redeeming past failures to win it all. Plus, the '78 race was a lot more intense than the '77 one, when the team won its division by double digits. From a fan's standpoint, of course, this made for some really exciting baseball.

Digging through my *Homerun Highlights* tapes, this aura of testiness reared its head on several occasions. Three of the franchise's most legendary meltdowns occurred that year: Steve Garvey and Don Sutton's tussle in the Shea Stadium clubhouse; the infamous "hip-and-run" obstruction play involving (who else?) Reggie Jackson that was the turning point of the World Series; and the sudden eruption of Mount St. Lasorda after an infamous game on May 14 against the Cubs.

I could have easily nicknamed this game "Dave Kingman's Three Homers," but "Mother's Day Massacre" is a much more accurate description for what a horrible day this was for the team . . . and for myself. The Dodgers were at home, playing the rubber game of a three-game set with the Chicago Cubs. It was the second Sunday in May—Mother's Day—and our family had decided to host a get-together at our house. Every L.A.-based relative on my mom's side came over to help celebrate the day with a barbecue and backyard games. I remember being a little bummed out that the festivities just happened to coincide with the start of the Dodger game that afternoon, which meant I wouldn't be able to record the game on the radio. (Mom, worried I was becoming anti-social, rightfully had put a stop to my recordings when we had company over.) Nevertheless, I made sure to bring my transistor radio outside so the game was always within earshot.

The Dodgers took a 3–0 lead, and after five innings, starter Doug Rau was cruising along with a four-hit shutout. Around that time, after we all had polished off our hot dogs and hamburgers, my mother made a casual suggestion that maybe I could turn the game off, seeing how the Dodgers had a comfortable lead. (Translation: It's Mother's Day, you ingrate! Kill the radio!) I assured her that I would . . . after just one more inning.

Always listen to your mother.

In the next inning, Dave Kingman walloped a two-run home run to cut the lead to 3–2. Anyone who remembers baseball from this era can recall the strange, towering menace that was Dave Kingman, who was in his first year for the Cubs after playing for four—*four!*—different teams the year before. For those unfamiliar, Kingman specialized in three things: hitting tape-measure home runs, leading the league in strikeouts, and terrorizing sportswriters—particularly female ones—whom he allegedly believed didn't belong in the clubhouse. Despite a career in which he hit 442 home runs, Kingman is probably best known for sending a live rat in a small box to Susan Fornoff of the *Sacramento Bee*. Given the choice, Lasorda would've gladly settled for a rodent in his post-game pasta salad rather than see any more of Kingman that day.

The last three innings were a seesaw affair. Unable to pry myself away from the suspense, I began a slow, stealthy withdrawal from the party, disappearing for long stretches of time to take in the action. By the top of the ninth inning, I was hiding out in my parents' darkened bedroom, quietly listening to the game on their glowing clock radio. Their bedroom opened onto the back patio, where everyone was starting to dig into pie and ice cream and hand out cards and gifts.

"Where in God's name is Paul?" I heard my dad say.

Mike Garman was on in relief. The Dodgers were ahead, 7–5. Ivan DeJesus led off with a walk. Not good. *C'mon*, I pleaded silently, *just close 'em out!* Outside, I could hear Mom telling my younger sister Monica to go find me. No one expected me to be in the room right next to the patio. Ha! Off went Monica in the other direction. The pitch to Ontiveros: fly ball to center. One out. Bill Buckner up next—their best hitter.

Mom was making threats to the effect of, "When I catch that kid . . ."

Buckner flew to right. Two out. My heart was pounding. I could barely listen, but I couldn't pry myself away. With one out to go and a runner on first base, up stepped you-know-who.

And the ball went you-know-where.

And I went I-don't-know-what. But I'm told it was *loud*, and it went something like: "@#$%#!"

Happy Mother's Day, Mom.

Dad stormed into the bedroom to yank the radio plug out of the wall. An awkward silence fell over the party. Relatives gathered at the doorway, eyeing me with a mix of pity and scorn. My parents could see I was not going to be good company for the rest of the afternoon. They encouraged me to spend it in my bedroom.

As bad as my day was going, I could only imagine the frustration that must have been building in Lasorda. In the 12th inning, the Cubs loaded the bases with only one out. Bobby Castillo pitched his way out of a jam. In the bottom of the inning, the Dodgers also loaded the bases, but they too couldn't score. Both teams went out in order in the 13th and 14th innings. In the top of the 15th, the marathon game was nearing the five-hour mark. Our guests had left our house long ago, and all of a sudden dinner was just about ready. I had never experienced a game that long before. Was I going to miss dinner, too? I was already in the dog house, I reasoned, so why not just stay in my room until the bitter end?

The end, it turned out, was coming soon enough, and it was indeed bitter. Rick Rhoden, normally a starter, began to lose it in his third inning of relief. With two on and two outs, Dave Kingman blasted a three-run homer to put the Cubbies up for good, 10–7. I couldn't tell you where the ball landed. I was too busy smothering my ears with my pillow and screaming into my mattress.

The Rat Man's final line for the game: 4-for-7, with one walk, three homers, three runs, and eight RBIs. Two of his homers came with two outs. One tied the game to send it into extras. The other won it in extras. Female reporters who were also mothers had to feel doubly insulted.

Of course, Kingman's act was just the warm-up for the show Tommy Lasorda put on after the game. Tommy's tirade is so legendary, it just might be the number-one post-game manager meltdown in baseball history. In Lasorda's office after the game, Paul Olden, a young reporter for a Los Angeles radio station, made the mistake of asking the infamous line, "What's your opinion of Kingman's performance?" To hear Lasorda tell it, it was the word "opinion" that set him off. Ask Lasorda his opinion about something,

Bullpen Session

Déjà Vu All Over Again

Stunningly, this was not the first time Dave Kingman had a three-home-run, eight-RBI game against L.A. at Dodger Stadium. The first came on June 4, 1976, when he was a member of the New York Mets. That game was decidedly more one-sided; the Mets won, 11–0. While Tommy was not the manager then (Walt Alston was), he did witness Kingman's one-man dismantling from the dugout as the third base coach. No records exist for what Tommy thought of that particular performance, but I'm sure it was fresh on his mind two years later when he was asked about Kingman's encore.

and he'll give you an honest answer—especially after a grueling game in which he had to dip into his starting pitching and saw his team leave 15 runners on base. Here's what Lasorda said:

> What's my opinion of Kingman's performance? What the [expletive] do you think is my opinion of it? I think it was [expletive] [expletive]. Put that in . . . I don't [expletive]. . . . Opinion of his performance? [Expletive] he beat us with three [expletive] home runs. What the [expletive] do you mean what is my opinion of his performance? How can you ask me a question like that? What is my opinion of his performance? [Expletive] he hit three home runs. [Expletive]. I'm [expletive] pissed off to lose the [expletive] game, and you ask me my opinion of his performance. [Expletive]. I mean that's a tough question to ask me, isn't it? What is my opinion of his performance?

Besides dropping a stink bomb on Mother's Day for Dodger fans everywhere, Dave Kingman's three-homer pageant presaged the frustration—and the fight—that lay ahead for the Dodgers in 1978, right up to the World Series.

5-FOR-5
FIVE GAMES THAT DEFINED THE 1978 DODGERS

#2—GARVEY SENDS A MESSAGE
Dodger Stadium, June 14, 1978

It would have been asking a lot for the 1978 Dodgers to repeat the red-hot start of the 1977 team, even though their roster was largely the same. The '77 Dodgers had a blazing 17–3 record in

April, spurred by Ron Cey's record 29 RBIs, and were never seriously challenged for the rest of the season. With Rick Monday assuming the Ron Cey "stud" role the following year, the Dodgers once again closed the month in first place, with a 13–7 record at the end of April. May, however, was a different story. The team played roughly .500 baseball and found themselves 3½ games out, in third place.

Their problems were just beginning.

The Dodgers proceeded to drop their first seven out of eight games in the month of June. The main culprit was the pitching staff, which compiled a 5.37 ERA during this stretch, a full 2¼ runs more than their final league-leading 3.12 ERA. Tommy John, in his last year with the team, was particularly ineffective, giving up five earned runs in 1⅔ innings in one start, then eight more in 3⅓ innings in another, both losses.

But then the staff settled down, keeping the opposition to five runs or fewer over the next seven games, all wins. Most of the games were closely contested battles. In the middle of this seven-game streak, on June 14, the Dodgers played another tight game during an uncharacteristically warm June night at home. The lowly Mets, under manager Joe Torre, were making their first visit to Dodger Stadium. Earlier in the month, they had taken two of three from the Dodgers, both tough, one-run decisions. If the Blue Crew was hot under the collar, it was certainly understandable.

The game featured two eventual 200-game winners. Tommy John, looking to redeem his last two disastrous starts, took the ball for the Dodgers. Jerry Koosman was starting for New York.

John got the Mets in order in the top of the first inning. In the bottom of the first, Koosman retired Davey Lopes and Bill Russell. Up stepped Steve Garvey. After fouling off a pitch, Garvey didn't miss on the next one. Vin Scully called it:

> And Garvey didn't foul *this* one off . . . a hiiigh
> drive into deep left field . . . it's gone!

Vin then let the crowd cheer for twenty uninterrupted seconds. (By the way, get used to me telling you *exactly* how long Vin let the crowd cheer after various home runs. It is, of course, one of his hallmarks, one that so many of us cherish—and one I wish more announcers emulated.)

Vin continued:

> So Steve Garvey hits his seventh home run of the
> year, his 37th run batted in, and the Dodgers now
> have taken a one-to-nothing lead.

But the lead didn't last long. In the top of the second inning, Mets catcher John Stearns came up with one out. Vin:

> Tommy into the windup and the 3–2 pitch to
> Stearns is a drive to left field. Back goes Baker to
> the wall . . . it's gone!

At this point on the tape, you can hear our dog Ginger jingling into the room and my sharp command for her to scram. If there was one thing I couldn't stand, it was someone or something puncturing my little bubble of perfectionism. Back then, I was still capturing the raw broadcasts by pointing a microphone at a radio speaker. I hadn't quite figured out yet how to record directly from the radio setting on my dual radio/tape recorder for a cleaner sound devoid of outside noise. Consequently, a sampling of early recordings reveal as much about my own emotional state as they do about the Dodgers. Some of my more common heat-of-the-moment reactions: sighing, clapping, whooping, telling people to shut up, telling the dog to shut up, and throwing objects across the room in disgust.

After the Stearns homer, Vinny made a point of bringing up the weather. As most Angelenos know, June is typically a time of year when a marine layer sets over the L.A. basin—"June Gloom," it's commonly called. Not this June:

> Boy, I'll tell you what—it's a pretty good guess if
> you want to talk about the June weather in Dodg-
> er Stadium, and how unusually *hot* and *dry* it is
> . . . *twelve* home runs in two games, plus an inning
> and half. Never seen anything like it.

Tommy John got nicked for another run in the second inning, and it looked like his recent funk was going to continue.
But he wiggled his way out of further damage, and it remained
3–1, Mets, going into the bottom of the sixth inning. After a
lead-off triple by Lopes and a run-scoring groundout by Russell
to make it 3–2, Garvey stepped up to face Koosman again.

Just to make it clear that he wasn't going to let Steve go deep
on him again in this situation, the old-school Jerry unleashed a
purpose pitch up near Garvey's face, prompting a chorus of boos
amongst the Dodger Stadium faithful. Garvey got up and methodically collected himself, as he always did. They say Garvey
was hyper-aware of his statistics as a player, a knock that seems to
suggest he was always about himself first. But when you put up
numbers like Garvey did year after year, it's not hard to see how
the team benefitted. Even in knockdown situations, Garvey kept
his own running tally—and, as usual, the stats were impressive. In
1989, he told Rick Reilly of *Sports Illustrated* that he remembered
being knocked down six times as a player in 1980. On all six occasions, he got back up and got a base hit. I don't have records for
how many times he was knocked down in 1978. But as Vin can
tell you, in that same at-bat, he was at least 1-for-1:

> Koosman back with a fastball and a *hiiigh* drive
> into deep left field. Back goes Henderson, a-
> *waaaaaaay* back . . . it's *gone!* And now Garvey
> sent *Koosman* a message!

Eighteen seconds of crowd noise. In the background, I am
audibly whooping.

Boy, can there be anything *sweeter* in this game of baseball than for a hitter to come up, take a fastball *close* to the *head*, get back up there, and hit one in the seats?

Vin, somewhat uncharacteristically, I thought, seemed to derive special satisfaction out of emphasizing Garvey's payback during this call. Who could blame him? It *was* immensely satisfying. Garvey's in-your-face heroics seemed to wake everybody up. If they were going to win another pennant that season, the team would need their Iron Man to deliver more clutch moments like that one. And he would, finishing second in the MVP voting to the Pirates' Dave Parker, while going on to win the MVP trophy in the National League Championship Series. This game, more than any other, made me a believer in Steve Garvey, the player. I was already sold on him as an ideal.

Joe Torre didn't mess around with Garvey in his next at-bat. Down 5–3 in the seventh inning, with a runner on second base—and two outs, no less—Torre had Koosman intentionally walk Steve in the ultimate sign of respect in order to pitch to Ron Cey, who struck out. Despite scattering 12 hits in

---

Who Knew?

Just how bad were the New York Mets in the late '70s? Jerry Koosman led the NL with 20 losses in 1977 en route to an 8-20 record. His ERA, however, was a nothing-to-be-ashamed-of 3.49 — almost a half-run better than the league average (3.91). As of 2011, there were 45 pitchers who lost a league-leading 20 games or more in a single season since World War II. Only two of them had an ERA lower than Koosman's — Wilbur Wood in 1973 and Phil Niekro in 1979. Despite their 20 losses, each pitcher, amazingly, had winning records in those years. So technically, that leaves Jerry Koosman as the most "successful" loser since 1945.

8⅔ innings, Tommy John held on for the win.

An ironic footnote: The Dodgers made up no ground in the standings during their seven-game winning streak. That's because the first-place San Francisco Giants were busy reeling off seven straight wins of their own. The Dodgers would have plenty of chances to take care of business against their rivals in the coming months.

THE CASE FOR GARVEY

Like many kids in the 1970s, I was a fan of the ABC Saturday morning cartoon series *Super Friends*, in which Superman, Wonder Woman, Batman, Aquaman, and other DC Comics icons rallied together as a sort of United Nations of Superheroes. Though I admired the unique talents each superhero brought to the table, they all had limitations. I mean, was Aquaman really any more threatening than me when he was out of the water? How many crimes actually took place deep in the ocean? (More than one might think, apparently.) Barring his nagging weakness against kryptonite, Superman was the only superhero whose powers were truly super, possessing all of his friends' talents and then some. Superman ruled. Or so I thought.

Steve Garvey was not Superman, but we could be forgiven for thinking he was, because he was one heck of an understudy. At 25 years old, Steve enjoyed a breakout season in 1974, when he won the National League's Most Valuable Player award and was the write-in starting first baseman for the All-Star Game (and rewarded his fans' faith in him by claiming that MVP trophy as well). The Garvey Mystique is legendary. He was already bleeding Dodger blue as a child, when he was a bat boy for the Brooklyn Dodgers in spring training, where his father was a bus driver hired by the team. To this day, nobody has ever looked better in the Dodgers' home whites. Garvey's chiseled face and Brylcreemed block of jet-black hair were truly the sort of things that could only spring from the pen of a comic book artist. His body was defined by Popeye-esque forearms and muscular thighs, with movements that were purposeful, smooth, and deliberate. Just as there was never a hair out of place when he hit, ran, or fielded, there seemed to be never a movement out of place, either. He was a model of consistency and durability, almost machine-like, developing the nickname "Iron Man." Iron or steel, when you added up the whole impossible package, *that* was Steve Garvey, whose sum total truly seemed like Clark Kent's doppelganger.

As an impressionable youngster looking for heroes, I fell hard under the spell of the Garvey Mystique. I was not alone. He was also the favorite player of my brother, Michael, and most boys I knew. I never bothered getting his autograph before games because the crowd was always too big. By 1977, Garvey's clean-cut image had elevated him to mega-role model status, resulting in a junior high school named after him in Lindsay, California. In 1978, he was the first player to rack up more than four million votes for the All-Star Game. Garvey repaid the fans by winning that All-Star MVP Award, too. He popped up in Aqua Cologne commercials and on *Fantasy Island*. He was crowned with a new nickname—"Senator"—a nod to the promising political career that no doubt loomed in his future. In 1981, he was included in a coffee-table book that I still have to this day: *The 100 Greatest Baseball Players of All Time*.

But behind the scenes, Garvey was dealing with his own kryptonite—teammates resentful of his popularity, troubles at home with his wife, Cyndy, and later, paternity suits brought against him after his own marriage dissolved.

There's an old adage in baseball: "You're only as good as your last at-bat." The public's lasting impression of Garvey was not the day he walked off the field as a San Diego Padre in May of 1987, but his admission that he fathered two children out of wedlock to two separate women in 1989. That same year, Cyndy, then his ex-wife, published a scathing tell-all book that exposed the alleged dark side of Steve Garvey.

I cannot overemphasize the repercussions all this had on Garvey's legacy at that time. Overnight, he became a national punch line. (Anyone remember those "Steve Garvey Is Not My Padre" bumper stickers?) Garvey's first year of eligibility for the Hall of Fame was in 1993. Needing 75 percent of the votes by the Baseball Writers Association of America for induction, Steve garnered just 41.6 percent. In 2007, his last year of eligibility, his vote count had shriveled to a paltry 21 percent.

So how did this "future Hall of Famer," as he was so often referred to in his playing days, lose his Get Into Hall Free card? It's a question many have pondered. I believe there are three main reasons why the Baseball Writers shut Garvey out of the Hall. Allow me to present . . .

EXHIBIT A

I recall that, early on in Garvey's eligibility, there seemed to be a lot of emphasis put on his sexual indiscretions from just a few years earlier. After all, we were told, character counts, too. But let's face it—nowadays, the idea of an entertainment figure getting slapped with a paternity suit is so commonplace, it has become almost quaint. So why was Garvey held to a higher standard than others? Countless other Hall of Famers had checkered pasts—some were connected to drug use (Paul Molitor, Ferguson Jenkins), others were ejected from games for allegedly doctoring baseballs (Don Sutton, Gaylord Perry)—and they still got voted in. One popular theory is that Steve had helped fashion his Mr. Clean image, so when it turned out that he wasn't so wholesome after all, it was considered the height of hypocrisy and left a bad taste in the voters' mouths. This seemed to perpetuate more piling on: he was a fake, a selfish player only concerned about his stats and his consecutive-games streak. I can still recall one sports talk radio host harrumphing that Garvey leading the league in Grounded-into-Double-Plays two different years was proof that he cared only for himself. I'm sure someone, somewhere, is blaming him for the 2008 financial meltdown and the endangerment of the Northern Spotted Owl.

As baseball progressed into the Steroid Era of the late '90s, chatter about Garvey's post-baseball dalliances began to recede. However, another troubling sign began to emerge whenever Garvey's name came up for consideration every year. Rather than creeping upward, his vote totals starting trending downward. Two of Garvey's contemporaries—catcher Gary Carter and outfielder Andre Dawson—received about the same number of votes as Garvey their first years on the ballot. But while Garvey would never get more than 42.6 percent of the votes, Carter and Dawson eventually got enshrined. Another recent Hall of Famer from Garvey's era is Jim Rice. The Red Sox leftfielder received only 29.8 percent of the votes in his first year of eligibility—*28 percent* lower than Garvey's first-year total. Fifteen years later, in his last year of eligibility, Rice surpassed the 75 percent threshold needed to enter the Hall.

So while Rice's percentage of total votes rose 150 percent from his first year of eligibility to his last, Garvey's *dropped* by 50 percent. Once again, what gives? I present Exhibit B for why Steve Garvey is not in the Hall—the one area where Garvey always seemed like a shoo-in during his era: his stats.

EXHIBIT B

During the fifteen years that Steve Garvey was eligible for Cooperstown, from 1993 to 2007, baseball culture underwent a sea change in the way writers and executives evaluated players. The conventional ways of rating a player of Garvey's caliber—batting average, home runs, extra-base hits, and runs batted in—had stood the test of time for close to a century. Then came the rise of sabermetrics, which uses objective evidence to analyze the game. Suddenly, we had access to a whole new set of statistics to measure a player's actual worth. Jim Rice's numbers stacked up nicely

under this new math; Garvey's, not so much. For the uniniti-
ated, some of the more famed sabermetric advocates include Billy
Bean, General Manager of the Oakland A's (featured in the book
and movie *Moneyball*); Theo Epstein, former GM of the Boston
Red Sox (who also hired the granddaddy of sabermetrics, Bill
James, as an adviser); and ESPN baseball writers Buster Olney
and Jayson Stark, Hall-voting members who have gone on record
stating that they didn't vote for Garvey. Stark went so far as to call
Garvey one of the most overrated first basemen in the history of
baseball in his book *The Stark Truth*. One of his arguments was
that Garvey's six 200-hit seasons did not produce any seasons in
which he scored more than 100 runs. In Stark's view, Garvey is
largely to blame for this due to his lack of plate discipline.

   In the sabermetric universe, one of the most important statistics is on-base percentage. A walk, it's rightly argued, is about as
good as a hit. Players with high OBPs tend to create more runs
for their teams. Garvey exceeded 40 walks only one time in his
career. So while he did indeed hit .300 seven times, many consider it an "empty" .300 because of his low walk total and runs
scored. Garvey's career on-base percentage hovered just above the
league average: 329. (You know that phrase "40 is the new 30?"
In sabermetrics, a .400 OBP is the new .300 AVG.) Still, a .329
OBP could almost be forgivable for a power-hitting position like
first base if one's slugging average exceeded .500 in some seasons.
Steve's never did (though he came within a hair in 1977 and
1978). Even Garvey's four Gold Gloves are considered illusionary
to many sabermetric followers, citing multiple defensive metrics.
The reason he made so few errors every year, they posit, is because
his range was so poor, it minimized his number of chances. He
also had a subpar throwing arm, which made him hesitant to start
double plays at second base and take risks.

   These are just snapshots of some of the arguments against
Garvey's inclusion in the Hall. There are, of course, a myriad
other metrics that many readers are likely already familiar with,

including Win Shares, Runs Created, and Total Player Ratings, which present a mixed bag of Garvey's real worth. There is even a Hall of Fame Monitor, created by Bill James, which breaks down a player's stats to decipher how likely that player is to get into the Hall of Fame. A score of 100 equals a "good possibility," while a 130 means a "virtual cinch." Garvey's score? 130. Another sabermetric advocate, economics professor Cy Morong, of the blog *Cybermetrics*, created a logit model that placed Garvey's odds of reaching the Hall at 94.7 percent probability. These analyses would seem to contradict all the other nontraditional data put forth by some Hall of Fame voters.

As a lover of stats, I am actually a huge fan of sabermetrics, but it should not be the end-all, be-all resource to evaluate a player's talent. Analyzing Garvey's career strictly through the prism of empirical analysis at the expense of more traditional stats does not give a complete picture of what Garvey accomplished on the field. It also discounts other intangible contributions he made to the sport that no metrics can ever measure. On July 28, 2011, ESPN Radio's Colin Cowherd brought up Garvey as a victim of the Hall's over-reliance on stats. "Jeff Kent is going to be a Hall of Famer," he said. "Steve Garvey's not. That's just *weird*."

EXHIBIT C

This final piece of evidence has some merit. Steve Garvey's career was never the same after the 1981 baseball players' strike. Prior to the 1981 season, Garvey was a virtual yearly lock for 100-200-300: 100 RBIs, 200 hits, and a .300 batting average, as well as at least 20 home runs. When the players shut it down on June 12, 1981, he was batting .279. No worries, he had often started slow but always worked his average up by the end of the year. But this season was different. Garvey struggled after the long, 50-day layoff, finishing at .283, his lowest batting average since 1972, when he was still a part-time player. He would never hit .300 again, and never came close to 200 hits or 100 RBIs, either. At the age of 32,

Garvey's best years were already behind him.

What accounted for this sudden drop-off at a relatively early age? Some speculate that his refusal to take days off ultimately wore him down. Garvey even admitted to hiding a hand injury that plagued him in '81, and you can be sure he played through lots of pain at other times. Whatever the case was, his skills were deteriorating. I can still remember the frustration I experienced seeing Steve bat in the early to mid-'80s. Pitchers started throwing him more outside pitches—balls he used to slap into right field, he was now grounding weakly to shortstop. For his final five full seasons (1982 to 1986, with '83 cut short by a dislocated thumb), Garvey averaged .279, with 15 home runs and 79 RBIs. He broke down for good in 1987, retiring after 76 at-bats and a .211 average. What we were left with was a player who had seven consecutive very good seasons (1974 to 1980), while the rest were, at best, ordinary with flashes of postseason brilliance.

Had Garvey been able to maintain his level of excellence for even two more seasons—say, pushing his 200-hit season total from six to eight, and maybe knocking in 100 runs a couple more times—I think his numbers would simply be too good for the Hall of Fame electorate to ignore. (Look no further than Hall of Famer Tony Perez to see how a player's longevity can help his cause.) Put another way, if Garvey had simply averaged a pedestrian 170 hits a year from ages 32 to 39—roughly a .280 average for him—including the 50 hits he minimally lost as a result of the 1981 strike (hey, I'm dealing in fantasy, so I can do that!), he would have eclipsed 3,000 career hits. This is a benchmark that, so far, has resulted in automatic inclusion into the Hall of Fame—at least, it has been for players not dogged by steroid allegations (or gambling).

It's ironic that, in an era before, ahem, "supplements" could prolong a player's career well into his early forties, perhaps Mr. Clean's biggest problem was that he really was too clean after all.

CLOSING ARGUMENTS

Steve Garvey was my favorite player as a kid, and I maintain a soft spot for him as an adult. I admit to owning an email address that includes his name in it. When Garvey gamely lent his appearance to the grand opening of a pet food store alongside a skateboarding bulldog on a gray, rainy day in Burbank in 2009 (god, did I ever think I would write *that* sentence about Senator as a child?), I was one of the first in line to shake his hand. Am I biased in my opinion about Steve Garvey being Hall-worthy? Yes. But I'm also a pragmatist who prides himself on being open-minded and not a slave to sentimental judgments. With that disclaimer out of the way, let me close out my argument with cold, hard, old-school facts. The evidence is irrefutable. Steve Garvey is guilty of greatness. I submit that he:

- Had 200 or more hits in six seasons

- Finished with a .294 career average

- Batted over .300 seven times

- Had over 100 RBIs five times

- Set a National League record for durability by playing in 1,207 consecutive games

- Finished with 2,599 career hits

- Finished in the top six in MVP voting five different times

- Won the National League Most Valuable Player Award in 1974

- Won the Roberto Clemente Award in 1981 (given to the player who combines on-field sportsmanship with community involvement—that's right, he got an award for character, people)

- Won the Lou Gehrig Memorial Award in 1984 (truthfully, I don't really know what this honors, but if it has Gehrig's name in it, you know it has to be good)

And that was just in the regular season. Garvey was even more dominant during All-Star Games and the postseason, when the stakes were higher and the competition even more fierce. In short, he hit when it mattered most. Observe:

- He was a 10-time All-Star.

- In those 10 All-Star Games (in which the NL went 10-0), he hit .393 with an .821 slugging percentage.

- Twice he was named the MVP of the Mid-Summer Classic.

- When he retired, he held the National League Championship Series record for most career home runs (eight) and RBIs (21) in a mere 22 games.

- He was named the MVP of the NLCS in 1978 and 1984.

- His walk-off home run in the ninth inning of Game 4 of the NLCS against the Cubs helped propel the Padres into their first World Series. The Padres retired Garvey's #6 uniform largely because of this momentous blast and his five RBIs that game.

- He hit .368 in the Divisional Series in 1981 (the year of the strike).

- He hit .319 in five World Series appearances, including

.417 with a .920 OPS for the 1981 World Series, the Dodgers' only title during his era. (Only his lack of RBIs probably cost him a share of the MVP Award that went to Steve Yeager, Pedro Guerrero, and Ron Cey. Could there have been a quad-MVP?)

- In 55 postseason games, he batted .338 with 11 homers, 31 RBIs, and 32 runs.

Of course, offense only tells one side of the Steve Garvey story. Here's a recap of his defensive prowess at first base:

- He led the league in fielding percentage five times.

- He tied the modern-era record for highest fielding percentage for any position player, minimum 1,000 games, at .996.

- He established an NL record by playing 193 straight games without an error.

- In 1984, he set a record for a starting player with a fielding percentage of 1.000.

- He won four Gold Glove Awards.

- While not blessed with a great throwing arm, *nobody* was better at picking low throws to first base out of the dirt. Shortstop Bill Russell had an erratic arm and was prone to bouncing throws to first. Garvey's adept scoops saved the Dodgers' pitching staff immeasurable unearned runs.

Still not sold? Consider this:

- Steve is one of only 17 players with at least six 200-hit

seasons in baseball *history*. Not including Derek Jeter and Ichiro Suzuki, who won't be eligible until five years after their retirement, only two of these players are not in the Hall of Fame: Pete Rose, for betting on baseball; and Steve Garvey.

I realize there needs to be more to a player's value than just racking up 200-hit seasons, which makes my final point all the more special. Courtesy of *JC Baseball Analysis*, an MLB blog:

> *Bullpen Session*
>
> **The Other Steve**
>
> In the chaos of the Dodgers celebrating their '81 World Series victory in the Yankee Stadium clubhouse, I seem to recall a member of the media saying "Steve" had won the MVP Award, along with Guerrero and Cey. Garvey, jumping up and down, was wrangled for a live TV interview . . . only to find out that they had meant Steve Yeager, not Steve Garvey. Garv was pushed aside to accommodate the other Steve. Somehow it seems only fitting that, in his one chance to taste the fruits of victory, he was asked to go away.

- Steve Garvey is the only player in baseball history to amass six 200-hit seasons, five 100-RBI seasons, and four Gold Gloves.

So why is Garvey the only player to meet the above criteria? I would observe that players who get 200 hits and hit for average typically aren't run producers who hit for much power. And Gold Gloves (which have been awarded since 1957) further narrow the list. The fact that Garvey—and Garvey alone—lays claim to this tri-achievement speaks to his multiple talents.

AND THE VERDICT IS . . .

So is Garvey Hall of Fame-worthy? I think he hurts his cause by stringing together only seven elite seasons. But he also makes up for that with the impressive contributions, outlined above, that he accumulated over an entire career. Even if you make a strong counterargument that Garvey does not belong in the Hall, he should at least be in the company of other very good, "on the cusp" players from his era, many of whom sneaked in toward the end of their eligibility (Gary Carter, Andre Dawson, Jim Rice, and even Bert Blyleven, who amassed only *17.55 percent* of the vote in his first year of eligibility in 1998 before the sabermetric revolution catapulted him above 75 percent in 2011). The fact that Steve never once got over 42.6 percent of the Baseball Writers Association of America votes—and ended with a withering 21 percent in his last year of eligibility—is, to me, the biggest injustice.

No, actually, I take that back. An even bigger injustice is the fact that Dave Concepcion—a lifetime .267-hitting shortstop (.322 OBP) who exceeded 20 errors in a season seven times, but whose legacy was inflated by playing on the Big Red Machine—got even more votes than Garvey when both were first eligible to be voted in by the Hall of Fame's Veterans Committee in December 2010. In an article about this latest Garvey slight, the *Daily News'* Tom Hoffarth couldn't help but pose this headline: "Who

Who Knew?

One of my first jobs in television was as a producer for E! Entertainment Television. During my tenure, my boss had an assistant, an attractive young woman with the last name of Garvey. It wasn't until I left E! that a former coworker told me she was one of Steve's daughters from his marriage to Cyndy. Probably just as well; I'm sure the last thing she would have wanted was someone hounding her with questions about what it was like to be the daughter of my childhood hero while also putting up with annoying interoffice memos about why he belonged in the Hall.

does Garvey have to sleep with to get into the Hall of Fame?" I'm not sure what editor approved this boo-hiss banner, but Hoffarth's point is well-taken. The Veterans Committee has certainly voted in players with far worse stats than the Garv (case in point: Bill Mazeroski).

In sum, Steve Garvey shouldn't have to live up to Superman standards to get into the Hall of Fame. Simply being Steve Garvey should be good enough.

2ND INNING
July-October 1978

Hello, and welcome back to *Homerun Highlights*, part two. The last tape had at least 30 home runs on it. This one and the one after should have more like 50! After this one will be home run tape three, four, and maybe five.

—Paul Haddad, June 21, 1978

Near the midway point of the Dodgers' 1978 season, I had completed one side of my first *Homerun Highlights* tape. Flipping the tape over, I was obviously starting to feel a little cocky about my project, with my bold prediction of 50 more homers in the Dodgers'—and my—near future.

I was determined to see my project through. To hit 50 home runs, I realized, I would have to make a few concessions. The first was to start including homers hit by opposing players. The first ones to make the grade on my tapes were blasts called by Vinny that were high on drama, like this one by Joe Ferguson (then with the Astros—he would be traded back to the Dodgers just a week later):

Hall-of-Fame broadcaster Vin Scully.

The pitch to Ferguson is lifted to right field and deep . . . back goes Lacy, way back, on the track, to the wall—*bangs* against the wall, falls face-forward in the dirt, and it's a home run for Joe Ferguson. And Lacy is *still* down on his hands and knees on the track in right field.

In a way, I'm glad I did start recording homers from opposing players; it provides a broader snapshot of what the baseball landscape was really like in the late '70s and early '80s.

Bullpen Session

Move Over, Mota

When he wasn't falling face-forward on warning tracks, Lee Lacy, as mentioned earlier, was an outstanding role player for the Dodgers and contributed key hits off the bench during his seven years with them. In 1978, he set a major league record when he hit three consecutive pinch-hit home runs.

Lee Lacy always reminded me of Racer X from the *Speed Racer* cartoon series. Strong, silent, enigmatic—the perfect reluctant hero for my childhood. Tommy Lasorda— whose point of reference was a tad older than mine—nicknamed Lacy "Hondo," after John Wayne's reluctantly heroic cavalry rider in the 1953 Western by the same name.

As we dive into the Dodgers' second half, I'd like to take a moment to issue my inaugural "True Blue Ribbon" Mic Award, given to the Dodger broadcaster with the most memorable call each season. These are not the most pivotal plays of the season—just the most exciting to hear on the radio. So roll out the blue carpet . . . and no cameras, please . . . this is all about the voice.

AND THE 1978 "TRUE BLUE RIBBON" MIC AWARD GOES TO . . .

Vin Scully! (I know—shocking.) Even though the Dodgers made it to the World Series in 1978, the greatest call I heard all year came in an innocuous home game against the Cubs on July 26.

The Dodgers were already leading 4–0 in the fourth inning when up stepped Davey Lopes, who hit a home run off pitcher Dave Roberts. Big deal, right? Well, it was for me. It was the first time in my life I had experienced an inside-the-park home run. Sure, that's how most homers are hit in Little League, but it never occurred to me that you could actually do that in the *major* leagues. I was so befuddled by this turn of events, I set up the audio clip by blurting that it was a "home run that is *in the stadium!*"—not quite grasping the terminology yet.

But let's face it, Lopes's round-tripper wouldn't have stood out as much if not for Vin's description. I love this excerpt because it features all the traits of a classic Scully call, with the added bonus of being wrapped up in one of those rare baseball moments, like a triple play or a steal of home. First, he perfectly set up the action:

> Joe Ferguson at second. Bill Russell at first. Four–nothing Dodgers in the fourth.
>
> Davey waiting as Dave Roberts . . . set at the belt. Looks at second, works the plate . . .

The crack of the bat. The crowd crescendoed, and Vinny along with them:

> And there's a drive to center for a base hit. Here comes Ferrrrguson—*and the ball goes aaaaaalll the way through to the waaaaaallll!* Jerry White tried to short-hop it and he came up *empty!*

By then, Vin was caught up in the excitement himself as Davey rounded third:

> Lopes is to third! They're *waaaaaaving* him in! The

throoooow to the plate—here comes *Daveeeeeey* . . .

Notice he didn't get specific about who was waving Davey in—it was just "they"—nor did he even say who was relaying the ball home. This was atypical for Vin, and it said to me that something special was going on, as in, we'll deal with specifics later!

He *scoooooooooooores!*

Not "He's safe!" but, "He scooores!" And then, in classic fashion, Vin shut up—for 32 seconds.

> Time out down on the field. Herman Franks is going out to the mound. Lopes hit a sinking line drive for a base hit into center field. Jerry White tried to short-hop the ball in order to get a throw off to the plate. And he ran right *by* the ball. It went all the way to the center field fence . . .

This clip also demonstrates Vin's lyrical quality of drawing out certain words in an alliterative way. "Aaaaaalll the way through to the waaaaalll" recalls his decades-long template for describing a key hit that clears the bases, as in: "Iiiiiinnnn comes Garvey, iiiiinnnn comes Cey, iiiiinnnn comes Baker on a double by Monday!"

I still feel that, not only is there nothing more thrilling than an inside-the-stadium—er, park home run, but an inside-the-parker the way Lopes hit *his* was even better: a dipping liner under the glove of an outfielder, which turned the whole escapade into a race between the runner jamming for home and an outfielder hustling toward the wall to get the ball back in. Of course, maybe I'd feel differently if Vin weren't behind the mic that first time I heard one!

5-FOR-5
FIVE GAMES THAT DEFINED THE 1978 DODGERS

#3—DODGERS/GIANTS SHOWDOWN
Candlestick Park, August 3, 1978

The Dodgers of '78 were a streaky, frustrating bunch. It seemed like every time they put together a winning streak, they would follow that up with a string of losses. At the end of July, they reeled off five wins in a row to move into a tie for first place for the first time in two months. How did they celebrate? By starting a new losing streak. As the team began a four-game series against the Giants at Candlestick Park, they were mired in a four-game skid, 2½ games behind the Giants, and two behind the second-place Reds. Don Sutton, the staff ace, took the ball to try to stem the bleeding and regain some momentum for the Boys in Blue. This was easily the most important series of the year up to that point.

Sutton had a lot of clutch performances during his Dodger career. This game was not one of them. He got raked for nine hits and four runs in only three innings, and very quickly the Dodgers found themselves in a 4–0 hole amidst a rowdy crowd of 42,084. But the team chipped away as Lance Rautzhan and Charlie Hough shut down a potent San Francisco lineup with five brilliant innings of one-hit relief. Pitcher Jim Barr took a 4–3 lead into the ninth inning and quickly got the first two outs. The Candlestick crowd swelled with anticipation, really giving it to "Dem Bums." Jerry Doggett took it from there:

> So two down now, the Dodgers are down to their last out. It'll be Lee Lacy coming on. Lacy to bat for Hough here in the ninth inning . . . the Giant fans now wanting Barr to get the last out,

> with Davey Lopes due up next. Lee as a pinch-hitter has done very well. Here's the pitch on the way . . .
>
> Fly ball to right-center field. This one might be in the gap. Coming for it is Herndon . . . *and Herndon and Clark collide!* They go down to the ground, we'll see where the ball is. Here's Lacy circling the bases, and Herndon comes up with the ball. Here's Lacy coming to the plate . . . *he's gonna score!* And the ballgame is tied, as the umpire raced out and ruled the ball was *not* in the glove.

I saw this play on TV, too. Center fielder Larry Herndon and right fielder Jack Clark converged on the play, resulting in a pretty brutal collision. I take no joy in saying that future Dodger-killer Jack Clark took the brunt of it, but allow me just to reiterate: Jack Clark took the brunt of it. I mean, he was just clotheslined by Larry Herndon. I seem to recall he was knocked out.

Jerry, you may continue.

> It was *not caught* by Herndon, as Herndon and Clark collided in center field. And Lacy kept running as the two were on the ground . . . they're gonna have to call for help for the two players who are prone on the outfield grass as Clark and Herndon smashed into each other head-on.

At this point, the field was strewn with orange and black personnel congregating like two swarms of bees—one presiding over the incapacitated outfielders, the others around umpire Jim Quick, who ruled that Herndon never had control of the ball.

> And now *Barr* is out arguing, *Evans* is out argu-
> ing—they all claim that the ball was *caught* by
> Herndon. But Herndon and Clark are on the
> ground and they *cannot* offer any *evidence* to it.

The defense rests, Your Honor.

> And Jim Barr is on his *knees*, pleading with the
> umpire, Jim Quick.

Throwing himself at the judge's mercy didn't help Barr. Once it became apparent the call was going to stand and the Dodgers had tied it on an inside-the-park, pinch-hit home run, the crowd shook itself out of its stunned silence and let loose its disapproval. Manager Joe Altobelli got himself ejected. And Jack Clark was carted off the field, to be replaced by Hector Cruz. The Dodgers were fired up. They had set themselves up for the comeback of the year against their bitter rivals.

But someone forgot to tell Terry Forster. With the score tied in the bottom of the ninth, the reliever worked himself into a jam. Darrell Evans laced a single to right field. The usually reliable Reggie Smith had a shot at gunning down the runner from second at home, but he couldn't get a good grip on the ball. Hated Ones 5, Dodgers 4.

This game defined the '78 Dodgers because it was a microcosm for how they played the season—always putting themselves in a hole, always coming back, always teasing us into *believing* as they consistently teetered between success and failure. This contest also seemed to drain the Dodgers' energy. They were dead on arrival the next night against Vida Blue, managing just one hit in eight innings in a 2–1 loss, their sixth loss in a row on the heels of their five-game winning streak.

Naturally, they would start a seven-game win streak the following day.

NOW HEAR THIS: THREE THINGS YOU SHOULD KNOW ABOUT VIN'S PARTNERS

Much of this book is a paean to Vin Scully, but his booth partners Ross Porter and Jerry Doggett were no slouches either. Over the years, I really began to appreciate Porter's craft in particular, even if my father always remarked, "It sounds like he has cotton in his mouth." I was shattered to see the Dodgers cut ties with him in 2004. Here are three things you should know about the "other" guys, who between them broadcast sixty years of Dodger baseball.

ROSS PORTER

1. He's the last announcer in L.A.—and maybe any-where—to use the word "skein" on a regular basis, as in, "Steve Garvey's hitting skein has reached 10 games." For years, I thought he was saying "hitting's game" or slur-ring the word "game." Even these interpretations made little sense to me, but I was unfamiliar with the word "skein." It wasn't until I was an adult that I came across the word in a sports magazine and realized it meant a "series of similar or interrelated things." Others must've shared in my confusion. For the last 10 to 15 years of his Dodger broadcasting career, I can't recall one instance of Ross uttering the word he once used so extensively. Which was a bummer, because now that I knew what it meant, I was looking forward to hearing it! He also had the quirky habit of occasionally describing clubs by at-taching possessives to their cities, like: Chicago's Cubs, Montreal's Expos, and Pittsburgh's Pirates.

2. One of the knocks against Porter, especially in the 1990s, was his overreliance on statistics. Ross was a

peerless researcher who seemed to delight in particularly obscure ones. A typical letter to the editor of the *L.A. Times* would sarcastically drip, "Thanks to Ross Porter, I now know the Dodgers have a 4-2 record against sub-.500 teams on the road on Tuesday nights when Mercury is in retrograde." I've long felt that this criticism was mostly unfair. Baseball, more than any other sport, is a game of numbers. As fans have grown more sophisticated with the advent of fantasy baseball and the rise of sabermetrics, they have come to expect advanced statistical analysis. Ross was always something of an old-school announcer embracing new-school ways, and I always appreciated that. So the real question is this: Did Ross's broadcasts *balance* stats with cogent play-by-play and maintain the equally appealing human element? And did he have a *point* to his stats—in other words, did he frame them in a context that had relevance to the goings-on? While nobody's perfect, more often than not Ross delivered on both accounts.

3. The following home run call is from July 2, 1980, in a game against the Padres at Dodger Stadium.

> 3–2 pitch to Guerrero is a fly ball to left field and hit deep. Richards going back, a-waaaaaaay back . . . on the track . . . at the wall . . . home run, Guerrero!

Sounds like a classic Vin call—only it wasn't. It was just one of many home run calls from the early years of Ross's career in which he emulates Vin's style . . . if Vin were from Oklahoma. (Ross's pronunciation of "back" and "track" have a slight twang.) But I don't think Ross, who was only in his second year of broadcasting for the Dodgers in 1978, ever set out to verbally plagiarize his partner. Just as Vin himself probably picked up a trick or two from Red Barber, his mentor in the booth in Brooklyn, Ross just seemed to know a good thing when he heard it. As a fan, just hearing "a-way back," "warning track," and "wall" in one sentence was enough to increase my pulse rate, regardless of who was saying it. Over the years, Ross's own personal style emerged—yes, including his penchant for obscure facts, like this gem that my buddy Rob remembers from a Dodgers-Pirates game in 1990: "Pittsburgh's Pirates have the word 'Pittsburgh' displayed on their road jerseys for the first time since—would you believe—1952!" Believe it!

JERRY DOGGETT

1. For his entire 32 years (1956 to 1987) as a Dodger broadcaster, Jerry had to play second fiddle to Vin Scully. But there was one thing Jerry announced better than anyone, and that was swinging strikes by opposing batters. Not one for theatrics, Jerry did allow himself to put a little spit 'n' polish on the word "swing" that I always found enjoyable:

   > Here's the 0-2 pitch to Morgan. There's a *swiiiiiiinnng* and a miss—he struck him out!

2. Where Ross and Vin were very specific about the action on the field with crisp descriptions, Jerry's style was more akin to a Harry Carey or Gerry Coleman, with an absent-mindedness that served as a refreshing counterpart to his colleagues (and that reminded me of my grandfather). In the heat of the moment, it was not uncommon to hear him say, "He hit it pretty good there" or, "The right fielder makes a great play," only to

tell you the right fielder's actual name a few seconds later, after he'd had a chance to presumably glance down at his scorecard. My favorite was his occasional oblique way of giving the score going into commercial breaks, like this one against San Diego on July 14, 1980:

> And the score at the end of four: Dodgers 3, the Padres have 4.

Not only did he break protocol by listing the higher number second (typically, an announcer would say it's 4–3, not 3–4), but he switches styles from one to the next, using the shorthand "Dodgers 3," then throwing in a complete sentence for "the Padres have 4." I'm sure both Strunk *and* White are rolling over in their graves.

3. Maybe it's because he shared a booth with Vin, who would make anyone sound humdrum, but the book on Jerry was that he was predictable, staid, and lacking in color. Not true. Like Vin, he too would occasionally break the fourth wall between himself and his listeners—like on this occasion, when

he spotted something unusual in the stands during a late-1980 home game:

> Santa Claus in a blue uniform walking up and down the aisle down the right field area in the lower stands, he's having a good time. [Laughs.] He's got a sack full of goodies he's passing out, too.
>
> Here's the wind-up and the pitch on the way. In a little high, ball one.
>
> My thought is, Tommy Lasorda will go to *any* lengths to get the Dodger image spread around Dodger Stadium. We have the Big Dodger in the Sky, and now we have the Big Dodger in a . . . *blue* Santa Claus uniform. [Laughs.] Let's call the bench and see if Tommy is down there, or if he's in that Santa Claus uniform.
>
> Two balls, no strikes [laughs].
>
> We're only kidding, Tom. You just keep managing down there, babe.

During a May 31, 1981 broadcast in which the Dodgers blew out the Reds, 16–4, his jocularity was again on display. After pitcher Dave Stewart *tripled* (his first major league hit!) to drive home Scioscia to make it 12–4 in the seventh, a weary Doggett sounded downright punch-drunk.

> 2-and-0 the count to . . . [laughs, can't finish the sentence]. Two runs in . . . [trying to contain himself] 12–4 Dodgers.
>
> We're laughing because [laughs] well, we started the day with a little sore throat, so we had seven runs in the third and now

[laughs] they got two runs in the seventh inning. [Chuckles.] Wheeeeew! Out of gas, out of sight!

Note the use of phrases like "out of sight" and "babe" in these two selections as well. Both Ross and Jerry were from the South, but behind Jerry, I believe a Rat Pack hepcat was always waiting to bust out. His awesomely loud plaid suits were another clue. They were always the highlight of Dodger pre-game shows on TV.

5-FOR-5
FIVE GAMES THAT DEFINED THE 1978 DODGERS

#4—DODGER/GIANTS SHOWDOWN, THE SEQUEL
Dodger Stadium, August 10, 1978

On August 4, the Dodgers lost 2–1 to Vida Blue and the Giants, dropping them 4½ back. One week later, the Dodgers improbably narrowed the gap to a single game as they prepared for a four-game rematch with the Giants, this time at Chavez Ravine. Unfortunately, the team was seeing Blue—as in Vida—for the first game. The Giants' ace came in with a 16–4 record and a 2.45 ERA. The Dodgers countered with 21-year-old rookie Bob Welch, who shut out the Giants in his last start for his first major league complete game. Was it a fluke? At stake were redemption against Blue and the chance to move into a tie for first place, all in front of 50,990 fans. No pressure or anything . . .

Any hope of Welch pitching back-to-back shutouts ended three batters in, when Jack Clark hit his 19th home run deep to left field to put the Giants up, 1–0. You could almost hear the crowd's groans through the radio. Fortunately for the Dodgers,

Reggie Smith picked that day to have his best game of the season. He began it with a two-run home run in the bottom of the first, then followed that up with another two ribbies in the fourth inning that effectively chased Vida out of the game. Vida's totals: seven runs, nine hits, three walks, and two strikeouts in 3⅓ innings.

The hit parade continued against the Giants' relievers—Garvey coming up a home run short of the cycle—but Reggie always seemed to be in the middle of things. He finished the game 4-for-5, with a home run, three runs, and five RBIs. By the seventh it was a blow-out, and Lasorda put in the scrubs to play out the game. Meanwhile, Welch was pitching another gem—a five-hitter through eight innings. Since his call-up from the minors on June 20, he had shown spurts of greatness that would portend big things for him as a reliever come October.

With their 12–2 drubbing of the Giants, the Dodgers moved into a tie with San Francisco for first place at 67–48, a half-game ahead of the Reds. The Giants were never really the same. Their record after that loss was 22–25, resulting in a third place finish. Except for one day when they fell out of first, L.A. led its division the rest of the way. As the next couple weeks would reveal, their biggest battle would be not the Giants, or even the Reds—but themselves.

OUR REGGIE WAS PRETTY GOOD, TOO

Their Reggie hit five home runs in the 1977 World Series. Our Reggie hit three.

Their Reggie was the self-proclaimed "straw that stirs the drink." Our Reggie once said, "I don't concern myself with what people say about Reggie Smith."

Their Reggie had a candy bar named after him. Our Reggie once gamely autographed the inside of a Dodger Dog wrapper for yours truly.

Their Reggie once got into a fight with his own manager in the dugout. Our Reggie climbed into the stands at Candlestick to beat up a belligerent Giants fan who later got arrested.

Two Reggies—born a year apart, both with long, productive careers that overlapped for 16 of them. Jackson is obviously the better known, a Hall of Famer who had transcendent moments that Americans love in their athletes: the three-homer game in the '77 Series; the prodigious moon shot in the '71 All-Star Game; the way he stood at the plate to admire his home runs (he was Barry Bonds years before Barry Bonds). Even his strikeouts were larger than life—physics-defying torque-fests in which his twisted trunk, facing backwards, seemed to end up on someone else's legs, crisscrossed in an "X" that resembled the limbs of Mister Salty.

From a public image standpoint, you couldn't find two more diametrically opposed players. But a closer look at their career statistics shows them to be more similar than you might think, with Smith actually coming out ahead in several categories. Here's a comparison of their 162-game averages.

Reggie Vs. Reggie—162-Game Average

	AB	R	2B	HR	RBI
Reggie Smith	573	92	30	26	89
Reggie Jackson	567	89	27	32	98

	BB	SO	AVG.	OBP	SLG.
Reggie Smith	73	84	.289	.366	.489
Reggie Jackson	79	149	.262	.356	.490

Both played right field, but Smith was the better defensive player, a Gold Glove winner with great range and a cannon for an arm. The switch-hitter also hit for a higher average and had better plate discipline, with a solid .366 OBP over his 17-year career. Another area where the Reggies differ: strikeouts. For all his power, Smith never fanned more than 95 times a single season, and only three times struck out more than 80.

Jackson? As you might expect for MLB's strikeout leader, he had his share of 100-plus strikeout seasons—18, to be exact, including five seasons in which he led the league. On paper, the only area in which Jackson clearly exceeded Smith was in power, and not even by a large margin. (Stolen bases are negligible.)

If I were to start a baseball team now and could only pick one of the Reggies in his prime, I'd have to go with Mr. Smith, just for his sheer versatility. So why is Jackson a first-ballot Hall of Famer, while Smith is pretty much relegated to the bargain bin of great players?

For starters, once Reggie Jackson got labeled with the nickname "Mr. October" in a large media market like New York, the Cooperstown gang was already picking out a wall on which to display his plaque. The only way Jackson could've screwed it up is if he had fallen off a cliff to finish out his career. To his credit, he not only didn't wither, he excelled. During the 1980 season, Jackson turned 34. He would go on to hit 186 homers from age 34 onward, finishing with 563 career homers and an automatic ticket into the Hall.

Reggie Smith turned 34 in 1979. He became even more injury-prone after that point, and never tallied more than 350 at-bats again in a single season, finally calling it a career in 1982. His home run total from age 34 onward was 44—just three more homers than Jackson had in his age-34 season alone. Like his teammate, Garvey, Smith simply didn't finish strong. Had he been productive throughout his thirties like Jackson—even with a 10 to 20 percent drop-off in performance—the two Reggies unquestionably would've been Hallmates. Ah, but that's one of the great joys of baseball, isn't it? The eternal game of "What If . . . "

Back to reality. Reggie enjoyed what was arguably the second-best season of his career for the 1978 Dodgers, his best being the year before, when he had an OPS of over 1.000. He would finish fourth in the MVP balloting in both 1977 and 1978.

Like many power hitters, Reggie often hit his homers in bunches, but that particular year, he set the gold standard for streakiness. From July 17–22, Reggie hit six home runs in six games. What does a guy like that do for an encore? How about try it again?

On August 12, the Dodgers were embroiled in another intense four-game series against the Giants, this time at home. As previously mentioned, Reggie came up huge in the first game. Two nights later, Vinny was behind the mic when Reggie stepped into the batter's box against Bob Knepper.

> Giants 2, Dodgers nothing, bottom of the fourth. Knepper into a windup . . . the 2-0 pitch to Reggie is lifted to left-center field. Back goes Herndon, on the track, to the wall . . . it's gone.
>
> [Twenty-five seconds of crowd noise.]
>
> A twenty-dollar book of Union Oil Auto Script to the Inner-Community Exceptional Children's Home in Long Beach.* And that makes it 2–1 in favor of the Giants. For Reggie Smith, he's hit four home runs . . .

At this point, Vin stopped mid-sentence. In the background, you could hear the Dodger Stadium crowd booing. I'm not sure what prompted what happened next, but this being a

---

* Raise your hand if you remember the Union Oil Auto Script plugs after Dodger home runs. I'll list some of the charities the oil company supported for every Dodger home run later in the book.

Dodger-Giant series—and the Giants ensuring a tie for first place with a win—I wouldn't be surprised if Giant manager Joe Altobelli was behind it.

> The plate umpire, Andy Olsen, went over and inspected Reggie Smith's *bat* after that home run . . . found it was perfectly legal.

Questioning Reggie's integrity only seemed to fuel his fire. The next night, he jacked two more home runs against the Giants, including one that tied the game, though the Dodgers lost in extra frames. But Reggie's rampage wasn't done. In the Dodgers' next game, in Philadelphia, Reggie smacked another long ball and hit a game-winning sacrifice fly. The following night, with a scoreless tie in the fourth, Ross Porter called the action as Reggie dug in with the bases loaded against the Phil's Jim Kaat:

> Smith hit a line drive to right fielder Bake McBride for the final out in the first inning. Reggie hit his 10th career home run here at Veterans Stadium last night. That was from the left side.
>
> Kaat's first pitch to Reggie is a change-up high.
>
> The only men who have hit more home runs in this stadium, from opposing teams: Dave Kingman and Willie Stargell, 12 apiece, and Johnny Bench, 11.

A quick aside—this is classic Ross, for better or for worse (naturally, I vote "for better"). In a time and age when a player's splits and home/away stats were rarely invoked, let alone known by the general public, it was refreshing to get this "inside baseball" information from someone who played to diehard fans' obsession with numbers. And I would like to point out he's not just showing off his knowledge of obscure stats here. Ross's point, by bringing up Kingman, Stargell, and Bench, is to show what exclusive company Reggie is in now.

Reggie waiting. 1-and-0. Kaat at the belt. The pitch. Breaking ball, a high drive to center field. Maddux going back . . . a-way back . . . to the warning track, to the wall. It's a *grand slam home run!*

Reggie Smith rips his *sixth* home run in *six games*—the third grand slam home run of his major league career. The first in the National League—the other two were with the Boston Red Sox—and the Dodgers lead four-to-nothing.

So there you have it. In the span of 30 days, Reggie had not one, but *two* six-game skeins (thanks, Ross!) in which he hit six homers. That's 12 home runs in a 12-game span—or 41 percent of his total homers for the *season*—including four against the Giants, and two apiece against those beasts from the East, Philadelphia and Pittsburgh. Both streaks included one 2-HR game and four 1-HR games. After a couple streaks like that, I guess I, too, would've inspected his bat if I were an opposing team's manager—not to see if it was illegal, but to find out the make and model so I could order others like it for my players.

Reggie, it turned out, would play a part in the final defining game of the 1978 season, even if it was indirectly.

5-FOR-5
FIVE GAMES THAT DEFINED THE 1978 DODGERS

#5—THE BRAWL
Shea Stadium, August 20, 1978

For a team rife with strife, the events of August 20 were no less shocking to us Dodger fans. The Dodgers of the Walter O'Malley era were the anti-Yankees. Airing one's dirty laundry simply wasn't a part of the Dodger Way. But prior to a game with the New York

Mets at old Shea Stadium, the Blue Crew momentarily turned into the crosstown Bronx Bombers. Clubhouse resentment over Steve Garvey had flared periodically ever since Garvey's arrival on the national stage in 1974, and on this particular day, it became a five-alarm fire.

From a fan's perspective, I hadn't even realized there was a problem until the next night. The Dodgers were preparing to play the Montreal Expos on ABC's *Monday Night Baseball* game of the week. During the broadcast—I believe it was part of the pre-game show—the announcers broke the news that Steve Garvey and Don Sutton had engaged in a clubhouse brawl prior to the previous day's game against the Mets. *Wait a minute*, I remember thinking. *Did he say Steve Garvey? A fight? My Steve Garvey? And against his own teammate? Come again?*

Sure enough, the producers cut to a pre-taped interview with Steve in which he addressed a scuffle he had had with Don Sutton. I'll never forget that image of Steve looking into the lens, his eye bloodied by an errant Sutton finger. It was hard to see my hero like that. For the first time, he appeared fallible and small. It reminded me of footage you'd see of American hostages overseas forced to endorse their captors on camera. Sutton, by contrast, did not have any visible bruises or scratches on his face. I found myself mentally defending Garvey: *Steve Garvey would never resort to scratching someone . . . that's how girls fight.* My rationalization was the only way I could preserve the Garvey Mystique—he was a martyr who wouldn't stoop to underhanded tactics.

The next day, I got into my own altercation over Garvey's fight. While riding my bike up our street, a neighbor kid named Jered, whose sole purpose in life seemed to be to mock anything I liked, took particular delight in the fact that Garvey had seemed to "lose" the fight, given that he had a visible injury and Sutton didn't.

Jered rode by on his bike, deriding Garvey in an obscene chant. There was never any point in trying to reason with Jered. He was a Giants fan.

So how did Reggie Smith fit into the Garvey-Sutton scrap? In an interview with the *Washington Post* several days before, Sutton had invoked his name to make a point about Steve Garvey:

> The best player on this team for the last two years —and we all know it—has been Reggie Smith. Reggie doesn't go out and publicize himself. He doesn't smile at the right people or say the right things. Reggie's not a façade or a Madison Avenue image. He's a real person.

According to numerous sources, Garvey confronted Sutton about the quotation before the Mets game. Sutton didn't deny it. The argument turned personal and escalated into a full-blown scuffle, both players rolling around on the clubhouse floor before players could pull them apart. I'll say this for Garvey: even though he apparently knew of the article for days, in typical people-pleasing fashion, he waited for Sutton to complete his last start before confronting him. And I'll say this for Sutton: at least he didn't hide behind anonymous quotes, as some Garvey bashers had done throughout the years. Still, having to now take the field with a newly scratched cornea, Garvey clearly got the raw end of the deal. On the flip side, he would have to be inhuman not to carry a little extra adrenaline into this August 20th game. And, as he so often did throughout his career, Garvey shone brightest under the glare of a spotlight.

Down 2–1, Steve singled home the tying run with two outs in the sixth. The Mets pulled ahead with a run in the seventh and one more in the eighth to take a 4–2 lead into the ninth. But Garv got a rally going with a single to left, then eventually scored the tying run on a Lee Lacy sacrifice fly. The Dodgers scratched out one more run to go up, 5–4. Terry Forster escaped a two-on, no-out jam in the bottom of the ninth inning to earn his 16th save.

A few days after the fight, I can recall a choked-up Sutton going before the cameras and reading from a prepared statement.

He did not publicly apologize to Steve Garvey, but he did, curiously, thank Garvey in a roundabout way for the role he played in teaching Don a valuable life lesson:

> I thank God for Steve Garvey and the role God has let him play him my life, and now I can thank him for the *Washington Post* article and for the disagreement in New York. Together they have helped to point out to me very vividly that as long as my life isn't right, then I can't be a good example for anyone.

The Garvey-Sutton saga hardly rivaled that of, say, Reggie Jackson versus Billy Martin in the Bronx. But maybe a page out of a championship team's playbook was just what the team needed. Even the Oakland team that beat the Dodgers in 1974 was as dysfunctional as they come. While the Dodgers were able to avoid more embarrassing sideshows, they did prove that you don't have to love one another to win. Case in point: In Sutton's next start, Garvey hit a homer and drove in three runs. The Dodgers won, 6–5.

DODGERS CLINCH; PORTER MISSES AN ARTICLE

I wasn't able to record the Dodgers clinching their second

National League West division title, but I can still vividly hear how it sounded on the radio at our kitchen table. Playing a three-game series at home against the Padres, the team secured at least a tie with a 5–3 victory at home on Saturday, September 23. The next day was a Sunday day game. Bob Welch pitched them into the NLCS with a five-hit shutout. With two outs in the top of the ninth and the Dodgers leading 4–0, Barry Evans hit a hard liner to left field that hung in the air. Ross Porter was behind the microphone, and as the ball made its way to Dusty Baker's glove, Ross blurted out:

> Baker coming up . . . *Dodgers win division!*

For whatever reason, Ross lapsed into what I call "head-line speak" and dropped "the" from in front of "division" (and "Dodgers," for that matter). Perhaps he was just caught up in the excitement, or rushed the call in order to complete it before Baker snagged the liner. Either way, Ross's omission of an article made it more memorable; here I am, talking about it more than 30 years later.

RABBIT SEASON, DUCK SEASON, POSTSEASON

The last month of the 1978 season was notable for two major events—one was on September 15, when the Los Angeles Dodgers became the first team in major league history to reach three million fans in attendance. The other, of course, was the day they clinched the division. However, the team didn't exactly build up a head of steam going into the playoffs, losing five of their last six. Given their tumultuous season, their subsequent letdown was almost understandable.

None of that mattered once the National League Championship Series began against the Phillies, winners of the Eastern division (back when there were only two divisions and no wild card). In front of 63,460 raucous fans in Philadelphia, L.A. took Game

1 of the Best-of-Five Series, 9–5, behind huge games from Garvey (two HRs, a triple, four RBIs, three runs), Lopes (one HR, a double, two RBIs), and pitcher Bob Welch (4⅓ innings of two-hit ball in relief of another shaky October outing from Hooton, this time surrendering four runs and 10 hits in less than five innings). The next two games, which the teams split, were similar one-sided affairs. Game 4 at Dodger Stadium was the first nail-biter of the series and went into overtime, tied 3–3. The bottom of the 10th inning lives on in Dodgers lore. With two outs, Ron Cey drew a walk against Tug McGraw. That brought on Dusty Baker, who hit a fly ball to center field that Garry Maddox, a perennial Gold Glover, appeared to lose in the sun (a similar play would plague Matt Holliday of the Cardinals during the 2009 National League Division Series). The ball glanced off his glove for an error, setting up a potential game-winning and series-clinching single by Bill Russell. Vin with the call:

> And there's a little dunker to center . . . base hit!
> Here comes Cey . . . Maddox doesn't have a play.
> The Dodgers *win* the pennant!

This was one of the few recordings I was able to capture in September. Not coincidentally, my audio archives pretty much stopped once I started seventh grade at a private school called Brentwood. The prospect of sitting down to produce and edit Dodger game highlights after three hours of homework every weeknight suddenly felt like . . . more homework. Once free to pursue my Dodger fandom with total abandon, I now glimpsed my future as a young adult, only to find it a hazy shade of blue.

Fortunately, I was energized by the World Series—another rematch with the New York Yankees—and made a concerted effort to revive my recordings using a new, novel medium. Just a year earlier, my dad had purchased our radio-cassette recorder. This year, he came home with another newfangled gadget called a video cassette recorder. It was an enormous Sony Betamax and weighed about as much as a fireproof safe. My brother used it primarily to record R-rated movies off Z Channel (a subscription movie channel, now defunct but much beloved by L.A. natives), while I started recording old Warner Brothers cartoons and snippets of televised Dodger games, often on the same tape.

Using a logic sprung from my twelve-year-old mind, I still equate the Dodgers of 1978 with a classic *Merrie Melodies* trilogy from the early 1950s that most are familiar with: "Rabbit Fire," "Rabbit Seasoning," and "Duck! Rabbit! Duck!" featuring Bugs Bunny, Daffy Duck, and Elmer Fudd. Something about Elmer constantly shooting Daffy, juxtaposed with Dodger games on the same VHS tape, formed an unconscious link between the two, though I'm sure a hunting sign played for laughs at the end of "Duck! Rabbit! Duck!" that read "Baseball Season" (instead of "Duck Season" or "Rabbit Season") had something to do with it.

The Dodgers of '78 were like Elmer Fudd. *They* were the hunters. All season long the Dodgers/Elmer took care of business by blowing the beaks off their opponents. Garry Maddox was the biggest Daffy Duck of all. His drop of that Dusty Baker fly ball in the NLCS was the equivalent of that scene where Daffy gets buckshot in his beak and dizzily croaks, "No more for me, thanks, I'm driving," before keeling over.

The first two games of the World Series continued the Dodgers' role as hunters. In a reversal of the '77 World Series, this time it was the Dodgers who went up, two games to none. The local angle was that they were inspired by the recent death of longtime Dodger great Jim Gilliam. In the history of the Series, only six teams had come back from 2–0 deficits to win the championship. It was now open season on the Yankees. Before the series was over, their beaks would be blown to smithereens.

But we all know that's not how the script ends.

A cruel twist of fate befell the Dodgers, just as it did Elmer Fudd in "Rabbit Fire." In the final seconds of that short, Elmer turns his gun on Daffy. In desperation, Daffy rips down a "Duck

Season" sign from a tree to reveal a "Rabbit Season" sign underneath. Bugs, in turn, tears down the "Rabbit Season" sign to reveal a "Duck Season" sign. Back and forth they go, trying to convince Elmer that it's actually *this* season or *that* season, until finally they reveal a sign that says: "Elmer Season." Stunned, the huntees turn around and train their sights on Elmer, who utters a meek "uh-oh" before running for dear life. The cartoon ends with Daffy and Bugs firing on the fleeing Fudd, stopping only to tell the viewer: "Shhh . . . be vewy, vewy quiet . . . we're hunting Elmers. Heh heh heh heh heh."

In Game 3 of the World Series, the Dodgers' season turned into Elmer Season. It seemed to come so suddenly, so out of the blue—but once it did, there was no stopping Daffy's revenge (with a little help from Bugs).

In keeping with the Elmer hunting trilogy, I offer my own trilogy of *Merrie Melodies* "shorts" that best sum up the 1978 World Series and turned the Dodgers from hunters to the hunted. Games 2, 3, and 4 provided all the source material I'd need.

EPISODE 1—"REGGIE SEASON"
Air date: October 11, 1978
Starring: Bob Welch, Reggie Jackson, and the Penguin

Synopsis: In this, Game 2 of the World Series, Ron Cey was a one-man wrecking crew and drove in all the runs in a win at Dodger Stadium. But the real drama came in the ninth inning. With the Dodgers up 4–3, the Yankees got two runners on base with one out against Terry Forster. Tommy Lasorda made a bold move in summoning 21-year-old fireballer Bobby Welch to face Thurman Munson and Reggie Jackson. Welch got Munson to fly out. That set up a battle for the ages—one that, 30 years later, still warranted inclusion among Dodger fans as one of the Top 50 moments in Los Angeles Dodger history.

Welch had only three major-league saves under his belt. Reggie was Mr. October. The at-bat lasted seven minutes but seemed to defy time. Welch threw all fastballs. If Reggie was going to beat him, it would be against his best pitch—heat versus heat. Jackson took a rip at four of them, fouling them off. After each blistering foul, he contorted his face and stalked around the box, muttering to himself.

As the count went full, I could feel the electricity from Dodger Stadium through my TV. I'm pretty sure I suffered a small stroke during this at-bat. Outfielder Bill North later compared the battle to the final round of a heavyweight fight, both fighters giving it their all.

Finally, on the ninth pitch, with the runners going, someone blinked. Joe Garagiola on NBC:

Struck him out! Ball game is over!

Untwisting himself from his Mr. Salty stance, Reggie stormed off the field in a rage, cursing and spitting. Daffy had been denied once again . . . but barely. The battle had exhausted Elmer, and he was out of "buwwets." He just didn't know it yet.

EPISODE 2—"FUDD'S DUD"
Air date: October 13, 1978
Starring: Ron Guidry and Graig Nettles's glove

Synopsis: The series shifted to the Bronx for Game 3. The last time the Dodgers had visited Yankee Stadium, Reggie Jackson was rewriting the offensive record books in the Yankees' series-clinching victory. This time, defense was the difference. Of course, it didn't hurt that the Yanks had their best starter on the mound. Ron Guidry was coming off one of the most dominant seasons ever for a pitcher (25–3, 1.74 ERA), and the Yankees got two runs for him early. Still, Don Sutton kept it close. In the third, the

Dodgers pushed across one run and had a chance to tie it if not for an amazing play by third baseman Graig Nettles, who made a belly-flopping smother of a shot down the third-base line and threw out Reggie Smith at first.

First-base coach Jim Lefebvre summed up our frustrations when Chris Chambliss flipped him the ball after recording the put-out. You could see Jim bob his head violently, like, "Damn!" In the fifth, Nettles made a nifty play on a Reggie Smith line-drive to keep the tying run from possibly scoring, and then with two outs and the bases loaded, he robbed Steve Garvey of a base hit with a sort of whirlybird pick to force the runner at second.

The Dodgers could have easily gone up 3–2 in this inning. In the sixth, they loaded the bases yet again. With two outs, Davey Lopes hit a bullet down the line. Another smothering stop by Nettles, another force-out at second, another two runs saved. ("I don't believe it!" announcer Tom Seaver yelped. "It's unbelievable the plays he's made behind the Yankees' pitching staff!" Tony Kubek: "He saves two runs!")

This can't be happening, I remember thinking every time Nettles leapt up with dirt on his uniform, holding the ball. *It's like there's a magnet in his glove . . . the ball is finding him!*

At the end of six, our hearts said 5–2 Dodgers, but the scoreboard still read 2–1 Yankees. L.A. didn't score any more runs the rest of the game, but New York added three more to win, 5–1. The Dodgers' deflated body language suggested that, if Elmer Season hadn't officially begun, the placards were at least starting to get nailed to the trees.

EPISODE 3—"HIP HIP HARE-RAY"
Air date: October 14, 1978
Starring: Reggie Smith, Thurman Munson,
and Reggie Jackson's hip

Synopsis: If you were to teach a course on classic literature and had to define "turning point," you couldn't ask for a better example than the infamous "hip-and-run play" in the sixth inning of Game 4. One could make a good argument that the true turning point was actually the day before, when Nettles's defense changed the complexion of the series.

But the Dodgers still led the series with a chance to reclaim their roles as hunters. In the fifth inning, they appeared to do just that, as Reggie Smith belted a three-run homer to put L.A. up, 3–0, teasing us with visions of a 3–1 series edge with the two final games back home. But the *other* Reggie had us right where he wanted us. In the bottom of the sixth, the daffy Yankees pulled off one of the most exasperating and despicable innings in the history of Dodgerdom. With two on and one out, Jackson singled in the Yankees' first run. The next batter was Lou Piniella, who hit a line drive to shortstop Bill Russell. Russell, perhaps getting too cute, appeared to purposely drop the line drive in order to step on second and finish the double play at first. What happened next threw NBC announcers Tony Kubek and Joe Garagiola for a loop:

> Tony: . . . Hit right at Russell, and he dropped the ball. Are they gonna get two? Ohhhh—he threw it away! Did it hit Reggie?
>
> Joe: It hit Reggie!
>
> Tony: There's *confusion* on the bases. Here comes Munson, he's gonna score for the second run. There's a lot of confusion. The ball hit Russell's glove. It then hit the

> ground. Reggie Jackson was forced out
> . . . on the throw to first base, they are
> saying that the ball hit Reggie. It is a com-
> plicated play because Reggie is out. Here it
> is, Joe . . .

Read—I'm not sure what happened. Joe, bail me out, will ya?

> Joe: [Watching the replay] Now there's the
>   force on Jackson right there. So Jackson's
>   out on the play, and it *hits* him, he's right
>   in line. And Jackson is *thoroughly confused*,
>   he's still at first base, he doesn't know *what*
>   to do.

Note three uses of the word "confused" and one "complicated." It's really not that complicated. Reggie cheated, plain
and simple. Replays conclusively showed him jutting his hip out
to deflect Russell's throw. Of course, it's only cheating if you're
caught, and in front of 56,445 amped up New Yorkers, the umps
folded their arms. Steve Garvey was closest to Reggie when he
hip-checked the ball and was aghast at the lack of interference
call. He was so busy crying foul to the umps that he neglected to
chase down the errant ball, which allowed Munson to score from
second. Lasorda also came out to argue the non-call, spewing to-
bacco juice on the ump as he cried runner interference, which
would've resulted in the third out of the inning.

But the play stood. Russell was charged with a throwing error, allowing the second run to score. The Yankees tied the game
in the eighth inning, after which the Dodgers plunked Reggie
Jackson with a pitch as if to get one final shot in. In the 10th,
Reggie keyed a rally against Bob Welch, and the Yankees won,
4–3.

The Dodgers were toast. The Yankees outscored them in
the final two games, 19–4, becoming the first team in World

Series history to sweep four games after being down two games to none. (Ironically, if just a couple plays from games three and four had gone their way, it's not so outlandish to think that the Dodgers could've swept the Yankees in four straight.) And so, for the second year in a row, Reggie Jackson thumbed his nose at the Dodgers and lived up to his Mr. October nickname, this time relying more on his brains than his brawn. And for the second year in a row, the Dodgers experienced a crushing defeat in six games to the Yankees. The results may have been the same, but one thing was different. This year, I kept a stiff upper lip and, proudly, did not cry.

I was too numb.

3RD INNING
April-September 1979

I f the 1978 season ended like a familiar Warner Brothers cartoon, 1979 was the equivalent of a horrendous one-car accident in the fast lane of the freeway. As spectators, all we could do was slow down and take in the damage of this once beautiful sports car, clucking our tongues and shaking our heads, yet strangely riveted as we wondered how all this twisted wreckage came to pass. After all, the team's starting eight was exactly the same as last year's. In addition to leading the league in homers (183) and RBIs (713), L.A. would have five players hit 20 or more home runs. Lead-off hitter Davey Lopes had a career year. Forty-one-year-old Manny Mota hit .357 off the bench. And they could certainly field and throw (well, except maybe for Bill Russell), committing the second-fewest errors in the National League. For a cause of the crash, look no further than pitching and injuries.

THE PLAYERS

During the offseason, Tommy John, an anchor in the starting rotation, signed a lucrative three-year deal with the Yankees (did it *have* to be the Yankees?). The Dodgers attempted to replace him

Davey Lopes doing what he did best—getting dirty.

with the cheaper Andy Messersmith, who hadn't won a major league game since 1977. He would finish an injury-shortened season at 2–4 with a 4.91 ERA and retire at the end of the year. Tommy John? He went 21–9 with a 2.96 ERA and finished second in Cy Young voting. That's a major ouch. At least Andy could take comfort in knowing he wasn't as bad as the normally reliable Doug Rau, who went 1–5 with a 5.30 ERA before he too essentially called it a career with a torn rotator cuff on his pitching shoulder.

Injuries like these forced a young Bob Welch into the rotation, but he was suffering from a sore elbow and his own demons; he would check himself into alcohol rehab when the season ended. Also pressed into the starting rotation was Charlie Hough. The good news was, he was healthy. The bad news was, he was healthy. The veteran knuckleballer walked about as many as he struck out and put up a 4.76 ERA, a full run higher than his 25-year career average. Meanwhile, closer Terry Forster was beset by arm problems and threw in the towel in early August after chalking up just two saves.

With relievers called into the starting rotation and the loss of their fireman, the Dodgers bullpen was a patchwork of untested rookies and journeymen veterans whose names were almost impossible to keep track of. Three of the pitchers—Gerry Hannahs, Lerrin LaGrow, and Dave Patterson—remain so unfamiliar to me that if you were to ask me if they were Dodger pitchers or Las Vegas showmen, I would probably vote "Vegas." But it wasn't all bad. Starting pitcher Rick Sutcliffe (17–10, 3.46) won Rookie of the Year honors, and Hooton had one of his better years (2.97 ERA).

General manager Al Campanis's shrewdest move during the off-season may have been his trade of Rick Rhoden to the Pittsburgh Pirates for Jerry Reuss. The big lefty started in the bullpen but became a fixture in the starting rotation. His ugly 7–14 record belied a decent 3.54 ERA, and he would figure prominently in the Dodgers' success in 1980 and 1981. Still, the team's ERA of 3.83—which would be pretty good nowadays—ranked seventh in the twelve-team National League. Worse, the pitching staff gave up more runs per game and more bases on balls than all but two teams in the National League—a shocking development for a team so rich in pitching tradition.

While the offense picked up some of the slack, the team's position players were equally snakebit. Nagging injuries had dogged right fielder Reggie Smith in 1978, but that was nothing compared to '79, when various ailments limited him to 68 games. Center fielder Rick Monday, batting .303, blew out his Achilles tendon the first week of May and was done for the season. Losing both for extended periods of time exposed the Dodgers' lack of depth. The team had replenished their role players during the off season, but the only significant contributors were Gary Thomasson (.248, 14 HR) and uber-utility man Derrel Thomas, who played the majority of games in center field. Otherwise, the likes of Von Joshua, Ted Martinez, and a green Pedro Guerrero and Mickey Hatcher hardly struck fear in their opponents.

Here's how the starting lineup looked on opening day:

- **2B Davey Lopes**—In his age 34 season, Lopes was a stud. He darn near had a 30/30 season with 44 stolen bases (only 4 CS) and 28 home runs. Not bad for a guy listed at five foot nine and 170 pounds in his playing days. By the way, he should've finished with 29 home runs, not 28. I distinctly remember a game at the old Houston Astrodome where he hit a ball above the orange "home run" line, but didn't get the call. It still bothers me . . .

- **SS Bill Russell**—Russell showed some surprising pop (a career-high seven home runs) but for a number-two hitter, his 24 walks and .297 OBP in 153 games were nothing to write home about, and his 30 errors marked the second year in a row he hit that ignominious number.

- **RF Reggie Smith**—Losing a five-tool (okay, 4½ tool) player for much of the season was a big blow for the team. If Smith had stayed healthy, the Dodgers easily would have had six guys (maybe seven, with a healthy Monday) with 20 or more home runs. As it was, Reggie hit 10.

- **1B Steve Garvey**—Tied with fellow infielders Cey and Lopes for the team lead in home runs with 28. By now, we had come to expect .300/200/100/20/162 (average/hits/RBIs/homers/games) from Steve every season. Once again, he'd deliver.

- **3B Ron Cey**—The Penguin quietly had another All-Star year, hitting .281 with an .888 OPS. His nine errors would be a career low for a full season.

- **LF Dusty Baker**—Dusty got his power groove back in 1979, with 23 HRs and 88 RBIs. Bakersfield fans were stoked.

- **CF Rick Monday**—You never want to pin your season's hopes on Rick Monday, but combined with Reggie's prolonged absence—and the team's lack of depth in the outfield—cracks in the Dodgers' foundation were starting to show.

- **C Steve Yeager**—Together, Yeager and Joe Ferguson split the catching duties and hit 33 home runs with 110 RBIs. While Yeager was superior defensively, Fergie's 20 home runs and .380 OBP (second among starting players) were welcome surprises.

From an archival standpoint, I was hit by a triple whammy in '79 that hindered me in keeping a consistent audio diary of the Dodgers' season, though the team's lackluster performance was the main factor in my flagging efforts. For most of April, I was indisposed due to after-school, crash-course cramming for my upcoming bar mitzvah. So while I really wanted to be studying box scores, I was stuck boning up on a little thing called the Torah.

The team then hit a serious wall in June, about the same time I did with my first-ever experience with final exams. Finally, in late July, as the Dodgers' record dipped 20 games under .500, I was spirited away to sleepaway camp at Calamigos Ranch for five interminable weeks. It all put a serious dent in my *Homerun Highlights* plans for 1979.

Yes, the '79 season was a wreck. So, like any good traffic cop, allow me to say we're gonna move this chapter along, folks . . . and keep the rubbernecking to a minimum.

5-FOR-5
FIVE GAMES THAT DEFINED THE 1979 DODGERS

#1—OPENING DAY
Dodger Stadium, April 5, 1979

It may seem odd to include the team's home opener as one of five games that summed up the season, but the way this game played out set the tone for the entire season. Junkballer Gaylord Perry, coming off a Cy Young-winning season at age 39, started for the Padres and blanked the Dodgers through 6⅔ innings before a two-run homer by Ron Cey tied it up, 2–2. In the eighth, the Dodgers went ahead on a clutch two-out single by Bill Russell. Starter Burt Hooton got into trouble in the ninth, so Tom

Lasorda called on the bullpen to preserve a 3–2 lead. Typically, this was where Terry Forster and his hard throwing slider would save the day. But with Forster on the shelf, that job fell to Lance Rautzhan. The first batter he faced was Kurt Bevacqua, who is probably best known to Dodger fans as the subject of a future epic Lasorda rant in which the manager, responding to accusations by Kurt of poor sportsmanship, claimed the .236 lifetime batter couldn't hit water if he fell out of a boat. Today, Bevacqua was happy to settle for a walk, loading the bases. Gene Richards tied the game on a single, with the go-ahead run being gunned down at home. The next batter was a young Ozzie Smith. Perhaps rattled, Rautzhan promptly uncorked a wild pitch, scoring Bevacqua from third base. Rollie Fingers came on to preserve the Padres' come-from-behind 4–3 win, and the Dodgers hung a nice fat "L" next to their name to start the season.

The team would go on to blow 16 saves this year. While their save percentage (percentage of saves versus blown saves) of 68 percent was about league average, the team had distanced itself from the pack the previous two seasons with percentages that ranked four percent and eight percent better than league average. As for Lance Rautzhan . . . at only 27, he would join a laundry list of Dodger pitchers who would hang up their cleats for good at the end of the year.

5-FOR-5
FIVE GAMES THAT DEFINED THE 1979 DODGERS

#2—SUTTON IS KING OF THE HILL
Riverfront Stadium, May 20, 1979

You know it's a lost season when I have to resort to individual achievements over team efforts to signify a key game. But I would be remiss if I didn't give serious props to Don Sutton somewhere in my book, and this date is as good a place as any. With his 6–4 win over the Cincinnati Reds, the Hall of Famer leapfrogged Don Drysdale to become the all-time Dodgers leader in wins with 210. What he might have lacked in pizzazz, Don made up for in durability and consistency, logging over 200 innings in 20 consecutive non-strike seasons, all but one with double-digit wins. In his 23-year career, his ERA exceed 4.00 only three times, and he never spent a day on the disabled list. By the time he signed with the Astros after the 1980 season (notwithstanding a brief return to the Dodgers in '88 before his arm gave out), "Black & Decker," as he was called, also held the team records for games started, strikeouts, innings pitched, and shutouts.

This latter category, to me, is the most impressive. Sutton had 52 complete-game shutouts for the Dodgers. Think about that for a second. For his career, he notched 58 (10th highest in major league history). To put that in perspective, in the first 13 years of his brilliant career, Roy Halladay had only 58 *complete games* (19 of them shutouts). In this age of strict pitch counts and multimillion dollar investments in pitchers' arms, Roger Clemens, with 46

Who Knew?

In the mid- to late-'70s, Don Sutton made numerous appearances on the celebrity panel for the greatest game show of all-time: *Match Game*. He was usually perched in the top left seat, next to Brett Somers. For someone who so famously chafed against Steve Garvey's slickster vibe, Don came across as somewhat of a slippery character himself. Decked out in quasi-leisure suits with giant fly collars and a gravity-defying man perm, he looked more like a swinger than a pitcher. From a fan's perspective, there was always something rather smarmy about Don. But, clearly, his smart-aleckyness—and his smarts—served him well on the show, which explains why Gene Rayburn and company always brought him back.

Bullpen Session

Best. PA Announcer. Ever.

With apologies to the Yankees' Bob Sheppard, there has been no greater public address announcer in baseball in the last 50 years than John Ramsey of the Dodgers. What Vinny was to the radio booth, Mr. Ramsey (it feels wrong to call him John) was to the PA booth. His booming, stentorian voice can be heard in the background throughout my *Homerun Highlights* tapes. Typically, when a player hit a home run, I didn't cut off the action until Vin had wrapped up what he had to say about that home run. Since Vin always clammed up so the listener could soak in the cheering crowd, that allowed for plenty of time to hear Ramsey announce the next Dodger batter on the radio. Case in point, after a late-game, Reggie Smith home run sent Dodger Stadium into a frenzy:

> Steve. [One-and-a-half-second pause.]
> Garvey. [Three-second pause.]
> First base.

Just hearing those clipped words with that impeccable timing is always enough to send chills down my spine. Like Vinny, Ramsey understood the power of restraint, letting the game sell itself without resorting to the cranked-up cheerleading that is so common today. While Ramsey was no homer, he did play to the fans in more subtle ways. It seemed that the greater the stakes, the longer his pauses between words, as if to really heighten the drama.

I know Yankee fans like to refer to Bob Sheppard as the "voice of God," but to me, Sheppard's gentle timbre sounded more like the soothing voice of your grandfather. Ramsey's voice—guttural, commanding, stolid—sounded straight out of *The Ten Commandments*. He even looked the part. At the stadium, you could often spot Ramsey standing behind home plate, a towering, Orson Wellesian presence with bouncing jowls and specs perched on the edge of his nose as he boomed announcements before Davey Lopes trotted out with the starting lineup.

Speaking of which, I would have to say my favorite part of attending Dodger games in the late '70s and early '80s was the way Ramsey introduced lead-off batter Lopes in the bottom of the first inning. It was a thing of beauty, powerfully deliberate and succinct, with just a hint of drama the way he dipped his monotone pitch for the phrase "second baseman" and raised it ever so slightly on the word "Lopes." Ramsey's fractured haiku always followed the same script:

Leading off.
For your Los Angeles Dodgers.
Number 15.
Second baseman.
The Dodger team captain.
Davey.
Lopes.

Mr. Ramsey died in 1990, but his voice lives on in *Two-Minute Warning*, a forgettable 1976 yarn starring Charlton Heston about a sniper wreaking havoc during a championship football game at the Los Angeles Memorial Coliseum. The game carries an air of credibility due to the fact you can hear him thundering out of the loudspeakers between plays, just as he also did for the then-L.A. Rams. Ramsey also served as the PA Announcer for the Lakers, Kings, USC Trojans, and the California Angels. But it was at Blue Heaven where this deity's voice resonated loudest.

shutouts, may be the last pitcher we'll see to even remotely taste Sutton's career 58.

5-FOR-5
FIVE GAMES THAT DEFINED THE 1979 DODGERS

#3—THE SEVEN-HOMER GAME
Dodger Stadium, May 25, 1979

In an otherwise dreary season, the Dodgers did have one laugher that provided their fans with a momentary reason to celebrate. As luck would have it, I was in attendance, thanks to my father going in on a partial-season ticket package that we would keep through the '84 season.

Future Hall of Famer Tom Seaver started for the Reds, facing Rick Sutcliffe, newly entrenched in the Dodgers' starting rotation. Seaver was runner-up in the NL's Win/Loss Percentage category in 1979, but he was pretty lousy for the first two months.

In the second inning, he gave up two home runs—one to Dusty Baker, the other to pitcher Sutcliffe (who had 17 RBIs in his rookie year at the plate). Manager John McNamara yanked Tom Terrific in the third when he couldn't get anyone out. Rookie Frank Pastore fared even worse. In the fourth inning, three Dodgers—Garvey, Thomasson, and Ferguson—pasted him for home runs, and in the sixth, Thomas and Lopes whacked two more. After six innings, the Dodgers led, 17–2, and poor Pastore saw his ERA balloon from 4.68 to 7.57. By that point, we fans were drunk on the long ball. Seven home runs was not enough. My friend David and I began a chant that took off in our section: "Hit Number Eight! Hit Number Eight!"

Alas, the team never hit another bomb, but their seven home runs did set a Dodger Stadium record. Final score: 17–6, Dodgers, who also collected 20 hits.

For one day, it felt great to be a Dodger fan again. The team pulled within two games of .500 and optimism was in the air. As David said in the parking lot after the game, "Sometimes you just need to see a good old-fashioned whippin'!"

BASEBALL'S DIRTY LITTLE SECRET

Amazingly, despite 23 runs and 34 hits in the Dodgers/Reds contest from May 25, both teams still managed to bring that game in under three hours. By way of contrast, in the year 2000, the Dodgers played a nine-inning game against the Mets in which only 15 runs were scored—and the game lasted four hours and nine minutes. Which begs the question: Why are major league baseball games so long now?

Forget pitching changes, visits to the mound, batters stepping out of the box, increased offense, global warming, or any other reasons the powers that be may trot out. Honestly, are we really going to make the games that much shorter by requiring a pitcher to deliver the baseball within 12 seconds upon receiving the ball? No.

The biggest reason—and the dirty little secret that the commissioner never likes to mention—is the increase in ad time between innings. According to *The Wall Street Journal's* David Biderman, Don Larsen's 1952 perfect game in the World Series contained only 9 minutes and 44 seconds of commercials—a sharp contrast to today's roughly 42 minutes. Combing through the raw footage from my *Homerun Highlights* tapes, I am a struck by how short the commercial breaks still were in the late '70s. Breaks are only one minute in length. Many times these breaks are taken up by a single 60-second Farmer John or Datsun commercial. Then it's right back to the action. End result: late-'70s games regularly clocked in around 2 hours and 25 minutes.

Sometime in the '80s, commercials running during baseball went from 1 minute to 2 minutes and 5 seconds (even longer for postseason) so television could get more ads in. Ka-*ching!* Right there you've just added almost 20 minutes to a nine-inning game. Throw in some of the aforementioned incremental delays like the increase of middle relievers, and it's no surprise that in 2011, 63 regulation Dodger games exceeded the three hour mark. Compare that with 1979, when only 10 regulation Dodger games were over three hours. (In 1978, there were six; in '77, only five.) Unless baseball and the networks work to scale back ad time between innings (don't expect that to happen for . . . well, ever), we'll never see games regularly dip under two and a half hours again. Now that you know the secret, pass it on . . .

EXTRA! EXTRA! DODGERS RULE!

Stop me if this sounds familiar. One of my favorite rituals to this day is turning to the *Los Angeles Times* sports section every morning during baseball season and poring over anything and everything pertaining to the Dodgers. If the Dodgers won the night before, I'll take twice as long to soak everything in.

The Dodgers of 1979 tested my allegiance. But like any True Blue fan, I continued to follow them religiously, even if my team resembled the Atlanta Braves more than a team that had just won back-to-back pennants. (For anyone born after 1980, there was a time when the Braves were synonymous with the word "suckitude." The team lost 92 or more games every year from 1975 to 1979.) Still, it got depressing to open the sports page and read about all the new ways the Dodgers were finding to lose. The solution? In June of that year, I started to create my *own* sports pages in which the Dodgers were steamrolling the rest of the National League and enjoying the type of season I wished they were having all along. I called my newspaper *Baseball Headlines* ('cause, ya know, *Baseball News* was obviously too dry) and emulated the font and layout of the *Times'* sports pages using nothing more than an IBM electric typewriter to create the columns and Sharpie felt pens for the headlines. Not that anyone would ever confuse my homemade job with the sports section of a major metropolitan daily. With uneven columns, no pictures, and coarse, watermarked typing paper from my dad's office stapled together at the corner, it looked more like a newsletter you'd pick up at a new age bookshop than a bona fide newspaper.

But man, oh man, was it cathartic! In my alternate universe, the Dodgers were not perfect, but they somehow always prevailed when it mattered most, usually winning slugfests with scores that resembled football games. Naturally, Steve Garvey was on track for an MVP-type season. And since I was engaging in wish fulfillment, I opened up my pages to other baseball stories. I wrote a long commentary on the downfall of the Oakland Athletics franchise from their early '70s heyday and implored them to move to Denver ("Maybe [owner] Charles O. Finley will take a vacation next year," I opined, "and when he is gone, the team can secretly move to Denver, where attendance could go up with the league, while in Oakland, it was going down by the bay.").* I penned a human-interest piece on Pete Rose under the eyeball-rolling title "Pete Rose: The Stem of the Game" (I don't even know what that means) and another on Davey Lopes under the heading "Mr. Threat!" I even added two expansion teams to the 1979 season—the Oregon Owls and the Miami Blue Sox—both of whom played in the National League in order to give the NL 14 teams just like the AL. (Fourteen years later, of course, the NL *would* add Florida/Miami and Colorado/Denver to the league. Was I a visionary? I wish. There had been talk of moving a team to both places, along with St. Petersburg and New Orleans, since at least the late '70s). For the record, the Owls had four players in the Top 10 in Batting Average,

---

* The Oakland A's drew 306,763 fans for the entire 1979 season at Oakland-Alameda County Coliseum, an average of 3,787 per game. In one game, their official attendance was 653—not so much a crowd as it was a gathering.

including one guy I named Anton McScranton who was not only challenging .400, but sounded suspiciously like one of the villains from a *Scooby-Doo* episode.

In all, I "published" four *Baseball Headlines* issues. Here's a snippet from a typical Dodger game, which was probably inspired by the Dodgers-Reds slugfest on May 25:

Los Angeles Dodgers Win in 11th:
S. Garvey Shows Power; Dodgers Win, 16–15

(Cincinnati)—It was an exciting night in Ohio as the Dodgers & the Reds rallied to go into extra innings. The Dodgers and Reds had many hits between them, but the Dodgers had 26 of them (setting a new major league record for 1979). Garvey had 6 of them. Baker had 5. Everybody on the Dodgers had at least one hit—with the exception of Steve Yeager, who went 0 for 5.

The win made the Dodgers sweep the 4-game series and pull ½ game ahead of the Reds, and 9½ ahead of the Giants. Tom Seaver was the loser (0–8) and has now lost 8 games in a row. His ERA is not very impressive: 7.65, the highest of his career and in the National League. "He's not the same Tom Seaver he used to be," Sparky Anderson said (Red's manager). Sutton won his 12th game (12–3). Sutton went all 11 innings. It was Don's 6th complete game, as he struck out 9 men and did not walk any. However, the 15 Cincinnati runs raised his ERA up to 3.97, highest on the Dodger staff. But 5 of the 15 Cincinnati runs were unearned.

When the Dodgers & Reds entered the four game series, the Dodgers were 3½ games behind the Reds. But because the Dodgers won all 4 games, they moved into first place by ½ a game. "We're playing

great ball, and we're going to win the pennant," Tom
Lasorda said. "And I'm sure of it too."

So you tell me—which Dodger team would you rather read about? The one in real life, or this one? Looking back, what most impresses me about this fictional game is Don Sutton sticking around for all 11 innings and giving up 15 runs (granted, *only* 10 earned). Was the bullpen on strike that day?

Below each Dodger article I included, of course, my own version of "Dodger Notes," just like in the *Times*. After the Dodgers whipped the visiting Phillies (thanks to two grand slams by Garvey) in another edition, I had this to say:

Dodger Notes:

Prior to last night's game, Reggie Smith was yelling at the Phillies' Bake McBride because he was using Smith's bat. Reggie threatened a fight, but Steve Garvey and Rick Sutcliffe calmed him down . . . Andy Messersmith will undergo more surgery on his elbow. Dr. Jobe will perform it tomorrow. . . . For the second day in a row, Phillies fans caused trouble.

No word on what that "trouble" entailed, but you can bet it wasn't just blowing up beach balls if it warranted a mention in the paper. Elsewhere in that issue:

Baseball Tales in Brief:

Dave Winfield told reporters that San Diego manager Roger Craig wanted to buy the whole team a drink after the Padres come-from-behind win 6–5 on Monday. The victory put the team in fourth place. "He'll never make a good manager being so nice," Winfield responded. It was a hot day anyway, so he took the drink.

Jim Fregosi, manager of the California Angels, was home in bed with a temperature of 101 degrees.

"I have Angel fever," he said.

Chub Feeney, National League president, is going to have a vacation in Colombia. "This pennant race is going to give me another heart attack for sure," he replied.

Feeney, older fans may recall, suffered a heart attack in June of '79 while president of the National League—a position that doesn't even exist anymore. As for that vacation in Colombia . . . let's just say if he was looking to avoid another heart attack, perhaps St. Barts would've been a wiser choice.

On the lighter side, I also "conducted" a fluff interview with Ron Cey. Of course, the Penguin could be a little crusty during real interviews, so some of that attitude seeped in here.

Hey, Cey, What Do U Say?

Q: Do you think you'll ever hit over .300?

A: How should I know?

Q: What do you like to do between seasons?

A: I relish doing exercises, raquet [sic] ball with my friends, and going to Jack LaLanne's with Steve [Garvey] and Cyndy.

Racquetball, Jack LaLanne, and Steve and Cyndy (who together did commercials for Lalanne's European Health Spas) . . . there's the 1970s in a one-sentence nutshell.

As liberating as it was to construct a successful Dodger team, I derived my greatest pleasure from some good healthy Yankee-bashing. In *my* alternate universe, the Yankees weren't just dysfunctional, they were dysfunctional *and* inept. The three players I despised the most—Nettles, Piniella, and, of course, Jackson—were given new identities as talentless hacks who couldn't be bothered, let alone live up to past dynasties. As in real life, Billy Martin was rehired (he had been fired during the 1978 season) to helm these losers. A sampling:

Billy Martin Is At It Again

"The whole team is in a slump for a year!" said the Yankees' manager Billy Martin. "When a team loses 12 in a row, and 25 outta 29, you know that something just has to be wrong!"

Reggie Jackson has a different point of view: "There is nothing wrong with our team or anythin' at all! We are just a bad team all the way around. We aren't the same team, like the team we were in the 1920s, '30s, '40s, or even '50s. We just aren't the same!"

Billy Martin says one of the reasons they are so far behind is because Mickey Rivers, Graig Nettles, Piniella, and Reggie Jackson are just too slow on defense. "They drop easy line drives, or let them drop in front of them for a lot of hits which could of easily been caught! A hit could cost the whole game!"

"No matter how good we are playing, he's [Martin] always going to complain at us," Willie Randolph said, the Yankee 23-year-old second baseman.

When the Dodgers returned to their winning ways later in the '79 season, I retired *Baseball Headlines* for good. Years later, I would feed my fantasy needs with Strat-o-Matic and Rotisserie Leagues, like millions of other baseball addicts. But for a few summer months in the middle of a fallow season, everything was coming up roses in Dodgerland.

5-FOR-5
FIVE GAMES THAT DEFINED THE 1979 DODGERS

#4—GIVE ME "AN ALL-STAR" BREAK
Veterans Stadium, July 15, 1979

So much for spring optimism. When June gloom hit the L.A. area, it permeated the Dodgers as well. The team coughed up a 7–20 record in June and plummeted another 12½ games off the pace—basically, almost one game lost for every two days. Their losing ways continued into July, when they began the month 3–11. The nadir came on the last day before the All-Star Break, a 10–3 drubbing on the part of the Phillies. The loss left them at 36–57, 17½ games out of first place, and typified their futility.

As usual, the Dodgers' pitching was the culprit, with Welch and Reuss giving up eight earned runs in four innings. Steve Yeager and Steve Garvey hit two meaningless home runs. The Dodgers were playing like a team of imposters. They looked like the players we knew but something was just "off." It was at this point in the season that I mercifully decided to pull the plug on *Homerun Highlights* for the 1979 season entirely. Losing was bad enough; having to wade through each raw broadcast trying to find "highlights" forced me to experience the pain all over again. I mean, how many more "The Dodgers Blow It Again" segments could I do, anyway? They were threatening to take over my whole enterprise. (As such, I don't have enough material to draw from to award my "True Blue Ribbon" Mic Award for 1979. I'll make it up to you for '80 and '81.)

In the end, it all proved moot because Mom and Dad exiled me to Calamigos summer camp for the end of July and all of August. With radios banned at the camp and the internet still a gleam in Congressman Al Gore's eye, I was subjected to a near-total media blackout, resulting in an extreme case of Dodgers

Withdrawal Syndrome. What I wouldn't have given to hear *just one inning* of Vin Scully's voice. However, I did get two baseball-related news items while I was there from two campers who got letters from home, both involving death: one was the plane crash that took the life of Yankee captain Thurman Munson on August 2, the other was the passing of Dodgers owner Walter O'Malley a week later. It really was one bummer of a summer.

AND NOW . . . A WORD FROM OUR SPONSORS

My sister, Monica, never one for baseball, could usually be talked into attending two or three Dodger games a year, primarily so she could sink her teeth into a Farmer John Dodger Dog and cap it off with a frozen Carnation Chocolate Malt. Monica is like a lot of non-baseball fans out there—I call them "attendees"—who go for the food (or beer) more than the games themselves. And Farmer John, which has been producing the team's signature Dodger Dog pretty much since the team moved into Chavez Ravine, is the sponsor most synonymous with the L.A. Dodgers. Even my grandmother, who never set foot in Dodger Stadium, knew all about the "footlong" dogs through sheer cultural osmosis.

But if I may be frank, Dodger Dogs are a below-average frank. Sometimes, when I bite into its mealy meat, I'll think, *This texture is what I imagine human flesh to be like.* It's lacking that skin, that snap, that burst of *flavor* you get from a good hot dog.

And yet, every game I attend, I still devour one or two Dodger Dogs. Is it because they are like that old axiom about why people climb Mt. Everest—"Because it's there"? Hardly. Even with Carl's Jr., CPK, or any number of other gastronomic choices available at the stadium, my preferred ballpark fare remains Dodger Dogs, with lots of mustard and onions. I think their popularity is a testament to the power of four things:

1. Like donuts and coffee, or peanut-butter and jelly, hot

dogs and live baseball just inherently go together. If Dodger Dogs were made of horse meat (and in no way am I trying to suggest they are), we'd still probably eat them. Consuming dogs is in our DNA as baseball fans.

2. Vin Scully. The saying that "Vin Scully could read a phone book and make it interesting" applies to pretty much anything. For decades, we were indoctrinated into liking Dodger Dogs by the mere fact that Vin waxed so eloquently about them in TV and radio spots under fiddle-laden jingles. I'm not sure I even understood what "Eastern-most in quality, Western-most in flavor" meant as a kid, but Vin had me at "mmmmm-hmmmmm!"

3. Alliteration. I'm telling you, never underestimate the astounding allure of alliteration by master marketers. Dodger Dogs benefit by the nice consonance created by both the team's nickname and the word "dogs" starting with the letter "D." At one point in their history, the franchise was known as the Brooklyn Robins. Somehow, "Robin Dogs" just doesn't have the same ring and, I'm sure, wouldn't have been as popular. Which brings us to . . .

4. Length. They aren't just Dodger Dogs—they're *"foot-long"* Dodger Dogs. (Never mind that they measure closer to 10 inches than 12.) The descriptor is another great marketing gimmick that just adds to their appeal.

Dodger Dogs may be an ingrained part of the team's culinary culture, but from 1977 to 1981, no sponsor permeated my Dodger experience more than Union 76 service stations (remember when the word "service" actually stood for something?). It started in the preseason, usually around February or March, when the stations would offer wallet-sized Dodger schedules for the upcoming season that were chock-full of handy-dandy information. Besides a calendar of the whole season, they included promotional dates and radio affiliates where you could catch the team's broadcasts outside

> ## Who Knew?
>
> A Dodger Stadium concessions manager named Thomas Arthur coined the term "Dodger Dogs" sometime in the early '60s. The wieners were originally made by the Morrell Meat Company before Farmer John took over.

of L.A. I swear that list of affiliates taught me more about California's geography than school ever did. During family road trips up and down the state, I would sit in the back seat with a map in one hand and the schedule in another, yelling out to Dad which AM stations carried the game as we passed through dark, lonely places like Victorville, Visalia, and Ridgecrest.

Then, of course, there was the oil company's presence at Dodger Stadium itself. Besides its strategic signage perched above the scoreboard and Diamond Vision, Union 76 held the distinction of being the only gas station on the premises of a major league ballpark. Located in the parking lot, its rotating 76 ball was visible beyond center field from almost any seat in the park.

However, it was over the airwaves that the "spirit of 76" was most strongly felt. Besides their radio spots during games, the company's TV commercials were little sagas on par with those old Miller Lite ads with Rodney Dangerfield and friends, creating a memorable world of characters whose fates you found yourself eagerly anticipating from one commercial to the next. But where the Miller Lite beer commercials were edgy and lascivious, Union 76's were wholesome, patriotic, even proudly square, a reflection of the Dodgers themselves. They were rooted by veteran character actor Richard X. Slattery playing the role of the grandfatherly Murph,

owner of the fictitious Murph's 76 Station. His employees included a cute tomboy named Jill, the smooth-talking Nick, and the
dude from *CHiPs*, Larry Wilcox. For such a hardworking bunch,
I always marveled at their uncanny ability to avoid grease stains on
their starched uniforms and grime under their fingernails.

Finally, as referenced earlier in this book, the 76 stamp made
its mark during radio broadcasts on almost every home run hit
by the Dodgers. Longtime fans will remember the template well:

> And on that home run by [Dodger player's name],
> the Union Oil Company is pleased to present a
> twenty-dollar book of Union Oil Auto Script to
> [fill in your charity here].

The following is a mere fraction of the charities mentioned
during broadcasts from the 1978 to 1980 seasons, when auto
scripts were worth 20 dollars, and in 1981, when the monetary
gifts were raised to 50 bucks. I was always bemused by the seemingly redundant descriptions of some of the places.

- Los Angeles Boys Club in Los Angeles (as opposed to
  the one in, you know, Duarte)

- Palm Springs Youth Center in Palm Springs (I mean,
  really. Was it not obvious the first time they said "Palm
  Springs"?)

- Brawley Boys and Girls Club in Brawley, California

- Gardena Valley YMCA in Gardena (enough!)

- Optimist Boys Home in Los Angeles (take *that*, Pessimist Girls!)

- Cri-Help Incorporated in North Hollywood (on one
  occasion, Vin erroneously referred to them as "Cry for
  Help Incorporated")

5-FOR-5
FIVE GAMES THAT DEFINED THE 1979 DODGERS

#5—THE DAVEY & MANNY SHOW
Dodger Stadium, September 2, 1979

The Dodgers of the late '70s had two of the best pinch-hitters in the game on their roster—Vic Davalillo and Manny Mota—fortysomethings who, to paraphrase Scully, could fall out of bed in the middle of the night and stroke a single to center field. It's amazing that the Dodgers could wholly commit to two players whose sole job was to come off the bench and sprinkle pinch-hit pixie dust to either win the game or extend a rally. These days, with complete games on the endangered species list and clubs carrying more pitchers, any GM signing two creaky players who didn't play the field would probably get himself run out of town, although *one* player isn't out of the question (see: Jim Thome, Dodgers, post-All-Star Break, 2009). This may sound like sacrilege, considering how beloved Davalillo and Mota were, but perhaps the '79 Dodgers would've been better served replacing at least one of them with another player with more athleticism, versatility, and pop (actually, the Dodgers *had* that player in Lee Lacy, but they let him get away after the '78 season). Nonetheless, there is no denying that something magical often happened whenever Manny Mota stepped up to the dish in 1979, especially in the second half, keying some miraculous Dodger wins.

On September 2, a Sunday home game, Manny was called upon to hit in the pitcher's spot in the eighth inning. He lined one of his patented flare shots to right field, tying Smoky Burgess's record of 145 all-time pinch hits, and leaving to an extended standing ovation. He would go on to break the record in the second-to-last game of the season (former Dodger Lenny Harris would go on to break Manny's record 22 years later). While

Bullpen Session

Script or Scrip?

A Dodger fan friend and I have had an ongoing debate about whether the announcers were actually saying Union 76 "Auto Script" or "Auto Scrip." He was convinced it had to be "scrip," since that's a term used to describe a form of credit in lieu of actual currency. But listening to Vin and company, I was convinced they were saying "script," with a "t" at the end.

An internet search only added to our confusion, as people remember it as "script" and "scrip," depending on *their* interpretations. I even called Conoco-Phillips, the owners of the Union 76 brand now. A spokeswoman replied, "I'm not even sure what you're talking about." I finally put the debate to rest by pulling up old Union 76 advertisements from the *Los Angeles Times* in 1973. The verdict: "Script." In one ad—a partnership with an Oldsmobile dealer—Union Oil offered 200 gallons of gasoline in auto script. Book value? Eighty bucks . . . or 40 cents a gallon.

Manny did not factor into the Dodgers' scoring in this game, his momentous hit did enable Davey Lopes—unquestionably the Dodgers' MVP that year—to get one more at-bat with two outs and the bases loaded in the ninth inning. All Lopes did was hit a game-winning grand slam for an improbable 6–2 win.

This game defined the Dodgers of the second half. Their 43–26 record was the best in the National League West after the All-Star Break. While this still wasn't enough to avoid their first sub-.500 record (they went 79–83) since 1968, it did give them something to build on going into 1980 . . . and gave me hope that next year would be a return to their championship ways.

MANNY BEING MOTA

From 1977 to the present day, after witnessing thousands of hours of baseball,

I have seen only a handful of players who seemed to have unlocked the secret to hitting—players whose wizardry with the bat was so complete, they played on a different plane than their contemporaries. The list is so short, I can almost count them on one hand:

1. Tony Gwynn
2. George Brett
3. Ichiro Suzuki
4. Wade Boggs
5. Rod Carew
6. Manny Mota

Interestingly, all of these hitters were left-handed batters, with one exception: Manny Mota.

Manny was one of those rare players (pre-Steroid Era, of course) who, like a fine wine, seemed to get better with age. His career had a fascinating arc. His last year as a semi-regular player for the Dodgers was 1972, when he hit .323 and had an OPS of .809 playing left and center field. He was 34 years old. In the three years after that, his batting average and OPS dipped each season as he became almost exclusively a pinch-hitter. In 1975, at age 37, he had his worst season outside of his '62 rookie year, batting .265. This is when a typical player might have called it a career. But clearly the Dodgers must have seen something that made them believe he could still contribute. Maybe it was the way he handled a bat. Like a right-handed Rod Carew, Mota had a preternatural ability to get wood on the ball and pretty much place it wherever he wanted. Also like Carew, the key to his bat control seemed to lie in his wrists. I would've loved to see those guys play each other in a mean game of squash.

From 1976 to 1980, Manny had clearly cracked the hitting code. On the next page are his yearly lines versus his career numbers for batting average and on-base percentage (his career spanned 20 years). Note that he beat his career averages eight out

Manny Mota—Ages 38–42

Year	Age	AVG.	AVG. (Career)	OBP	OBP (Career)
1976	38	.288	.304	**.367**	.355
1977	39	**.395**	.304	**.521**	.355
1978	40	.303	.304	**.361**	.355
1979	41	**.357**	.304	**.400**	.355
1980	42	**.429**	.304	**.429**	.355

of ten times, and was not too far off with the other two.

True, each season was represented by a small sample size, but during this span, he did accumulate 201 plate appearances—enough to prove that his hitting acumen was no fluke. A particularly impressive year was 1977. In 50 plate appearances, Manny went the entire season without striking out. He also walked 10 times, even more amazing when you consider that 90 percent of his hits during this five-year period were singles. Far from looking like Barry Bonds, Manny was about as threatening as your dad out there—and frankly, he looked like Dad, too. But then, through his combination of guile and good hands, he would invariably come through, much to the delight of the home crowd. After 1979, Manny was promoted to hitting coach but remained on the active player roster for his pinch-hitting prowess. Three decades before Manny Ramirez triggered Angelenos' zeal, Mota was the original "Manny being Manny."

Mota's legacy, of course, extends beyond his pinch-hitting exploits for the Dodgers. In 2011, he celebrated his 42nd anniversary with the organization, for which he has worked in various coaching capacities since retiring from active hitting duties—hitting coach, first base coach, assistant coach, bench coach, even player-coach. Most of all, he seems to play the role of confidant for young Latin players, and Yoda-like guru for all the players. Perhaps most importantly, with all the changes the team has undergone on the field, Manny has been the only continuous link in the dugout to the 1977–1981 nucleus.

4TH INNING
February-July 1980

Me: Hello there again, everybody, and welcome to *Homerun Highlights*, part four. The following home runs and highlights are recorded from Dodger games from the 1980 season. The first home run you are about to hear on this tape is by Steve Yeager, who hit the first round-tripper of 1980. It came in the third game of exhibition play. Here's Jerry . . .

Jerry: Here's the look and the pitch on the way. Fly ball to left field, he hit it deep. It's up in the breeze, going, going, this ball is all gone! Home run, Yeager, to tie it up.

I t was February 1980. Listening to this opening intro of *Homerun Highlights* tape four, three things are apparent:

1. Sometime over the winter, my voice (finally!) changed like Peter Brady's in *The Brady Bunch*. On the downside, this also meant the impending appearance of a disturbing caterpillar mustache.

Dusty Baker stroking one to "Bakersfield."

2. I wisely scrapped aiming for home run quotas and decided to memorialize home runs and "highlights," meaning Dodger rallies, pitching gems, devastating losses . . . in short, my baseball IQ had evolved to a point where I was seeing each season as having its own storyline beyond just the long ball.

3. It had obviously been a *long* off-season for me with-out the Dodgers, made even worse by their lost 1979 season. How else to explain the fact that I sat glued to the team's spring training broadcasts from Florida, waiting to see who would hit the first home run of the pre-season?

As for the Dodgers themselves, the previous off-season had sparked a winter of negativity, both in the press and on talk radio. Their players were getting old. They relied too much on their farm system. They needed to be like the Yankees. They'd never win a World Series unless they signed splashy free agents. Who was *their* Mr. October? And so, whether it was because of pressure or an actual desire to change with the times, GM Al Campanis did sign two high-profile free agents for around five million dol-lars: starter Dave Goltz, who had won 14 games five years in a row for the Twins; and reliever Don Stanhouse, who had chalked up at least 20 saves each of the last two seasons for the Orioles. Both would factor prominently into the 1980 season, but for all the wrong reasons.

THE PLAYERS

Offensively, the opening day lineup looked like this:

• **2B Davey Lopes**—1980 began a discernable two-year decline for Lopes as he began to break down with nag-ging injuries. It was as if his tank simply ran out of fuel after his explosive 1979 season. He had career lows in steals and on-base percentage. For a guy who used to regularly steal at least 40 bases a year, his 23 swipes were alarmingly low. You'd have to think that even an average season from Davey would've seen the Dodgers cruise into the playoffs.

- **CF Rudy Law**—A rookie with only 13 plate appearances before this season, Law got the nod over Rick Monday and played the majority of games in center field this year. Although he stole 40 bases, he didn't walk much and slumped badly in the second half. He never played for the team again afterward.

- **RF Reggie Smith**—Reggie was enjoying a nice bounceback year, hitting .323 with 15 homers through the end of July, despite a bum shoulder. But the shoulder did not improve, and after just one at-bat in August, he underwent surgery and was done for the year. Again, playing the "what if" game—what if Smith were healthy in September?

- **1B Steve Garvey**—Yawn . . . Another season of at least .300/200/100/20/162. Next . . .

- **LF Dusty Baker**—Moved up to the fifth spot, Johnnie B. Baker enjoyed his finest year since 1977, hitting .294 with 29 home runs and 97 RBIs, finishing fourth in MVP voting. He was Player of the Month for June.

- **3B Ron Cey**—Though he matched his 28 homers from the year before, Cey had a bit of an off year (for him), offensively. Still, he played almost every game and was his usual anchor at third base. Came up huge in the season's last series.

- **SS Derrel Thomas**—Russell was still the Dodgers' regular shortstop but wouldn't start until the third game of the season. Derrel once again proved his worth by playing every position this year except first base and pitcher. I loved watching him play, especially his daring basketcatches in center field on routine flies that would make your (and his manager's) heart stop. My brother and I nicknamed him "Spider" because of his spindly limbs flailing all over the place when he batted.

- **C Steve Yeager**—Lasorda's loyalty to Steve Yeager ran deep, but could only go so far. Despite his above-average defense, Steve was always struggling to stay above the Mendoza line (.200). He would once again platoon with Joe Ferguson and new kid on the block Mike Scioscia.

The team's reserves were a stronger, deeper bunch in 1980. Besides Derrel Thomas, Pedro Guerrero could play infield or outfield and had another year of maturation under his belt, batting .322 with an impressive OPS of .856. Jay Johnstone, signed as a free agent, batted .307, had some big games in September when Reggie went down, and emerged as a crowd favorite. And having the powerhitting Rick Monday (10 home runs) off the bench was certainly a nice weapon to have around. Mota and Davalillo were still in the picture, but, perhaps wisely, the Dodgers waited until September to activate them once rosters expanded, with Mota pulling double duty as the team's first-base coach.

The pitchers shored up their game again; the staff was second only to Houston in ERA. Don Sutton, in his last full year as a Dodger, couldn't have picked a better time to enter the market. He was outstandingly consistent and led the league with a 2.20 ERA. Jerry Reuss won Comeback Player of the Year honors, going 18–6 with a 2.51 ERA. (How does one "come back" from a respectable 3.54 ERA, by the way? Was the pool of candidates that weak?) Hooton was back with another solid year, and Welch rallied from his alcohol rehab to go 14–9 as a starter before injuries dealt him a setback. However, Rick Sutcliffe (3–9, 5.56) followed up his award-winning rookie season by suffering a nasty sophomore jinx. After a few awful starts, he was marooned in the bullpen much of the year. Dave Goltz (7–11, 4.31) was not much better, but because of his high contract, he had a longer leash to work with and made 27 starts, including the pivotal one-game playoff at the end of the season. That start, along with Niedenfuer pitching to Jack Clark in the '85 playoffs, rank as the two top Lasorda decisions we Dodger fans wish we could hit "undo" on.

Out of the pen, Don "Stan the Man Unusual" Stanhouse, who had T-shirts with his Stan Musial-inspired nickname emblazoned on them, seemed more intent on bringing the funny than fastballs. (Imagine how much Kirk Gibson would've disliked this guy.) He remains one of the biggest free-agent busts in franchise history. Pitching only 25 innings because of injuries, he blew almost as many games as he saved (5 to 7), threw up an ERA over 5.00, and had a 3:1 strikeout-to-walk ratio—*the wrong way* (16 walks to 5 strikeouts). If his walk rate was alarming to the Dodgers, it shouldn't have been. Don's save totals in '78 and '79 were a mirage. In both of those years—and in five of his first eight seasons—he actually walked more batters than he struck out, with markedly low strikeout totals. The Dodgers decided to cut bait on the second year of his deal, figuring he could do less damage by simply not playing at all. Fortunately, the closer void in '80 was filled by a brash Steve Howe, a much-heralded former first-round draft selection who always seemed kind of bratty— but, as they say, he was *our* brat. The 22-year-old lefty had 17 saves and was named Rookie of the Year. Like Welch before him, Howe would go on to battle addiction, only with far more tragic results.

AN ALMOST-MIRACLE

I'm loath to fall back on a passage from Charles Dickens that's been used to death, but 1980 truly was the best of times and the worst of times, for the team and us fans. While the 1981 squad would endure its share of eviscerating losses, it was at least offset by the team winning the whole enchilada. In 1980, we didn't have the satisfaction of a trophy, just a big plate of empty at the end of the season. This was the same year of the U.S. Hockey team winning the gold in the Winter Olympics, memorialized by Al Michaels's classic call, "Do you believe in miracles? Yes!" For much of '80, the Dodgers, too, had us believing. For every devastating loss, they countered with dramatic, come-from-behind wins. Then, just when it looked like they were dead, they swept a three-game set with the first-place Houston Astros, rallying in every game to force a one-game playoff at home. The only thing standing between them and their own miracle was an aging knuckleballer named Joe Niekro. The Dodgers, of course, lost when it mattered most. Miracles rarely happen more than once a year. We were left with an Almost Miracle.

It wasn't just the season that went right down to the wire, but the games themselves. The Dodgers tied the Padres for number of contests decided by one run (31–33), and established their high-water mark for the 1977–1980 period. Because so much was decided by so little, it's hard not to look back at every close game with extra scrutiny and wonder how things could have played out if, say, the normally reliable Cey doesn't make that error in the ninth inning in a loss against Atlanta on August 5th . . . or if Bobby Castillo gets the benefit of a borderline call and strikes out Jack Clark instead of walking him in a loss to the Giants on October 2nd . . . or if Fernando would've pitched the sudden-death game against the Astros instead of Dave "Gopher Ball" Goltz . . . or if . . . well, you get the picture. It wouldn't have taken much to flip that one-run record from 31–33 to a mere 32–32, which would've had them playing the Phillies in the NLCS. But it's all academic. Or as Vin would say, "So close . . . yet oh so far."

What's also amazing about 1980 is how evenly matched the Dodgers were with the Houston Astros (then in the NL West). From June until the first week of October, it was pretty much a two-team race. The teams switched places between first and second at a dizzying rate, neither climbing more than 3½ games in first place or falling more than 3½ back. Each was unable to get on an extended winning "skein" to pull away. Even the Dodgers' longest game of the season was with Houston—an early-season, April 12 affair in the Astrodome that hinted at an intense rivalry that would play out all year. The game took 5 hours and 35 minutes to play before L.A. finally prevailed in the 17th inning, 6–5 (highlights: *five* shutout innings of relief pitching by rookie Howe; a save by starter Hooton; and a pinch-hit single by pitcher Sutcliffe).

The Astros were a team custom-made for the cavernous Astrodome, with lots of speed (six guys with over 20 stolen bases, but not one with over 13 homers) and a stellar starting staff led by the one-two punch of heat meisters Nolan Ryan and J.R. Richard. To be fair, you have to wonder how far in first place the Astros might've been at season's end—and how the rest of the '80s would've played out—if J.R. Richard hadn't collapsed in the Dome that summer due to a stroke that ended his career as he was entering his prime. Nolan Ryan's legacy was already firmly entrenched by this point: four no-hitters, a seven-time strikeout champ, and a place in the *Guinness Book of World Records* for fastest pitch ever recorded (100.9 mph). But J.R. was downright scary. There were rumors that some Dodgers would come down with "J.R.-itis" and claim to be sick before games in which he was scheduled to pitch—and can you blame them? At six foot eight and 222 pounds (I remember he had Goofy-sized feet), standing on a mound 10 inches high and unleashing wicked sliders that could reach the mid-90s and find their way under your chin (he led the league in walks and wild pitches three times), he must've looked like a clumsy, lethal giant. But what made him even more scary in 1980 was that he had found his control while still maintaining his strikeout total of at least nine K's per nine innings. Richard was the NL's Pitcher of the Month for April, started the All-Star Game, and had a 10–4 record with a 1.90 ERA when he went down. The loss of their behemoth left an even bigger void in the Astros' rotation—he was replaced by Gordie Pladson (0–4, 4.35) and Joaquin Andujar (3–8, 3.91), best known for his Meltdown of the Century against umpire Don Denkinger in the 1985 World Series as a member of the Cardinals.

I recall not having much sympathy for the Astros when my partner-in-crime David called me about the J.R. news. Our conversation went something like this:

> David: Dude, did you ya hear?
> Me: What?
> David: J.R. Richard collapsed while pitching warm-ups.
> Me: Wha—? Is he dead?
> David: He's at the hospital, but even if he makes it, dude's done for the season.
> Me: [Fist pump] Yessssss!

As a young fan, all I cared about was knocking their ace out of a tight division race. I gave little thought to the actual tragedy itself. Now, of course, I would think of the person first. But I'm pretty sure that my gleeful reaction is what karmically blew the 1980 season for the Dodgers.

5-FOR-5
FIVE GAMES THAT DEFINED THE 1980 DODGERS

Because 1980 was such a topsy-turvy year, I cannot possibly boil the regular season down to five games. The last four games of the season alone each warrant their own section. That said, I'm going to play commissioner here and enact a one-time rule change in the best interests of this book. I'm going to lump games 160, 161, and 162 against Houston—which I bill on my tapes as the "Big Three"—under the heading of one "game." So you'll get seven games for the price of five. Ernie Banks would be thrilled.

#1—JERRY IS ALMOST PERFECT
Candlestick Park, June 27, 1980

In keeping with the "almost" theme, it's only appropriate that Jerry Reuss came about as close as you can get to joining the elite few allowed entry into the Hall of Fame with perfect games next to their names. Without a doubt, the six-foot-five, blond southpaw was the most consistently dominant starter for the Dodgers in the 1980 and '81 seasons, coming up big in late-season, pressure-cooker games. And yet even his no-hitter "almost" never happened. Reuss started 1980 in the bullpen, and were it not for Dave Goltz coming down with the flu on May 16, he might've still been in the pen for much—if not the rest—of the year. But he won that spot start and secured his place in the rotation by hurling four shutouts in his next eight starts, the last culminating in his no-hitter. Despite his size, Reuss was not a strikeout pitcher. He relied on a deceptive delivery, changing speeds, and a nasty sinking fastball to get a lot of ground-ball outs. "Big Bird" was The Man, and never more so than on a June 27 match-up against Vida Blue and the Giants at Candlestick Park.

Going into the contest, the Dodgers, as usual, were hovering around the top of the division—two games out of first, to be exact. The Giants were circling the drain of last place, an odd bag of spare parts with one young stud (Jack Clark), one respectable veteran (Darrell Evans), and a seemingly endless assortment of broken-down (Rennie Stennett), weak-hitting (Johnnie LeMaster), or weak-hitting-cum-flash-in-the-pan (Rich Murray, Joe Strain) infielders. Veteran Vida anchored a staff comprised of middling pitchers like Montefusco, Ripley, and Hargesheimer. Throw in Karloff and Lugosi and you've got what sounds like the perfect all-horror-movie starting rotation.

Early on, it was clear that Reuss brought his A-game. The Giants were killing worms, as they say, against his sinker, with five of their first six outs on the ground. But it was a grounder in the first inning that loomed largest as the game went on. Jack Clark (who else?) hit a routine ground ball to Bill Russell. The veteran shortstop always had a serviceable glove, and he fielded this one cleanly. But he often side-armed his throws to first, which would cause them to dip or sail and force Garvey to bail him out on the other end . . . when he could. This was one of those throws. Russell's slingshot to first bounced in front of the first-base bag. Garvey short-hopped it, but the ball fell out his glove like a scoop of vanilla ice cream out of a cone. Steve made a small motion of frustration—like, "I had that!"—and 95 percent of the time, he did. But on this one occasion, perhaps because the ball was *too* far in front of the bag and therefore not conducive to the patented Garvey scoop, Steve couldn't hold on. Back home, watching on TV, I merely shrugged. A Russell error was nothing new. He had made at least 28 in each of the last four seasons.

By the fifth inning, the Dodgers were cruising, 7–0, allowing Reuss to pitch more aggressively. His sinker seemed to be on an invisible string attached to wherever Yeager's mitt set up. According to a 1980 *Sports Illustrated* article, Reuss recalled throwing only five curveballs all night—he simply didn't need it. With his impeccable control, he didn't really come close to walking anyone all night. Vinny and company kept reminding us that a first-inning error by Bill Russell was the only thing standing between Reuss and a perfect game. How much do you want to bet, as Jerry's no-no reached the later innings, Russell stood out at shortstop thinking, "Please walk this guy please walk this guy please walk this guy please walk this guy . . . "

For the bottom of the ninth inning, I contemplated turning off my tape recorder in order not to jinx Reuss's no-hitter. But history was waiting in the wings; I had an obligation to keep rolling. I noticed that Vin Scully was now doing the television broadcast on Channel 11. I *had* to get Vin's call, so for the first time on *Homerun Highlights*, I pointed the microphone toward the TV speaker. The first batter up for the Giants was back-up catcher Mike Sadek. As he did so famously with the Sandy Koufax perfect game in 1965, Vin set the stage (though, because this was TV, he didn't need to be as descriptive):

> So in the 70th game of the nineteen hundred and eighty season, on a Friday night, June the 27th, 1980, Jerry Reuss, three outs away.
>
> Ground ball . . . to Cey . . . over to Garvey.
>
> And he is *two* outs away. And the first time any emotion at all shown by Reuss. He had his back to home plate, he made a little fist with his left hand, and you could see how happy he was that he had gotten *one* of them.
>
> Now, Rennie Stennett, coming off the bench as a pinch-hitter, to bat for Lavelle.

Stennett, a former Pirate, was known for two things in his career. On September 16, 1975, the second baseman became the first player in the modern era to go 7-for-7 in a 9-inning game. Two years later, he was hitting .336 with a chance for the batting crown when he broke his right leg in August. He wound up just 12 plate appearances shy of qualifying for the Top 10, and teammate Dave Parker won the title with a .338 average. Stennett was never the same player after breaking his leg. He played two years for the Giants and was out of baseball by age 30.

> Ball one . . . and Reuss might've pitched beyond himself that time, trying to get a little something extra.

The count went to 1-and-2.

> The Dodger outfield, shaded ever so slightly to right field. That's the defense for Stennett. Stennett, a tough out, even though he has lost his job momentarily to Joe Strain. One ball, two strikes.
> Bouncer down to Russell. He has the hop . . . he is *one* out away from a no-hitter.

By this point the orange-and-black fans were implausibly roaring their support for Reuss, many of them standing. Me? I was probably more on edge than Reuss himself. You can hear me exhaling nervously on the tape, the microphone picking up my every reaction.

> Jerry Reuss, who was *denied* a no-hitter eight years ago against Philadelphia when Larry Bowa singled in the ninth, is now one out away from a no-hitter, the first one we have seen by a Dodger pitcher in 10 years, the first no-hitter at Candlestick in 12 years. But he *has* to get Bill North. North has grounded out twice, flied to left. A veteran who is a threat to bunt.

Wouldn't that be just like the Giants to bunt on a Dodger pitcher to break up a no-hitter? Fortunately, North was an ex-Dodger, so he had some Blue blood in him.

Even the Giant fans now, you can sense, are

> rooting. Reuss got an ovation when he went to
> the hill to start the inning. Ball one. Eight–noth-
> ing Dodgers, but it is Jerry Reuss.

North swung away and ended up with a swinging bunt, as it were.

> Little nubber, back to Reuss. He picks it up, he's
> got a no-hitter! Jerry Reuss, at thirty-one years
> old, has done it! A no-hitter!

In the background, I clap my hands together and try to stifle a "#$%@ yeahhhhh!"

> He missed a perfect game *only* by an error by *Bill
> Russell* in the first inning.

Oh, yeah. Him. Sigh.

> What a magnificent moment for the Big Blond.
> Rick Sutcliffe, throwing his arms around him, and
> all of the Dodgers happy for their player-represen-
> tative, who put on a magnificent show!

Reuss induced 17 ground balls while striking out only two. But as magnificent as he was, the Russell error left a bitter af-tertaste in my mouth. To vent, I spent the next thirty seconds spontaneously lambasting Russell—my first *Homerun Highlights* commentary, more spiteful than insightful—as the post-game Farmer John and Union 76 commercials blared out of the TV in the background.

I eventually did get to hear Vin call a perfect game. Unfortu-nately, that was bittersweet, too—it was the 1991 gem by the Ex-pos' Dennis Martinez against the Dodgers. Bill Russell watched it all as a bench coach.

SCIOSCIA JACKS CLARK

Look, I'll readily admit that I'm taking shots at Jack Clark whenever I can in this book. It's nothing personal. (Okay, it's a little personal.) Even before he hit that crushing home run in the 1985 NLCS—the one where everyone except Lasorda felt he should've been intentionally walked—Clark was a ready-made villain. He was a Giant. He was talented. He had big games against the Dodgers. And he was cocky. Put it all together, and he was my National League equivalent of Reggie Jackson. So I can hardly pass up an opportunity here to convey Vin Scully's July 6th call of Mike Scioscia's first major league home run, which in itself was of historical significance. But it's how the home run went down that made it something special.

> No balls and one strike. John [Montefusco] into the windup and the strike-one pitch, a chaaaange . . . *whacked* to right field . . . back goes Clark, a-waaaaay back, to the wall . . . leaps up . . . it's gone!
>
> [Dodger Stadium crowd noise for 22 seconds.]
>
> Mike Scioscia got a change-up from Montefusco, and almost knocked Jack Clark out of the ballgame. Clark went *crashing* into the right field fence, *banged* his head, sat down, a complete *disgusted* ballplayer as he sat on the warning track. The Giants started coming out of the dugout thinking he was hurt.

Unlike Lacy's inside-the-park homer in '78, when Clark knocked himself out of the game, he remained in this one.

> For Mike Scioscia, his first big league home run. Clark has put himself together. That might be the last change-up that John Montefusco will give Mike Scioscia. Oooooh, did he blackjack *that* thing!

Turns out it was the only thing rookie Mike blackjacked that year. He ended up with one home run in 152 plate appearances.

HIGH FIVES FOR THE ALL-STAR GAME

The 1980 All-Star Game was held at Dodger Stadium—the first time Chavez Ravine played host. Fittingly, the team was represented by six players: Garvey, Lopes, Russell, Smith, Welch, and Reuss, who was also the game's winning pitcher. It was the National League's ninth straight win. Overall, it was a pretty dull game. I remember it was almost upstaged by a couple of things

Bullpen Session

Last Train to Clarksville

In 1975, former Giant Juan Marichal, reviled among Dodger fans for going caveman on Johnny Roseboro with a baseball bat, joined the Dodgers as a free agent. It was perhaps the most shocking signing in the history of the L.A. franchise. The second-most? It's got to be Jack Clark signing on as the Dodgers' hitting coach in 2001. Blogs buzzed with anger when the news was announced. For fans who vilified him for delivering the crushing blow in the '85 NLCS (the same year he knocked Scioscia out on a play at the plate a few months earlier), this was like sleeping with the enemy.

The only thing that could've redeemed Clark was if the Dodgers made the playoffs during his tenure. They didn't. In fact, the most notable thing that happened wasn't even on the field. During 2003 spring training, the injury-prone Jack Clark, not wearing his helmet, almost got killed in a motorcycle accident. He landed in intensive care, had to have staples inserted into his head to close wounds, and missed the first few weeks of the season. He recovered just in time to get fired that summer, ensuring that his legacy among Dodger fans remained forever intact.

that had nothing to do with the contest itself: a small brush fire that broke out on a hill behind the stadium, and the Dodgers trotting out their new Diamond Vision color scoreboard in left field, which I believe was the first of its kind in the majors.

For me, the most memorable moment came right after the NL team clinched. Vin Scully was calling the game for CBS Radio with Brent Musburger. Here's how Vinny described their celebration:

> And a happy scene for the National [League team], as they are now doing what has become a Dodger trademark—a high five. You don't shake hands straight on, you have to hold your arms *fully* extended over your head, *leap* as high as you can, and touch skin. A *high* five!

It wasn't the birth of the high five—in baseball, at least, that came after Glenn Burke high-fived Dusty Baker after Baker hit his 30th home run on the last day of the 1977 season—but it *was* a formal introduction of this newfangled salute on a national scale. There is something quaint and sweet about Vin's thorough explanation of the high five for the listeners at home. It also got me thinking . . . I would love for Vin to have been there when the first handshake went down in ancient times:

> As has become common among Grecian soldiers, they are engaging in what is called a handshake. Each party grasps the other's hand, preferably the *right* hand, in a firm gesture of friendship. They then move their locked palms up and down, almost like clenching a pump handle. And there you have it: a handshake!

5-FOR-5
FIVE GAMES THAT DEFINED THE 1980 DODGERS

#2—THE DODGERS EXHALE
Dodger Stadium, July 29, 1980

The Dodgers treaded water in June and July, going 27–28 for the two months combined. Davey Lopes was having a particularly rough go of it, and when he slumped, the team seemed to follow. On July 26, with the Dodgers down by four in the bottom of the ninth inning and the bases loaded, Lasorda pinch-hit for the Dodger captain, mired in a 3-for-18 skid and nursing an injury. His replacement, Pedro Guerrero, responded by singling in a run against Bruce Sutter. Tommy proceeded to sit Davey for the next three games (though he did pinch-run), with Pedro starting all three games at second base (shocking in itself), and rookie Rudy Law batting leadoff.

As the team prepared for its 100th game on July 29, they sat in second place, 3½ games behind the Astros, their biggest deficit since April 25, with the third-place Reds a mere half-game behind. Their record was only seven games above .500. Was this the beginning of a free fall that would ostensibly end the Dodgers' season, just like the year before? Or would they find it in themselves to put it all together for the last two months and play like they were capable? Something had to give.

With Lopes on the bench, the Dodgers busted out with five runs and eight hits through three innings against the first-place Pirates and starter Bert Blyleven. In the bottom of the eighth, the Dodgers had a 7–2 lead. Rod Scurry was on in relief of Blyleven. With two outs and a runner on second, Scurry intentionally walked number eight hitter Steve Yeager to get to Burt Hooton, who was well on his way to winning his 10th game in 13 decisions. Typically in these situations, it's not unusual to see a pitcher take three quick strikes so he can get back out there to finish what he started without tiring himself. But Happy worked the count full. Vin Scully called it from there:

> 3-and-2 to Burt Hooton. Runners again ready to go. Scurry turns and looks at second . . . Rod looks into Ed Ott . . . now the lefthander ready and the 3-2 pitch is swung on and *belted to left field* . . . if it's fair, it's gonna go! It's goooooone, home run for Hooton!
>
> [Crowd noise for 43 seconds.]
>
> Boy, they're going *wild* here, as Burt Hooton hits a 3-2 pitch into the lower deck, to the left of the Dodger bullpen, and the crowd is insisting that he come out and take a bow, and he does.

As the crowd began a chant of "Hooooot!" Vinny informed us it was the pitcher's third big league home run. Leadoff hitter Rudy Law was the next one up.

> So it is 10–2 Dodgers, here is Rudy Law—*and the pitch hit him!*

The "Hoooots" quickly turned to "booooos."

> And why [Scurry] would ever throw after a pitcher hits a home run . . . and immediately [home plate umpire Ed] Montague goes out to the mound . . . and that's crazy.

Almost as crazy as what happened next from the Dodger dugout.

> Davey Lopes is gesturing to Rudy Law—steal! Even though it is 10–2 Dodgers, Lopes is so incensed, that he wants Law to steal bases. And

> [Bill] Madlock is trying to talk to young Scurry
> and smooth his feathers a little bit.

I know it left Vin chagrined, but I could almost understand Scurry's frustration. The Dodgers were up by five runs, there were two outs in the bottom of the eighth, a weak-hitting pitcher was up—the "book" says he should roll over. "Who the heck does this guy think he is, working me to 3-and-2, *and then hitting a 3-run homer?*" Not that I'm excusing Scurry's behavior. Hooton was right to battle him, and the Pirates were certainly a team capable of coming back. I was at Dodger Stadium the night of August 21, 1990 when the Dodgers blew an 11–1 lead against the Phillies after seven innings and lost, so I'm a firm believer in playing till the last out and not throwing away at-bats!

> So Rod Scurry throws a 3-and-2 fastball, Burt Hooton of all people hits a home run, and Scurry then wings Rudy Law. Ed Montague has cautioned Scurry and has also warned Lasorda.
> 'Course, the Dodgers feel thoroughly blameless, and to a man they're incensed. Now we'll see whether Rudy Law will try to steal after Lopes made everyone in the ballpark aware of it: he hits you, so run on him, even though we're leading by eight runs.

Law never did steal that base, but it ultimately didn't matter. With the Dodgers' 10–2 victory, this game perfectly exemplified Lopes's leadership, even when he wasn't playing. I can't recall another example of a player in the dugout who demonstrably encouraged a teammate to steal a base after being plunked, can you? Maybe he was frustrated after riding the pine for a few days. Then again, Lopes always played with somewhat of a chip on his shoulder, which, for a team that wasn't exactly known for fire or cohesiveness, was probably a good asset to have. If the other players ever became immune to Lasorda's motivational mechanisms, at least the Captain was always there to kick them in the pants.

Davey started the next night against the Pirates and had his best game in two weeks: 2-for-4 with a stolen base, a run scored, and an RBI in a Reuss 3–0 shutout that lasted only 1 hour, 43 minutes. But the July 29th game was a turning point. It provided a nice springboard for a successful August and set Team Blue off on a mini four-game winning streak that saw them make up four games in the standings and move back into first place. Again, to reiterate my buddy David's immortal words, sometimes you just need a good old-fashioned whippin'. Curiously, they would never score in double-digits again the rest of the year.

Who Knew?

I always like when major league teams have team captains. It reminds me of the playground. There were definitely more team captains when Davey Lopes played. From 1977 to 1981, Lopes, Willie Stargell, Carl Yastrzemski, Thurman Munson, Sal Bando, Pete Rose, and even Jerry Remy of the Angels were just some of the players wearing the figurative or literal "C" on their unis.

As of the 2011 season, there were only three official team captains in the major leagues, and none in the NL: Derek Jeter of the Yankees, Jason Varitek of the Red Sox, and Paul Konerko of the White Sox. The one thing they all have in common? Each had spent at least 13 years with his team. Longevity with one team is not always a prerequisite to be a captain, but it helps. Given the modern era's transient player, don't expect a captain revival any time soon.

5TH INNING
August 1980

First, the good news about August. The Dodgers went 18–11 after flatlining in June and July. I also somehow convinced my parents *not* to send me to the Calamigos sleep-away camp this year, so I wouldn't miss out on weeks and weeks of games like I had last summer.

As they say, be careful what you wish for . . .

5-FOR-5
FIVE GAMES THAT DEFINED THE 1980 DODGERS

#3—THE "IT'S OUTTA HERE!" GAME
Atlanta-Fulton County Stadium, August 5, 1980

"It didn't seem possible, but it happened!"

Pop quiz: Okay, Dodger fans . . . who uttered the above line, and what Dodger event was it in reference to?

    A. Vin Scully, right after the Kirk Gibson walk-off homer in Game 1 of the '88 World Series.

    B. Vin Scully, after the Dodgers finally beat the Yankees

Jerry Reuss, aka "Big Bird."

in the '81 World Series.

C. Ross Porter, after the Dodgers improbably swept the Astros at the end of the '80 season to force a one-game playoff.

D. Me, setting up a random August 5, 1980 game against the lowly Braves.

The correct answer, of course, is "D," though you're forgiven if you picked "A." I could see where you'd get momentarily confused between my line and Vin's immortal one: "In a year that has been so improbable, the *impossible* has happened." Don't feel too bad. I once picked "Lady Gaga" on a pop culture internet quiz when the correct answer was actually "Shakespeare." The truth is, I just wanted any excuse to put my name in a quiz next to Vin Scully's.

The Dodgers enjoyed a lot of come-from-behind wins in 1980. Two of the more memorable, played out on *Homerun Highlights* under the heading "Another Dodger Rally," are when they scored four runs in the fifth inning against the Padres to turn a 7–4 deficit into an 8–7 win, and another when they were down to the Cubs, 6–2, only to turn that game into a 7–6 victory. And, of course, we haven't even gotten to games 160, 161, and 162 against Houston yet. So naturally, the *"IT'S OUTTA HERE!"* must refer to an amazing Dodger home run to win the game, right?

Ah, but remember, this year was also the worst of times. And on August 5—under the category "The Dodgers Blow It Again"—the Dodgers played a game whose end result still haunts me to this day. If you're a passionate fan like me—of any team, in any sport—I'm sure you feel the same as I do, that winning is great, but *nothing* stays with you longer than an agonizing loss. It comes with the territory of being a fanatic. You *expect* your team to have amazing comebacks. But the gut-wrenching defeats always seem like such a betrayal of faith, even though they're a normal part of the game.

Which reminds me . . . hearing someone say, "Well, it all evens out in the end" is no consolation. Number one: statistically, that's not always true. Number two: even if it were true, we fans don't want to hear rationality enter the equation, no more than a priest wants to listen to an atheist popping off at Midnight Mass. There is a certain dogma to losing. Wallowing is one of the basic tenets. And after this particular game at Atlanta-Fulton County Stadium, I hit new heights (or were they lows?) of martyrdom.

I guess I should've known there'd be trouble when the fate of this game hinged on the Dodgers' two big free agent busts—Dave Goltz and Don Stanhouse. But great losses, like great wins, are team efforts, and there was plenty of blame to go around. Facing 41-year-old knuckler Phil Niekro, the offense managed only three singles and one extra-base hit through eight innings, yet somehow squeaked out four runs. Goltz, carrying an ERA over 5.00, got into trouble in the sixth and was replaced by Rick Sutcliffe, whose ERA was even higher. But Rick kept the Braves in check. Going into the bottom of the ninth inning, the Blue Crew led, 4–1. This was where the real fun began.

The first two batters for the Braves were Bob Horner (35 homers in '80) and Dale Murphy (33 homers in '80). Sutcliffe retired them on a fly out and strikeout. Two quick outs, bases empty, the big dogs out of the way. My finger was resting on my radio's off switch. The next batter was Jeff Burroughs. He hit a routine ground ball to Ron Cey. He booted it for an error—only his ninth of the season. Still, the game should have been over. Bobby Cox (then in his first tour of duty with the Braves) sent Mike Lum up to pinch hit for catcher Bruce Benedict. Lum drew a walk, putting the tying run on base. That brought up Rafael Ramirez, a future fixture at shortstop for the Braves in the '80s who was making his debut in this game.

Cox summoned lefty Brian Asselstine to pinch-hit for Raffy. Lasorda countered by replacing Sutcliffe with the lefty Howe. Cox countered that by calling Asselstine back to the bench and sending in right-handed pinch hitter Charlie Spikes (a great baseball name if there ever was one). Spikes greeted Howe with a single to left field, which scored Burroughs. Dodgers 4, Braves 2.

Listening to the game in my bedroom, I was surprisingly calm. Steve Howe had been lights-out all season and had emerged as the Dodgers' preeminent stopper. He had not given up an earned run in all of July, and was working on a scoreless streak of 16⅔ innings. Then I heard Ross Porter announce:

So the Dodgers will go with Don Stanhouse . . .

Nooooooooooooooooooooooooooooooo! Don Stanhouse, who had pitched all of 4⅔ innings since April 16 because of injuries? Don Stanhouse, with an ERA almost four runs higher than Steve Howe, whom he was replacing? Don Stanhouse, with a mustache resembling Gabe Kaplan from *Welcome Back, Kotter,* and taken about as seriously by opposing batters? *That* Don Stanhouse? I could almost understand the move if Howe had been overworked. But the rookie was well-rested, having thrown only an inning and a third three days earlier. Keep in mind, this was the same pitcher who had thrown two or more innings nine times already, including two stints of five innings. Even more baffling, Stanhouse had just pitched two innings himself the day before. Granted, he got the save (and maybe Lasorda wanted to play a hot hand), but he walked two. If anyone could have used the rest, it would have been Mr. Kotter.

Okay, so maybe Lasorda didn't want Howe to face a powerhitting right-handed pinch hitter coming off the bench for pitcher Rick Camp. That would be understandable if the Braves were reactivating Hank Aaron. Instead, they sent up Jerry Royster. That's right, Steve Howe was replaced after one batter so he wouldn't have to face a utility man hitting .231 with no home runs on the year. With Stanhouse in there, Lasorda wasn't playing percentages; he was playing Russian Roulette.

All Royster did was single home a run to make it a 4–3 ball-game. There were maybe 2,000 fans left from the official 10,187 at the start of the game. With so few people in attendance, you could hear actual isolated insults hurled by crazed fans. Now, with two runners on base, up stepped a 150-pound, fuzzy-faced pipsqueak, Glenn Hubbard, who had worked himself into the starting second baseman job, replacing (you guessed it) Jerry Royster. If you followed baseball during this era, it's hard to forget Hubbard, who resembled a garden gnome. Despite his diminutive size, he was always a thorn in the Dodgers' side.

In an at-bat that seemed like an eternity, Hubbard worked Stanhouse to a full-count. On the radio, even Ross Porter couldn't mask his nervousness. There seemed to be a franticness to his delivery. By this point, I was on the floor of my bedroom, curled up in a fetal position. I felt like I had swallowed poison. Short of Stanhouse slamming the door, death would have been a welcome relief.

> The Braves have scored two with two out in the ninth inning and nobody on. An error, a walk, and two singles. And the Dodgers have had that lead pared to 4-to-3.
> Mustachioed Don Stanhouse facing bearded Glenn Hubbard. The ball game on the line. 3-and-2. Here's the stretch . . . and Stanhouse backs off the rubber.

Stanhouse's nickname with the Orioles was "Full Pack." They say that's how many cigarettes manager Earl Weaver smoked whenever he pitched. His nickname to me became "Full Box"— that's how much Kleenex I went through over the 1980 season, wiping away tears of rage and angst.

> All right, Stanhouse, back up on top. Goes to the stretch. The runners go, and the pitch is . . . a fly

> ball to left field and hit deep. Baker going back,
> a-way back, he's at the *waaaaalllll* . . .

Wouldn't it be great if we could freeze-frame time and change the outcome of certain events in our lives? For me, I would change:

- The day I called up a platonic friend to take to the senior prom when I *could've* taken a girl I had the hots for, and who, I found out later, really wanted me to ask her.

- The day I got duped into buying sizable chunks of shares of WorldCom and Nortel Networks, only to lose everything after both companies went belly-up.

- This outcome:

IT'S OUTTA HERE!

There was an overmodulated shrillness in Ross's voice that I hadn't heard before. Think about that line itself. Usually, announcers reserve the phrase "it's outta here!" for the home team after they hit a game-winning homer. But with those three words, Ross turned what was normally a phrase of excitement into one of unfiltered, unmitigated shock, akin to a scream queen shrieking, "Get outta here!" in a horror/slasher movie.

Don't believe me? Ross didn't talk for a full *40 seconds* after Hubbard hit his game-winning homer. I think he was trying to pick his jaw up off the floor. Finally, he broke his dazed silence:

> Glenn Hubbard belts his sixth home run of the year on a 3-2 pitch, a three-run homer, and the Braves score five runs with two out and nobody on in the bottom of the ninth, to pull one out over the Dodgers, 6–4.
> The Dodgers let one get away.

You think?

> Instead of winning, 4–1, the Braves come back
> and beat the Dodgers, and Don Stanhouse sur-
> renders his second home run as a Dodger. And in
> dramatic fashion, little Glenn Hubbard rifled one
> to the left-center field fence.

Why is it that the fact he was "little" just makes my blood boil
even more?

> Baker went back, leaped high and could not get
> it. And the Braves with ninth inning magic, pull
> it out tonight.
> And this is one of the tough Dodger losses of
> the year.

On my *Homerun Highlights* tape, the recording ends there, at
which point I come back on as the narrator and say: "Now, as a
little extra, I've extended the Hubbard homer, as called by Ross
Porter." I then cue up the Hubbard homer all over again, only this
time, doing a little audio editing, I repeat the last line. Not once.
Not twice. Not even 10 times. But, well, you'll see . . .

> All right, Stanhouse, back up on top. Goes to the
> stretch. The runners go, and the pitch is . . . a fly
> ball to left field and hit deep. Baker going back, a-
> way back, he's at the *waaaaaalllll . . . IT'S OUTTA
> HERE!*
> > *IT'S OUTTA HERE!*
> > *IT'S OUTTA HERE!*
> > *IT'S OUTTA HERE!*
> > *IT'S OUTTA HERE!*
> > *IT'S OUTTA HERE!*
> > *IT'S OUTTA HERE!*
> > *IT'S OUTTA HERE!*
> > *IT'S OUTTA HERE!*
> > *IT'S OUTTA HERE!*

IT'S OUTTA HERE!
IT'S OUTTA HERE!
IT'S OUTTA HERE!
IT'S OUTTA HERE!
IT'S OUTTA HERE!
IT'S OUTTA HERE!
IT'S OUTTA HERE!
IT'S OUTTA HERE!
IT'S OUTTA HERE!
IT'S OUTTA HERE!
IT'S OUTTA HERE! . . .

You get the idea. I repeated Ross's line a total of 56 times. Toward the end of the sequence, the call speeds up in an out-of-control frenzy, as if the Chipmunks had taken over, before all suddenly falls silent. This was an epic loss that demanded an epic response. I didn't do it for comedic effect. My own survival depended on it. The only way to purge a poisonous snakebite is to take on some of the toxin itself. Strangely, I started to feel a little better almost immediately. I had taken Ross's shock-and-awe line and deconstructed it, taken some of the sting out, like someone adding an infectious rap beat under Mel Gibson's volcanic rants against girlfriend Oksana Grigorieva or Christian Bale's diatribe on the set of *Terminator Salvation*.

The Braves would end up beating the Dodgers, 7–6, with *another* three-run homer in the ninth inning just a week later at Dodger Stadium. And, as we'll get to later, Team Blue would lose even more late-inning heartbreakers in the last two weeks of the season. But when the dust cleared on 1980 and the team lost by one game, the *"IT'S OUTTA HERE!"* game is what stood out to me as the real difference-maker.

Red Sox fans will always bemoan Bucky @^%$# Dent. Me? I'll never forget Don #@^%& Stanhouse. And Glenn Mother Hubbard.

ALL-STAR BASEBALL NAMES

"Donnie Baseball." "Teddy Ballgame." "Charlie Hustle." The name of the Braves' Charlie Spikes would seem to fit right alongside those other great nicknames for Don Mattingly, Ted Williams, and Pete Rose, respectively. Charlie Spikes. One pictures a hard-charging base-stealer, spikes flying menacingly in the air à la Ty Cobb.

But in reality, Charlie Spikes was neither a base-stealer (he was thrown out half the time over a nine-year career) nor much of a hitter (3,687 hits behind Cobb). Instead, all that can be said of Charlie Spikes is that he makes my list of coolest-sounding baseball names from the 1977 to 1981 seasons. Here's a position-by-position lineup of my favorites. The best part: the majority of these names are their birth names, not nicknames.

- **1B—Champ Summers.** Imagine how wonderful it would be to be called "Champ" every day. The cheerful surname is an added bonus.

- **2B—Garth Iorg.** Seems like his name would make a good anagram, but the best I could come up with is Hot Art Rig.

- **SS—Dickie Thon.** Try to say it without giggling.

- **3B—Doug DeCinces.** The double "D" and double "S" sounds please the tongue.

- **OF—Sixto Lezcano.** Harvey's Wallbangers' Brewers had lots of great names. This one was the best.

- **OF—Drungo Hazewood.** Sounds like a character from a Cheech & Chong movie.

- **OF—Charlie Spikes.**

- **C—Bif Pocoroba.** I thought I read somewhere he was part Native American. Or maybe I just wished he was.

- **STARTING PITCHER—Gaylord Perry.** Like his name, Gaylord always seemed as old as the Ancient Mariner (which, of course, he became when he pitched in Seattle in his twilight years).

- **RELIEF PITCHER—Rollie Fingers.** Could you come up with a better name for a pitcher, especially one with a waxed mustache?

- **RESERVES—**Kent Tekulve, Dan Quisenberry, Jamie Quirk, Rance Mulliniks, Ron LeFlore, Max Venable, Joe Charboneau, Johnny Oates, Bob Owchinko, La-Marr Hoyt, and of course, bringing up the rear—Mario Mendoza!

AND THE 1980 "TRUE BLUE RIBBON" MIC AWARD GOES TO . . .

I'm going to keep the Ross Porter skein going here and go with . . . Ross Porter! (On the heels of the heavy Hubbard game, something lighter seemed in order.) On August 25 at Veterans Stadium in Philadelphia, I got to experience three rarities in one game. The first was a Jerry Reuss home run in the second inning that put the Dodgers up, 3–0. Reuss had exactly one home run in 22 seasons—1,024 at-bats—and it came in this game. So I heard something occur whose odds were literally one in a thousand. The other events were just as unusual and were called by Ross Porter, who proved he didn't need to cite statistics to call a great game.

The Dodgers broke a 4–4 tie in the top of the ninth inning when Baker and Cey hit run-scoring doubles off Warren Brusstar.

Hoping to stem the bleeding, manager Dallas Green brought in his ace, Tug McGraw. Ross took it from there . . .

> So Tug McGraw will come on and face pinch hitter Joe Ferguson here in the ninth inning. First base is open. Bill Russell would be next. One out. The Phillies have to keep the infield in. Garvey's the runner at third, Cey is at second. Baker and Cey with run-producing doubles in the ninth inning.
>
> And the Phillies are going to take the bat out of Ferguson's hands immediately and walk him to load them up. So, looking for a double play that could bail them out of the inning without further damage, Philadelphia will put Ferguson aboard.

I'd like to point out how masterfully Ross set up the scenario, with a succinct economy of words. Like Andre Ethier years later, Ross was always a good finisher, hyper-focused at the end of tight games.

Simply put, the Phillies, down by two runs, were going to try to set up a double play to get out of the inning down by only two runs. Nothing unusual about that. But then, as Tug casually threw one of his intentionally wide pitches to catcher Bob Boone, something unexpected happened . . .

> And [Ferguson] swings and grounds one to right field for a base hit! McGraw didn't get it far enough outside! *One* run will score . . . here comes Cey . . . *he* scores, and the Dodgers lead, 8–4!

It was the Kelly Leak play from *The Bad News Bears!*

> How about *that?* Joe Ferguson, with an *alert* play. Tug McGraw just *lobbed* on up there, high and away, he thought. And Ferguson reached out and

spanked it into right field for a two-run single.
The Dodgers have made it a four-run inning, and
they're leading the Philadelphia Phillies, 8–4.

One could go his entire lifetime and never witness another
event like this in a baseball game. I know it's happened before and
since, but personally I can recall only one other instance of a major league batter swinging and connecting during an intentional
base on balls—Miguel Cabrera, on June 22, 2006—though I
didn't experience it live. (*Baseball Tonight* showed highlights of
Miguel poking home the eventual winning run for the Marlins
during a failed free pass. Joe Girardi, the Marlins' manager at the
time of Miguel's hit, admitted he had never seen that before. This
was a man who had seen a lot of baseball.) The odds must be one
in the hundreds of thousands when you amass all the games. Even
Ross suggested he was witnessing it for the first time.

> [Laughs] Weeeeelllllll, I'll tell ya, the more you're
> around this game, the more you realize that there's
> a *lot* that you haven't seen when you follow base-
> ball. I don't care *how* many years you watch the
> game. That was academic!

After Derrel Thomas pinch-ran for Ferguson, who received a
hero's welcome in the dugout, Bill Russell, batting seventh that
day, stepped up. Then things got even nuttier . . . and Russell did
something that, I believe, was *his* only time in 18 seasons:

> Pitch hits Russell, and *Russell will charge McGraw!*
> And we have a *brawl* in Philadelphia!

Not just a "brawl," but a "brawl in Philadelphia." Brilliant!
Sounds like the title of a *Rocky* sequel. In true boxing fashion,
Ross gave a blow-by-blow account:

> Russell *swings* and misses, Pete Rose *tackles* Russell!

> There goes Baker, there goes Thomasson, they're
> after McGraw, and we've got both benches empty-
> ing.

After a lot of pushing and shoving, during which Dusty Baker
led a "beeline toward McGraw," yet another atypical event caught
Ross by surprise. Again, the Finisher did not miss a beat.

> And now, here comes one of the Phillies out of the
> dugout without his *shirt* on! Somebody was back
> in the dressing room and heard about the fight
> and *ran out!*

To this day, I've always wondered who that shirtless pugilist
was. My best guess would be pitcher Dickie Noles, who pitched
three innings before being replaced by Brusstar, four batters before Russell. That would give him enough time to get in the clubhouse and start hitting the showers. Who else would be getting
undressed before the game ended if not him? Maybe starter Nino
Espinosa? Maybe it was little-used infielder John Vukovich, in-
terrupting a massage in the trainer's room. Alas, the only detail
Ross left out was that of the unidentified naked torso. Was this
latecomer hairless or hirsute? Sinewy or broad-shouldered? What
color skin did he have? Did he have back hair?

> So Bill Russell took it on the hip. And if you know
> Bill Russell, you know how mild-mannered he is.
> It takes a lot to get him fired up. And he imme-
> diately dropped the bat and charged McGraw. He
> took at swing at Tug, I don't think it landed.

Poor Bill . . . the one time he charged a pitcher in his career,
he couldn't even land a blow, as Ross was all too quick to point
out not once, but twice now.

Russell, of course, was ejected, but McGraw was allowed to

remain in the game, which incensed Tom Lasorda, who rushed the field and, in Ross's words, went "cheek-to-cheek" with crew chief John McSherry. I think he meant to say "jaw-to-jaw," but "cheek-to-cheek" sounded so much better, since I could imagine their generous jowls jiggling back and forth.

All in all, Ross's account of this sequence of events was a highlight of the 1980 season. It wasn't just incredulous; it was funny. Ross got *so* into it, you couldn't help but be entertained. Fergie spanks a free pass! A fight in Philadelphia! A shirtless thug! Blow-by-blow! Cheek-to-cheek! Someone stop me from using so many exclamation points!

The Dodgers once again showed they wouldn't be pushed around, but the Phillies would get the last laugh. They would go on to win the World Series that year.

THE BAD NEWS BEARS VS. THE WORLD

Okay, since I've invoked Kelly Leak and *The Bad News Bears* (the original 1976 version), I have a moral obligation to pause here and outline my case for why it is the best baseball movie of all time. How can a movie about a bunch of foul-mouthed youth league twerps trump such cinematic giants as *The Natural, Bull Durham,* even *The Pride of the Yankees*? The real question you should be asking is, how can those movies even compare to *The Bad News Bears*? There's only one way to settle this, and that's on the playing field.

Mirroring the nine positions of a baseball field, I'm going to field nine baseball movies (outside of *The Bad News Bears*) that are generally considered the "best" by fans and critics alike. Yes, I know some of these were good books before they became movies. Take it up with a librarian.

1. *The Natural*—More syrupy than an IHOP; Roy Hobbs is a bore. Commits the one crime of most baseball movies—putting the sport too much on a pedestal. Blech.

2. *Field of Dreams*—Fathers and Sons and Holy "Shoeless Joe" Ghosts, all nice touches that have their moments. But it too suffers from TPS (Too Precious Syndrome).

3. *Bull Durham*—This one at least captures the right spirit of the sport. I like my baseball movies messy, like life itself. But the scene where Kevin Costner says to Susan Sarandon, "I like warm, wet kisses, and walks on the beach, and Tutti-Frutti ice cream, and Sloe Gin Fizzes" or whatever the heck he says just ruined it for me. Sorry, there was no turning back after that.

4. *Major League*—C'mon, I said "best" baseball movies. Out-and-out farces don't qualify in my book. And *Platoon* notwithstanding (that was more about Oliver Stone), Charlie Sheen cannot be the best of anything.

5. *Bang the Drum Slowly*—Zzzzzzzz. Seriously, ever tried to watch this when it comes on cable on a Sunday afternoon? I'm going to start my own film festival one day called SnoozeFest, and *Bang the Drum Slowly* is going to premiere on opening night.

6. *The Pride of the Yankees*—Okay, high marks, obviously, for Gary Cooper's depiction of Lou Gehrig. And you'd have to be Montgomery Burns not to be moved to tears by the end. But the storyline and filmmaking are a little too pat, some of the performances a little too wooden. For the most part, you are always

aware you are watching a *movie*. And it's the Yankees. Phooey.

7. *A League of Their Own*—I liked this movie. But its only real legacy is that it launched a timeless catchphrase: "There's no crying in baseball!" By the way, whatever happened to Lori Petty's career? She was great in this. And remember when Rosie O'Donnell was funny?

8. *Eight Men Out*—I remember being bored senseless seeing this in my early twenties. Could've just been my unhappiness over a recent break-up, not to mention the fact that I always find John Sayles movies difficult to follow. But seeing it again recently gave me a newfound respect for his treatment of the 1919 Chicago Black Sox Scandal, and I found it okay. Thankfully, although Charlie Sheen is in it, he rarely says much.

9. *The Rookie*—I watched this on a plane, saw that it suffered from TPS, and fell asleep during it. Okay, that's a double-header for SnoozeFest. Watch this and *Bang the Drum* and wake up with drool on your shoulder.

I'm going to counter the above with nine reasons why *The Bad News Bears* is number one. Some quick backstory: I was 10 years old when I saw the movie for the first time in a Westwood, California theater. I seem to recall that it was my fourth PG-rated movie, after *The Poseidon Adventure, My Name is Nobody*, and *Jaws*. But it was the first movie I had ever seen that was so *honest*. It almost felt like I was watching a documentary. Having spent much of my childhood in the San Fernando Valley, where the movie is set, I *knew* these 10- and 11-year-olds. They spoke like kids speak, acted like kids act. As I got older, I started to see some of the truths the movie spoke about baseball, to the point where I became convinced that no other movie captures the *essence* of the sport quite like *The Bad News Bears*.

Here are nine reasons why *The Bad News Bears* takes home the molded-plastic gold:

1. **The Bears lose the big game**—I have a theory that the best sports movies are the ones where the team or hero we are identifying with loses the big event. *Rocky* is the classic example. Rocky Balboa loses the big match against Apollo Creed at the end, but do we think of him as a loser? Of course not. He proves that a heavy-lidded butcher-turned-fighter can hold his own against a world heavyweight champ and in so doing earn the respect of himself, the world, and Talia Shire. It's the little life lessons along the way that matter, not the final outcome. Heck, losing only makes our hero more empathetic and relatable. The main problems with *Rocky II, III,* and *IV*, besides the fact that they pitted Rocky against cartoonish opponents like Mr. T, was that he *won* all those matches. And we knew he would, too—there was never anything at stake except how much money Sylvester Stallone would rake in with each film's grosses.

2. **Walter Matthau**—Matthau brings his usual hangdog persona to his role as perpetual burnout Morris Buttermaker, the Bears' alcoholic manager and part-time pool cleaner who reluctantly agrees to coach a team of rejects. In the game of life, this man's a forfeit. While pitching batting practice, he passes out drunk. But as the movie goes on, his gruff exterior peels away, revealing a wounded soul who still has unresolved issues about being a lousy father figure to Tatum O'Neal's Amanda and his own baseball career, which flamed out

in the minors after so much promise. A scene where he tosses beer in Amanda's face in the dugout is particularly shocking, leaving both in tears. (The film has jarring moments of drama—the type where you audibly go, "Whoa!") Buttermaker falls into the trap many do, thinking that if his team can just *win, baby, win*, his own life will be better, and he gradually turns into the type of hothead Little League coach he always loathed. In the championship game, he realizes his mistake, plays the worst players on his team, and becomes a better man for it. His message to his players: Just have fun. Isn't that what baseball was always meant to be?

3. ***Carmen* soundtrack**—Director Michael Ritchie's and music supervisor Jerry Fielding's decision to use a 19th century opera written by Frenchman Georges Bizet as the basis for the movie's musical score is a stroke of genius. The opera's classical flourishes elevate these Little League games to high drama. (Likewise, eschewing a soundtrack made up of music from the '70s also helps make this movie timeless.) Baseball *is* like great opera—it has highs and lows, and moments of tension followed by moments of release. The stirring orchestral passage—uplifting, then tragic—as the Bears try to tie the championship game on Kelly Leak's potential inside-the-park grand slam (after slapping an intentional pass to right field) still gives me goosebumps whenever I hear it. The closest comparison I can come up with is Carl Stalling's classical signatures that are such an integral part of the Looney Tunes cartoons. Imagine a Roadrunner/Coyote cartoon without the Warner Bros.' playful orchestra under the animation. You can't.

4. **Tatum O'Neal**—My first movie star crush was Tatum O'Neal. Looking back, she might've been the tipping point of what got me interested in baseball. She was close to my age when this movie came out, looked good in a halter top and puka shells, and threw a mean curveball. In the movie, Tatum's Amanda Whurlitzer represents that "out-of-the-box" wild card that many successful franchises sometimes turn to to draw interest—and win. The Chicago Bulls had Dennis Rodman. The Dodgers had Manny Ramirez. The Durham Bulls had "Nuke" LaLoosh. The Bears have a (spit it out) *girl*, who just happens to be their ace.

5. **The Characters**—The Bears are made up of unforgettable characters who are fighting a wide array of demons. Among my favorites are Ahmad Abdul Rahim, who sheds his uniform and sits in a tree wearing nothing but underwear because he'll never be as good as his idol Hank Aaron; Tanner Boyle, who hates losing so much, he picks a fight with the entire seventh grade; Timmy Lupus, the "booger-eating spaz" who goes the whole season unable to catch a fly ball . . . until it matters most. Then there's Kelly Leak, who's too cool to join any organized sport, let alone the Bears. Played by Jackie Earle Haley (who enjoyed a revival starting with *Little Children* thirty years later), Leak is that classic rebel you find in '70s movies who courts danger, keeps cigarettes in his ear, rides a Harley—and plays a mean game of air hockey. The filmmakers perfectly set up his iconic yet untouchable status in the Valley. When a ball gets loose during a Bears practice, Kelly gets off his bike and guns it 175 feet back to the infield on the fly. Buttermaker, intrigued, comments on his great arm. One of his players says, "Of *course* he's got a great arm, Buttermaker. He's

the best athlete in the area. But you don't understand. *That's* Kelly Leak." Kelly eventually joins the Bears, puts on their dorky uniform sponsored by Chico's Bail Bonds, and learns how to be a team player.

6. **Quotable dialogue**—The best movies have lines you can quote with your friends. "*That's* Kelly Leak" is just one of dozens of memorable lines from the movie. But don't take my word for it—check out www.imdb.com, the internet movie data base. It features several pages of quotable dialogue. Only *Major League* can compare. Tanner wins the prize for Most Un-PC Line Delivered By A Kid in Any PG Movie when he sizes up his team of minorities and misfits with a flurry of epithets that I'd prefer not to repeat here. Matthau, of course, delivers his lines with impeccable timing, including a classic salvo near the end when he tells a councilman to "get back to the stands before I shave off half your mustache and shove it up your left nostril." After the Yankees win the championship, the Bears, instead of being good losers, essentially tell them to stick it where the sun doesn't shine, and oh yeah, "Just wait till next year." How many times have we uttered *that* truism as baseball fans (the second part, not the first)?

7. **It's a microcosm of MLB**—A dominant Yankees team with a "winning at all costs" mentality. Backroom politics and shady owners. Player jealousies and racial tension. Out-of-control managers. Sounds like another day in Major League Baseball. But it's also the universe that *The Bad News Bears* inhabits. As I said before, baseball, like life, is messy. Just as Charles Schulz's *Peanuts* characters were mouthpieces for an adult world, so too are the potty-mouthed kids and their manipulative parents in

the North Valley Little League. Which brings us to . . .

8. **It *nails* youth sports culture**—I know this deviates a little from big-league ball, but prior to *The Bad News Bears*, there had never been a mainstream movie about the corrosive culture of youth sports. This movie shone a light on the disturbing trend of moms and dads who instill in their children the idea that winning is a matter of life and death—a trend that has only gotten worse. The manager of the Yankees, Vic Morrow, who sadly is best known for being decapitated in the *Twilight Zone* movie helicopter accident six years later, epitomizes the kind of ironclad dad who won't settle for second-best. His motivational speech to his players before the championship game is more intimidation than inspiration: "I'm not going to talk about winning. I'm going to talk to you about *losing*. 'Cause if you guys lose this game, each and every one of you, you're gonna have to live with it." George Steinbrenner couldn't have put it any better.

9. **The championship game**—The title game between the Yankees and the Bears is by far the most entertaining and engaging match-up you'll see in any baseball movie. The filmmakers don't just give us snippets and highlights. They devote the last 30 minutes of the film to it. We get to see much of each inning, so that the drama unfolds almost in real time and we become invested. Along the way we see a classic baseball brawl, players flipping the bird, a beanball pitch at a batter's head, Vic Morrow clocking his pitcher-son on the mound, Matthau throwing players against the dugout wall in a rage . . . if you're looking for a feel-good movie like *The Natural*, you've come to the wrong place. And

that's why *The Bad News Bears* takes the prize. After all their scrapping and clawing, the Bears *still* lose. But, as they douse each other with beer (!) anyway, at least they are glorious losers, proving that they belong on the same field as the Yankees, just as Rocky proved he belonged in the ring with Apollo Creed. To me, the true spirit of baseball—and ourselves—resides not in Roy Hobbs, but in Morris Buttermaker.

Winner: *The Bad News Bears*. (Now, let's just pretend they never did any bad sequels starring Tony Curtis, or a remake with Billy Bob Thornton as Buttermaker, which I will never, ever watch, even if you tape back my eyelids *Clockwork Orange*-style.)

BOO ON VIN

Back when Vin Scully did the bulk of the radio broadcasts, one of the cool things about going to a Dodger game was hearing his voice reverberating through the stadium from fans' transistor radios. His voice was so

---

Bullpen Session

You're Outta Here!

Worst baseball movie ever? That's easy: *The Fan*. This one is so bad, it's good. When I saw a premiere of it at the Village Theatre in Westwood, the audience was rolling in the aisles. Not good for a movie that's supposed to be a drama. Everything about this 1996 stalker movie starring Robert DeNiro (who seems to be spoofing his own Travis Bickle creation) and Wesley Snipes (he's essentially playing Barry Bonds) is unbelievable and overwrought, right down to the fact that the umps let a game go on despite a torrential downpour that has rendered the field so flooded, you half-expect a family of ducks to go wading by. Maybe someone should have clued in British director Tony Scott about the concept of "rain delays." I'm convinced DeNiro lost a bet when he took this role.

ubiquitous, many times I wouldn't even bother to bring a radio. I could get up, hit the restroom, grab a pretzel, and return to my seat without missing a beat, his voice echoing off the steel and concrete around me.

Vin was well-aware of this fact and sometimes had fun with it. The most famous example occurred back in the days the Dodgers played in the Coliseum, when Vin got the entire crowd to yell out "Happy Birthday, Frank" to umpire Frank Secory in 1960. Flash-forward to August 31, 1980. In the second game of a doubleheader that the Dodgers were winning handily (which might explain a few things), Vin got into a little more mischief when he uttered what I refer to on my tape as "a horrendous, ear-plugging joke." Unfortunately, I don't recall what this "num-Scully" joke was, but it was so lame, it actually elicited vociferous boos from many of the 48,000 fans in attendance. Vin *loved* the response and had fun with his minions.

> Boooooyyy . . . [laughs]. And Derrel Thomas hits a fly ball to Andre Dawson in center field, and he makes the—
>
> Are you people *terrible*?
>
> And going to third is Ferguson, and he beats the throw! And *that* gets the applause.
>
> So Derrel Thomas hits a fly ball to center field, and all of you should be *ashamed* of booing. Do you realize Derrel Thomas thinks you were booing *him*? And he's playing so hard down there?
>
> So a runner at third [laughs]—that is a *terrible* joke, isn't it?
>
> A paper airplane on the field, so time-out . . . that will allow us time to *clear* the air, huh?

If you ever want to win a bet, tell someone Vin Scully was once booed at Dodger Stadium, and refer to this anecdote. They'd never believe you in a hundred years.

ROSS PORTER—A TRIPLE PLAY

Clearly, I'm into some serious Ross overdrive in this chapter, but no analysis of the Dodgers' 1980 season would be complete without referencing a recurring segment that appeared on KABC 790 called "Ross Porter's Viewpoint." I never knew when a new "Ross Porter's Viewpoint" was scheduled to air; they seemed to pop up at random times just hours before a game. They were essentially two-minute commentaries in which Ross was given airtime to climb aboard his soapbox and speak his mind about the Dodgers and baseball—heavy on statistics, natch, to bolster his points. Really, it was almost like an audio blog (as I've alluded to before, Ross was ahead of his time).

I always looked forward to Ross's commentaries because they showed me another side of him, one who couldn't summon such strong opinions in the context of doing Dodger play-by-play. Ross's proclamations were bold and often ominous:

> The Dodgers are doomed *unless* their pitchers can get the staff ERA under 3.50 . . .
>
> The Dodgers will win *only if* Dusty Baker breaks out of his 3-for-29 slump . . .
>
> *If* the Dodgers don't improve their record in one-run games, they will probably *never* catch the Astros . . .

Every "Viewpoint" ended with Ross's signature phrase: "I'm Ross Porter. And that's my viewpoint." After a while, I started to look forward to these segments not so much for what Ross had to say, but for the fun I could have with them. As you probably figured out by now, I had discovered the joys of re-editing clips to form my own audio mixes. Ross Porter's segment afforded me opportunities to cut up his commentaries and insert myself asking him often inane questions. Granted, this is very amateurish by today's standards, but to a 14-year-old armed with a radio and multiple tape recorders, this was sheer comic genius.

My baseball buddy, David, insisted on getting cassette copies of these reinvented "Viewpoints," and by the '81 season, he was making guest appearances in them. In one instance, I phoned David at his parents' house and, recording our conversation, asked him if Ross was home, whereupon David yells at Ross to pick up the phone. The real Ross "gets on the phone" and starts lamenting how the Dodger starters are all hitting under .250 on a current road trip. I get impatient with his "negative attitude" and blow up his house (and presumably David's) using a prerecorded explosion from Jim Healy's wacky KMPC radio show (don't ask). The capper: underneath this noisy explosion, you can just barely make out Ross uttering, "I'm Ross Porter. And that's my viewpoint." And . . . scene.

In any event, here's what Ross had to say when I "interviewed" him about the state of the Dodgers after an August 17 game left them two games back.

> [Cue the Knack's "My Sharona."]
>
> And now, as a *Homerun Highlights* special edition, an interview with Dodger announcer Ross Porter . . .
>
> Me: Ross, rolling into the third week of August, the Dodgers went from a half game up to two games out in the National League West in just a week. Do you think they're in trouble?
>
> Ross: The Dodgers are clearly a team in trouble.
>
> Me: Oh. I see. Why do you think the Dodgers are declining? Give me, say, two reasons.
>
> Ross: Two of the Dodgers' glaring faults were accentuated yesterday in the loss to the Reds. First and foremost, the Dodgers do not have a bullpen stopper.

Me: Well . . . how about Don Stanhouse or Steve Howe? Joe Beckwith?

Ross: The Dodgers have *no one* they can rely on in relief for a consistent stretch.

Me: [Defensive] Sorry! Jeesh . . .

Ross: It's hard to win a title without a relief ace.

Me: Well, how 'bout offense? Has that been a factor in their decline?

Ross: The Dodgers are hitting out of sync. In only two games last week did they score more than two runs. And they continue to leave too many runners in scoring position.

Me: Which players have led the Dodger offense, if any?

Ross: Steve Garvey and Dusty Baker.

Me: Well, even with Reggie Smith out [with injuries], I think Johnstone and Monday have done a legitimate job.

Ross: It's not the same club without Reggie. And he may not be back until September, if then. Injuries are affecting the oldest men on the Dodgers—Smith, Don Sutton, Davey Lopes, and Bill Russell—when their contributions are badly needed . . .

Me: [Interrupting him] Okay, okay, let's switch the subject. Do you think the Dodgers, overall, have a shot of winning the pennant?

Ross: The Dodgers still have a shot at the West flag *if* they survive this [road] trip.

Me: What's that supposed to mean?

Ross: That means *not* falling more than five games out of first place in the next nine days. *If* that happens, the Dodgers will likely be finished.

Me: Oh, come on, what kind of a viewpoint is
      that?

Ross: [A beat] I'm Ross Porter. And that's *my*
      viewpoint.

Happily for all of us, the Dodgers never did fall back more
than five games in the next nine days. In fact, the furthest they fell
the rest of the season was three games.

But those three games can look like Mount Everest when they
occur with only three games left in the season.

6TH INNING
September-October 1980

DESTINATION: FALL CLASSIC . . .
OR CLASSIC FALL?

O n September 2, the Dodgers sat tied with the Astros for first place. But neither team could put the other away. They continued to play a game of "take it . . . no, you take it . . . take it . . . no, you take it" for most of the month.

On September 24, a win would move the Dodgers back into a first place tie with the Astros with only 10 games left. L.A. was playing San Francisco at home. The game went into extra innings, 4–4. In the bottom of the 12th, with two outs and runners on first and second, the pitcher's spot came up. Dodger Stadium began to stir, as called by Jerry Doggett:

The fans are *pleading* for Mota, and here he comes!

Suddenly, exuberant cheers as everyone's favorite pinch-hitting savant left the first-base coaching box to grab a bat. At 42 years old, Manny had not played for most of the season, but the team activated him (and Vic Davalillo) this month when the rosters expanded to 40 players. Jerry wisely stepped aside to let his radio audience hear PA announcer John Ramsey's introduction of player-coach Mota:

Ron Cey, the "Penguin," going deep.

> Your attention please.
> For the Dodgers.
> Batting.
> For Castillo.
> Number 11.
> Manny.
> Mota.

Even the normally monotone Mr. Ramsey seemed to get caught up in the moment, discernibly raising his register on the word "Manny," then even higher on "Mota." It was the most emotion I'd ever heard from the man. Mota was facing righty Mike Rowland and worked a tough at-bat. Then:

> Mota, a ground ball up the middle, base hit to center field! Here comes Garvey, and he will scoooooore, on a base hit by Mota!

The crowd sounded as if they had just won the World Series.

> He gets a hug from Lasorda, a handshake and a pat on the back from everybody . . . the Dodgers are tied for *first place* here in the National League West with the Houston Astros!

The hit was Manny's first of the year.

After wrapping their series with the Giants with a loss, the Dodgers headed to Jack Murphy Stadium in San Diego for a three-game set. The teams split the first two games, setting up the rubber match on Sunday afternoon, September 28. Meanwhile, the Astros were in the midst of winning six out of seven and had reclaimed first place by two games with seven games left. The Dodgers weren't in "must win" territory yet, but they were certainly getting close. Every pitch, every play, every at-bat garnered ever-increasing scrutiny. And whatever I was doing in my life increasingly took a backseat to these late-season games.

After only one inning, the Dodgers found themselves in a hole, 3–0. Starter Welch had to be replaced due to a groin injury. But in the top of the fourth, Rick Monday stepped up with two men on. Ross:

> Here's the 0-1 pitch to Rick Monday . . . high fly ball to left field and hit deep, Richards going back, a-waaaay back, this ball is goooone! Home run, Monday. Dodgers tie it, 3–3!

The Dodgers added two more runs in the top of the eighth to go up, 5–3, but blew a golden opportunity to score even more when Cey got caught in a rundown between third and home. Still, word got out that the Astros had just lost their game to the Reds. If the Dodgers held on to win, they would be only one game back.

In the bottom of the eighth with one out, the Padres came within one run when Don Stanhouse, doing what he did best, walked in a run. Lasorda quickly yanked him after one batter and put in 19-year-old Fernando Valenzuela, making only his sixth major league appearance. The batter was pinch hitter Barry Evans. Doggett made the call:

> Popped up . . . near second base . . . Davey Lopes is there . . . waiting, waiting, waiting, backs up— *DROPS IT!* He lost it in the sun!
>
> Here's the play at second base, and the run scores. Davey Lopes had the ball *drop* at his side, and the Padres take the lead. *Unbelievable!*

Believe it—the Dodgers lost the game, 7–5, and remained stuck two games behind the Astros. As I did during the *"IT'S OUTTA HERE!"* game, I inured myself by deconstructing a key call—in this case, Jerry's cry of *"Unbelievable!"* which I sliced and diced until it finally disappeared and seemed to lose all meaning, sounding something like this:

Unbelievable!
Unbelievable!
Unbelievable!
Believable!
Believable!
-Able!
-Ble!
-L!
!

At which point I say: "Don't feel too bad, folks. Some folks find Dodger baseball quite amusing!" Cut to a medley of crazy laughter, including a loop of one of Jerry Doggett's giggling fits. Under these layers of laughter I intone, "Dodger baseball—it will tickle you to the crazy house."

Once again, I resorted to humor as a coping mechanism to keep from going insane myself. I *had* to—there was a lot of doom and gloom going around L.A. that last week of the season. Stu Nahan, the sports anchor for KNBC Channel 4, was virtually throwing in the towel on the season. Referring to the base-running error by Cey and the botched pop-up by Lopes, Stu said, "The whole mess cost them a run, what can I tell you." He said it would take a "miracle" for them to win the division. Ross Porter was a little more reflective. On his "Ross Porter's Viewpoint" that week, he pointed to several losses in recent weeks that loomed even larger, including the Padre game:

> That extra inning game that got away in Houston three weeks ago, and the ones the last two Sundays against the Reds and Padres they seem to have won and didn't, have to be *especially* galling to the Dodgers right now . . . I'm Ross Porter. And that's my viewpoint.

After San Diego, the team headed to San Francisco for their

final road series of the season. The Dodgers took the first two games at Candlestick, thanks to two unlikely heroes. The star of the first game was Pedro Guerrero, who helped tie the game in the ninth, then hit a three-run, game-winning bomb to right-center field in the 10th inning that was one of the longest home runs to the opposite field I had ever seen. As he made his way back to an ecstatic dugout, I remember thinking, "This guy is a superstar . . . his time has arrived."

The winning pitcher in relief was Fernando Valenzuela—his first major league win. Joe Ferguson, who got hot at the end of the year, was the hero of the second game, with six RBIs. Unfortunately, all these heroics could buy was the right to keep pace with the Astros. The Dodgers, of course, have a history of late-season implosions against the Giants, dating back to Bobby Thomson. With just one game left at Candlestick, that familiar gnawing in my stomach grabbed me.

In fairness to the Dodgers, injuries forced a lot of their starters to the bench for that final game. Three-quarters of their starting infield consisted of reserves Mickey Hatcher, Pepe Frias, and Derrel Thomas. Nonetheless, they led the Giants going into the bottom of the eighth inning, 2–1. The Dodgers had already blown a lead in the eighth inning just three games earlier. Everyone was acutely aware that the Astros had already won their game. If the Dodgers tanked this one, they would be three games out with the final three games against the Astros back at home, having to sweep all three to force a one-game playoff.

Needless to say, the Giants scored two runs to take a 3–2 lead. Despite an announced crowd of only 11,693, it sounded like at *least* 15,000 fans in the house. (Seriously, don't laugh. The next day against the Padres, the Giants drew a whopping 2,740.) In the top of the ninth, to the tired chants of "Beat L.A.," Manny Mota singled with two outs. Alas, our last hope lay with Steve Yeager, digging in against Al Holland. Jerry:

Here's the stretch, here's the look, and here's the pitch . . . struck him out. And the Dodgers lose as Yeager strikes out, as they are now *three games back*.

It would be a mere two years later that Joe Morgan would hit his infamous home run off Terry Forster to ruin L.A.'s divisional chances in 1982. In both years, the Dodgers would lose the division by a single game.

But nobody knew the outcome of 1980 yet. Returning to L.A., according to quotes in the papers, the Dodgers actually seemed like a relaxed bunch, confident in their ability to sweep at least three games at Dodger Stadium and force a playoff, also at home. But to sweep all four games? They would need more than a miracle. They would need to make history. That sort of thing had never been done in the annals of major league baseball.

5-FOR-5
FIVE GAMES THAT DEFINED THE 1980 DODGERS

#4—THE BIG THREE
Dodger Stadium, October 3, 4, and 5, 1980

Now it's time for another *Homerun Highlights* Special Exclusive . . .

[Cue Devo's "Whip It."]

And now it's time for the Big Three, the Dodgers' last three games with the Houston Astros. And they are forced to win the three games or else they are *dead*, because beginning this three-game series, they are *three* games back of the Houston Astros. Actually, they have to win *four* straight games to

> win the Western Division. If the Dodgers sweep, a
> one-game playoff would be necessary. Their work
> is cut out for them, and they know *exactly* what
> they have to do.

This was how I officially began tape six of *Homerun High-lights*. I particularly like this last sentence. Why throw in one sports cliché when you can have two? As for "Whip It," it became my theme song for all three games of the Big Three. The Dodgers had a problem, and they had to whip it. What more need be said?

It seemed only appropriate that the number one and two National League pitching staffs would square off in a final showdown. Fortunately, in a season riddled with missed opportunities and coulda woulda shouldas, the Dodgers more than made up for it by playing their hearts out for three games in a row at a raucous Dodger Stadium and reminding us all over again why we loved this team. From a fan's perspective, I would argue that these three regularly-scheduled games (160, 161, and 162) represent the greatest non-playoff series the Los Angeles Dodgers have ever played, and I don't think you'd get much argument from Dodger historians, either.

Notice I qualified that with "regularly scheduled" games. As a refresher, one-game playoffs as a result of ties for first actually count in the standings as Game 163. So technically the teams played a four-game series, but only three of the games were on the schedule. I know I'm quibbling here, but the more I can trick myself into forgetting that fourth game ever happened, all the better. But let's not jump ahead of ourselves . . .

Here is the first of three games that the Dodgers needed to sweep in order to force a one-game playoff against Houston.

GAME 1—OCTOBER 3, 1980

Game 1 was played on a perfect Friday night in L.A. I was stoked that these final three games fell on a weekend when school work wouldn't interfere. The game featured two dependable veterans—Ken Forsch versus Don Sutton. As expected, the game was a tight, crisply played affair that was tied 1–1 after seven. In the top of the eighth, however, the Astros went ahead 2-1 on a sacrifice fly by Alan Ashby. The Dodgers did not score in the bottom of the frame. In the top of the ninth, Fernando took over for Sutton and got into a little jam before wriggling out of the inning.

Ken Forsch remained in the game to face the Dodgers in the bottom of the ninth. With one on and one out, Dusty Baker hit a ground ball to Rafael Landestoy, in as a defensive replacement for the 37-year-old Joe Morgan. A double play would end the game—and the season. But Raffy booted it. A huge break for L.A. Now they had a runner in scoring position—Rudy Law, in as a pinch-runner.

Manager Bill Virdon stuck with Forsch, who induced Garvey to fly out to center. Two outs. The fate of their season came down to one batter: the Penguin. I remember liking the match-up. Cey wasn't hitting a lick against the Astros (.167 all year), but he always seemed to come through in the clutch, hitting .333 in the ninth inning onward (about 80 points higher than his overall batting average). Jerry Doggett was behind the mic. Just through his words, you could practically visualize the sweat against the back of his plaid jacket.

> And the tension *continues. Oh*, what a game . . .
> Forsch hanging tough. The Astros, 2-1 lead.
> Okay, one ball, one strike. Here's the stretch
> . . . the look . . . and the pitch to Cey.
> Ground ball *up the middle . . . base hit!* Here
> comes Law, around *third . . . he-will-score-tie-game.*

The run-together words at the end of Jerry's call is intentional. He sounded spent, like he just wanted to get it all out there. His voice disappeared under the cacophony of the crowd. Doggett's call may not win any style awards, but it scores points for its human element.

Still, where was Vin Scully? On television, it turns out. The Dodgers and KTTV made a rare concession by adding all three home games to the TV schedule. That was welcome news to Dodger fans, but it also meant that, at the close of games, we would be hearing Ross or Jerry on the radio. Again, no offense to either, but when the season is on the line, not hearing Vin is like not having your ace closer in there to finish a game. And so, breaking out my second tape recorder, I made sure to simultaneously capture the same game-tying single by Cey, this time called by Vin on television:

> And down in the clubhouse, you can understand the feeling for Houston. *One* out away. One ball and one strike to Ron Cey.
>
> [Cey bounces the ball up the middle, just past the pitcher.]
>
> Ground ball, it's going to go *up the middle* . . . Rudy Law will score to *tie it up*. The *Dodgers* are still *aliiiiiiiiiiiive!*

Vin seemed to bump the microphone after this call. Whatever happened, it resulted in a distinct jostling sound. As a kid, I liked to imagine it was because Vin was so excited, he took the microphone and slam-dunked it to the floor, like "$#%^ yeah!" The image was so deliciously incongruent. Of course, the game was only tied. And with the winning run on second base, Forsch got Guerrero to ground out and end the inning.

In the top of the 10th, Fernando returned for his second inning of work. You could feel the momentum shift the Dodgers' way as he retired the Astros in order, including two strikeouts. He left to a standing ovation.

Amazingly, Forsch went back out to the mound for the bottom of the 10th. Having starters work that deep into games seems like something out of the Dark Ages, now, doesn't it? Obviously

Virdon figured his veteran had enough stuff to face the Dodgers'
bottom three spots in the lineup. Jerry:

> Crowd standing again, trying to get the Dodgers
> rolling one more time.

The first batter for the Dodgers was Joe Ferguson. He saw
only one pitch.

> Long fly ball, left field. A-wayyy back, Cedeno at
> the warning track, up in the air . . . *can't-get-it-
> home-run-Dodgers-win.*

As with Cey's game-tying single, Doggett's call ended with a
stream of words that ran together like a verbal necklace. Let's re-
set this momentous occasion, shall we? Here's how Vin sounded
on TV:

> The crowd on its feet *again*, in the bottom of the
> 10th.

Fergie whacked the first pitch—a high fastball.

> High drive into deep left-center, back goes Cede-
> no to the *waaaaaaaaaallll* . . . it's *gone!*

Vinny then treated us to a full *1 minute and 16 seconds* of
solid crowd noise to let us soak in the spectacle. In somewhat of
a surprise, that was officially 10 seconds more cheering than the
1 minute, 6 seconds of crowd noise that followed Vinny's "she is
gone!" call of Gibby's legendary homer, making Joe Ferguson's big
moment the unofficial record-holder for Longest Uninterrupted
Crowd Noise Among Scully's Classic Dodger Calls.*

---

* The longest span of uninterrupted crowd noise from any Vinny call—Dodger or
opponent—that I know of came after Hank Aaron hit his record 715th home run
against the Dodgers in Atlanta. Vin clammed up for 1 minute, 44 seconds.

Speaking of Kirk Gibson, there is an eerie similarity in the way Vin uttered "gone" in both Gibson's 1988 World Series homer and this one. In both cases, the word had a satisfying, guttural grind to it—a spontaneous burst of exuberance that Vin reserved for truly special occasions.

Meanwhile, on the field, Ferguson wasn't rounding the bases so much as he was floating around them. In what was the single greatest image from the 1980 season, the cameras captured that magical moment when Fergie tossed his helmet into the air as he came around third base, grinning from ear to ear in seeming disbelief at what he had just done before falling into a sea of hugs, slaps, and high fives. Joe then lifted Lasorda about three feet off the ground—no small feat. As Helen Dell broke into "Happy Days Are Here Again" on the organ, we heard Vin again:

> Joe Ferguson hits his ninth home run of the year. His 29th run batted in. And the Dodgers, who looked to be *beaten* in the ninth, have *won* it in the 10th.
>
> The winning pitcher is *Fernando Valenzuela*, who is now 2-and-0. The loser is tough-luck Ken Forsch. And this crowd of 49,642 absolutely *delirious*.
>
> Now there is *tomorrow*. And it will be Nolan Ryan . . . we'll just have to wait and see about who will be the pitcher for the Dodgers.

That night, Ferguson's game-winning homer was the lead story on the local news. I must've relived it at least five different times while channel surfing, and another few dozen in my dreams. Fergie's childlike reaction was so intoxicating, I couldn't get enough. Just as important, with the Astros' magic number remaining at one and the Ryan Express on deck, I wanted to savor every great Dodger moment before they ran out of tomorrows.

GAME 2—OCTOBER 4, 1980

The next day it was announced that Jerry Reuss would start on three days' rest against Nolan Ryan. Normally, Bob Welch probably would've started, but he was out for the remainder of the season with his groin injury. For the year Reuss's ERA was actually a full run better when he went three instead of four days between starts, the theory being that his sinking fastball sank even more because his arm was not at full strength. I didn't care who was starting—I just knew that, due to the way our shared season seats were distributed, we happened to have tickets to that day's game, to be played under sunny skies. My brother, Michael, now in possession of a driver's license, got us and our two friends there at least an hour before first pitch.

Of course, attending ball games always presented challenges when trying to record key moments off the radio for my *Homerun Highlights* tapes. Fortunately, Dad had succumbed to one of his impulse buys a few months earlier when he came home with an early model JVC boombox. This was just the latest addition to his fanciful finds, which would soon include an Atari game console, a moped, an African Grey parrot, a medieval sword kit, and a fat-jiggling "weight loss" machine.

With six D batteries, you could take this JVC unit anywhere, if you didn't mind lugging around something that weighed as much as a small icebox. In addition to having a radio and cassette recorder, it had a small black-and-white TV screen that could tune in local VHF and UHF over-the-air stations. This was a godsend on long road trips, where we could actually make out ghostly images in the car.

For Game 2 of the Big Three against the Astros, I came to the stadium prepared, jamming my JVC with fresh D Batteries, a blank 90-minute cassette to record the game, and another blank tape in my pocket. There was an anticipatory buzz around the stadium. I always got an additional charge out of getting to see

Bullpen Session

Magic at Dodger Stadium

By far the best use of our little portable TV came on May 16, 1980, when I was attending a Dodger game. Laker fans will recognize that date as the game in which rookie Magic Johnson famously led the Lakers to the NBA title against the Philadelphia 76ers. I was a huge Laker fan by then, too, but no one—and I mean no one—thought they stood a chance in that Game 6 in Philly with-out Kareem Abdul-Jabbar, who didn't even travel with the team due to a severely sprained ankle. Consequently, rather than stay-ing home to watch the Lakers lose, we joined the 47,929 in at-tendance at Dodger Stadium that night, since we had tickets to the game.

It soon became apparent that half the stadium was listening to Chick Hearn on their transistor radios—the only time I can re-call Vinny being upstaged by another announcer at a ball game. Whenever the Lakers made a great play, the crowd would react, which was oddly out of sync with the comparatively mundane ac-tion on the field. As the Dodger game rolled along, the operator of the newly installed Mitsubishi Diamond Vision began flashing updates of the Laker game, drawing cheers from the crowd and even clapping from the Dodgers. When the final score flashed to a euphoric crowd, John Candelaria, the Pirates' funnyman pitcher, was on-deck. He seized the moment by playfully bowing and doff-ing his cap.

But the real action was around our seats, where we were able to faintly tune in the Laker game on Channel 2. Nowadays, we'd just pull the game up on our iPhones, but on that night, the ability to watch a live NBA game in our seats was like discover-ing fire. Wondrous fans from adjacent seats hovered around our JVC like moths to a flame. And that's how I saw the Lakers clinch the title—on a portable, flickering, black-and-white TV with a dozen strangers from Aisle 14 breathing down my neck during a Friday night Dodgers-Pirates game. (Who won the Dodger game? Who *cares*?)

Nolan Ryan, his first year in a National League park after eight seasons with the California Angels. Just like when your favorite basketball team went up against Michael Jordan and his Bulls, there was nothing quite like having to face a living legend in Ryan to ignite a fan's passion. With the single-season strikeout record and four no-hitters, Ryan's legacy was already written. Nolan had also inherited a bull's-eye for hecklers after being the first free agent in baseball history to sign a contract for (cue Dr. Evil) *one meeeellion dollars!* While he was especially tough in the spacey Astrodome, on the road Ryan was 3–8 with a 4.67 ERA in 1980. He was certainly beatable . . . but so was Jerry Reuss.

Fortunately, the Dodgers relieved some of the pressure by striking first. After singles by Garvey and Guerrero in the second inning, Derrel Thomas, playing in place of Bill Russell, came up with two outs. Jerry Doggett:

> 2-and-2. Ryan ready, here's the pitch . . . looped into left field, along the line, base hit. Here's Garvey, around third, Cruz with the throw to the plate, it's gonna beeeeeee . . . *late!* Dodgers lead on single by Thomas.

Meanwhile, Reuss settled into a groove after a rocky start. But he got a bad break in the fourth, when Cruz singled, stole second, and went to third on a groundout. With two outs, Art Howe came up and hit what looked to be the third out of the inning. Vin:

> 1-and-2 to Art Howe, who struck out in the second inning. Reuss eyeballing Ferguson. Jerry to the wind-up and the 1-2 pitch is hit to straightaway center. Guerrero has a play—*lost it in the glare* and it *drops!* He *lost* the ball in the shirtsleeve crowd, couldn't find it, and by the time he saw where it was, it was on the *green grass.* So *there's* a break.

I particularly like Vin's emphasis on the "green grass" (as opposed to simply "grass"). Just another example of how little things can speak volumes. In this case, the "green grass" strikes a nice color contrast to the "shirtsleeve crowd," which is typically white.

But then, just as soon as he said that, he switched gears and leveled with us, the listeners, in a moment of candor:

> We will tell the people across the country he lost
> it in the shirtsleeves. *You* and *I* know where he lost
> it . . .

Vin's last comment was a reference to L.A.'s notorious smog, and all game long, he and Jerry noted how ugly the air was. Anyway, it was now Dodgers 1, Smog 1.

The score did not remain tied for long. Steve Garvey was the first batter against Ryan in the bottom of the fourth and promptly hit a mammoth home run—his 26th. It happened so quickly, I didn't have time to put down my soda and flip the cassette over in my JVC to capture Vin's call. Thus, my recording picked up with the crowd going berserk, followed by Vinny doing the obligatory Union Oil plug:

> Boy, Steve Garvey got *all* of it as he hit it back into
> the Dodger Bullpen. A 20-dollar Book of Union
> Oil Auto Script to the Impact Drug Rehabilita-
> tion Houses in Pasadena, and the Dodgers lead,
> 2–1.

Garv wasn't done against Ryan. Of the Dodgers' six hits against Nolan, half of them were from Steve. The third one came in the sixth, with the score still 2–1, Dodgers. Vinny again:

> You can bet Ryan knows all about Garvey—Steve
> wearing him out. And Ryan trying somehow to
> *get* him out.
> The 2-2 pitch is . . . a line-drive base hit. So

> Garvey is hitting *.500* against a *million-dollar*
> *pitcher* . . . he is *9 for 18*. But even more than that,
> with three hits today he now has *199*. Incredible!

The "million-dollar pitcher" lasted only one more inning before being lifted, but Reuss was getting better as the game went on. After striking out the last two batters of the seventh inning, the crowd gave him a standing ovation. Caught up in the excitement, I flipped the JVC to a live mic and decided to record the entire stadium singing "Take Me Out to the Ballgame" as a "special exclusive" for *Homerun Highlights*.

Hearing it now, it's a charming little moment in time. It starts with John Ramsey imploring, "Let's all join in," as he always did, followed by Helen Dell pumping the first few notes to lead us in. As the crowd sings along, you can also hear me, Michael, buddy David, and Michael's friend Jack earnestly belting our lungs out. Much has been written about the Seventh Inning Stretch and its uniqueness in the world of professional sports. Suffice to say, for that fleeting minute, I didn't care who won or lost. I was at a baseball game with friends and family, soaking in the vibe at the world's most beautiful ballpark, without a worry in the world.

Coincidentally, Vin was thinking pretty much the same thing on the radio. Late in the game, he took in the spectacle and paused to offer this perspective:

> Boy, isn't this great? Win or lose, isn't this *great*?
> How *lucky* we are to have all this excitement.
>
> Do you realize it's sleepy time in most cities
> in the big leagues? But not here. And year after
> year—*not here.*

These words resonate even more today. It only takes a couple of "sleepy time" seasons to *really* make you appreciate what you once took for granted.

In the end, Garvey's home run was enough to hold up. Reuss

went the distance, retiring the last 10 in a row, and the Dodgers won, 2–1. How much of a Vinny freak was I? I made sure to switch my boombox to TV mode in order to hear him deliver the last out on television. In between the signal fading in and out, we heard:

> And [Woods] hits a ground ball to the hole, Percante comes up with it, throws to Garvey!
>
> [One minute of crowd noise.]
>
> And now the Astros know it will be *very* difficult. As the Dodgers, somehow, tenaciously fight back . . . come from behind last night to win it in 10 innings. And come back and *win* it today!

As I was leaving the stadium, cradling my mustard-stained JVC in my arms, I was struck by the odd sight of an animated usher telling two departing nuns, "Two miracles down, sisters, two more to go!"

GAME 3—OCTOBER 5, 1980

The third game of the Big Three—Game 162—featured Burt Hooton against Vern Ruhle in the season's final Sunday afternoon game. Back at home, I had my tape recorders cued up for both the radio and TV broadcasts. But as I would find out later, Vin was nowhere to be found that day, having to fulfill obligations for CBS by announcing a Rams-49ers game in Anaheim. I couldn't help but feel crushed by his absence. It was like attending your graduation and not seeing your parents in the stands.

While the TV and radio duties would be relegated to the Dodgers' B team, you couldn't blame us Dodger fans for feeling confident about the game itself. We had already beaten their most feared pitcher the day before. Faced with the prospect of a one-game showdown in an opposing team's ballpark in front of 56,000 rabid fans, the Astros had to be feeling the pressure.

Also, in a freak accident, Ruhle—the Astros' best pitcher in the second-half (7–2, 2.03 ERA)—had cut his finger in the dugout during Friday night's game and required stitches. He would pitch but certainly not be 100 percent. This was a huge break for the Dodgers.

Still, while Hooton was having another solid year, we all knew about Happy in big games and losing his cool. This time, he didn't even wait until all the fans had settled into their seats. In the top of the second in a scoreless tie, Hooton gave up a bunt single to Cesar Cedeno, which seemed to unnerve him. Cedeno stole second. Art Howe laid down a sacrifice, but Hooton butchered the

Bullpen Session

Some Kind of Another Great Year

There was one highlight in the early innings for the Dodgers. Jerry was behind the microphone when Steve Garvey stepped up:

> Bunt try, third baseway . . . here is Cabell . . . can't play it. Garvey beats it out. And he gets his 200th base hit on a bunt single!

> The crowd stood to honor Garvey, and the cheering went on for over a minute.

> Standing ovation, Garvey at first base, takes his helmet off, salutes the crowd.
> Oh, he has had some kind of another great year.

Garvey detractors would argue that this surprise bunt was a calculated attempt by the numbers-conscious Steve to reach 200 hits on the last day of the season. I would counter that, while I'm sure he valued 200 hits, he was much more interested in winning the ballgame. Steve was an excellent bunter. With Cabell playing deep, he probably saw an opportunity to get on base and start a rally. If anyone else pulled this off, it would be a "smart" or "alert" play. When Garvey did it, it was "selfish."

play for an error. Alan Ashby then drove in the game's first run. That brought on the .219-hitting Craig Reynolds. Jerry:

> Two on and Reynolds back in there. Here's the look now and the pitch on the way . . . drive into right field . . . Monday coming up for it, it drops for a base hit. And it's two to nothing in favor of the Astros as Reynolds, a weak-hitting shortstop, singles into right field . . . and here comes Lasorda.
>
> So Hooton has had a mess here in the second inning. Two on, two in, and nobody out.

Tommy, wisely, brought the hook. Bobby Castillo took over and the Dodgers escaped further damage. Ruhle, as expected, did not last long himself. With his stitches coming undone, *he* was pulled in the bottom of the third. The battle of the bullpens had begun.

In the fourth, Terry Puhl doubled home a run to make it 3–0 Astros. When the inning ended, David called me and asked who I thought would win in the NLCS—the Astros or the Phillies. I hung up on him. Dying a slow death in front of the TV, I was in no mood for jokes. Later, he told me he was trying "reverse psychology," hoping to reverse the Dodgers' fortunes. Uh-huh.

Then again, I couldn't deny the results. Davey Lopes got the Dodgers on the board with a single in the fifth inning. In the bottom of the seventh and losing, 3–1, the Dodgers got runners to second and third, with one out. Player-coach Manny Mota was relieved by Don Sutton in the first-base coaching box so that Manny could pinch-hit for Fernando Valenzuela (who had pitched two scoreless innings in relief—a key decision by Lasorda that would lead to a lifetime of second-guessing for reasons that would soon become clear). Mota was facing Joe Sambito, a tough lefty who had some excellent years for the Astros out of the pen. Jerry:

> Two balls, two strikes, one out. Guerrero at third,

Ferguson at second. Manny Mota looking for a big one. The infield is back, they'll give up a run on a ground ball.

Here's the 2-2 pitch on the way . . . looped into right field, it's gonna fall, base hit. Here comes one run in, Ferguson will be held at third! Mota's gonna try for second and he *makes* it with no play, as Ashby thought the runner was coming to score.

Mota came out for a pinch runner and returned to the bench "for a hug and a kiss from Lasorda." The Dodgers' ageless wonder had struck again. His RBI single would turn out to be the last base hit of his storied career. Next to his two-out, pinch hit double off Greg Luzinski's glove to key a Dodger comeback in the '77 play-offs, it would also be his biggest. It was now 3–2 Astros after seven.

As I said before, whenever Mota had dramatic pinch hits, the Dodgers always seemed to come up with a little magic of their own. In the bottom of the eighth, with shadows creeping across the Dodger Stadium infield, Steve Garvey led off with a grounder to Enos Cabell at third. Cabell booted it. It was shades of Game 1, in which an error by an Astro infielder led to a game-tying hit by Ron Cey. Once again, Cey was center stage, this time representing the go-ahead run. What followed was arguably one of the greatest Dodger at-bats in the history of the Los Angeles franchise, a heroic battle certainly worth mentioning in the same breath as Steve Finley's walk-off slam in '04, with echoes of Kirk Gibson's gimpy-legged game-winner.

First of all, Cey was questionable to even start the game. He had been battling a sore hamstring, but given the stakes, there was no way he was sitting out. With Garvey representing the tying run on first base, Lasorda ordered Cey to sacrifice Steve to second, which would bring up Pedro Guerrero. Cey, with no sacrifices the year before, failed to get the bunt down—not once, but twice.

With the bunt called off, Cey hacked at an offering from reliever Frank LaCorte and fouled it hard off his left foot. Time was called as Cey keeled in obvious pain. Now we had a real mess on our hands—two strikes and a hurt Penguin. But he climbed back in the box and somehow worked the count to 3-and-2. If memory serves, I believe he then fouled off three *more* pitches. In front of the TV, Michael and I had been reduced to human jellyfish peeking through interlocked fingers in front of our eyes. The tension level was akin to the Welch-Jackson at-bat from '78. Jerry Doggett, on the radio, called it from there:

> Astros all seated quietly in their dugout. The Dodgers, some of them standing, Lasorda pacing. I'll tell ya, if Tommy survives this weekend, boy, he's a man of steel. 3-and-2!
>
> Garvey ready to go. Cey waiting at the plate. Here's the pitch . . . fly ball to deep left field . . . this one is going, going . . . this ball is *goooooooo-oooooooooooooooooooooooooooooone!*
>
> [Fifty seconds of crowd noise.]

Doggett may not have been in peak form with his calls at the end of Game 1, but here he knocked it out of the park himself. His set-up was crisp, colorful, and well-drawn. When the ball left the stadium, rather than run out of steam, he unleashed the longest prolonged vowel this side of a soccer match—his "gone" went on for almost three seconds! To these ears, it was his greatest call ever.

> Well, the noise is deafening and you can understand why. The Dodgers lead 4–3 . . . they want Cey to come for an encore—here he is!
>
> With a sore left foot and a bad right leg, Ron Cey hangs in there on a 3-2 pitch, hit it deep into the stands and there was no doubt about it.

Cedeno gave up on it almost instantly.

    You *can't believe it!* You just *cannot* believe it. *Utter* dejection on the Astro bench. *Jubilation* on the Dodger bench.

Like with Ferguson's homer, Cey left us with a memorable image upon approaching home plate. And yet their reactions couldn't have been more different. Ferguson's homecoming was like a giant frat party—everyone laughing, celebrating, throwing their arms in the air. Cey had struggled—literally struggled—just to stay on his feet. His whole at-bat was like a mini-Greek drama, complete with a beginning (two failed bunt attempts), middle (allowed to swing, he almost knocked himself out of the game), and end (a redemptive home run). When he greeted Garvey and Guerrero at home plate, there were no smiles. His was a reaction of competitive relief—almost *anger*. You could clearly see him mouth two swear words as he high-fived them so hard, he almost dislodged their hands from their wrists.

If there was one disappointment about the whole at-bat, it was that no one knew what the in absentia Vin Scully thought about it. Still, one good call deserves another, and over on the TV side of things, Ross said just enough to let the pictures carry the story:

> Garvey goes . . . a drive to left-center field and hit deep . . . it's gone, I think . . . *DODGERS LEAD!*

But, this being the Dodgers, you knew nothing would come easy. With the Dodgers up, 4–3, in the ninth, Jay Johnstone perhaps staved off elimination on a ball hit by lead-off batter Jeff Leonard. Ross on the radio:

> Check swing blooper along the right field line in foul ground, coming over Johnstone, fighting the sun, reaches up, crashes into the barrier . . . caught the *baaaaaaaaaall!* A sensational catch and they show it again on Diamond Vision. *Wow!*

That play loomed even larger when Steve Howe gave up two singles to put runners on first and third. Lasorda, using a tactic he would successfully employ in postseason games, called on starter Don Sutton to get *one last out* (hey, his other first-base coach had come through for him that day, why not Don?). Ross again:

> Sutton at the belt and the 0-1 pitch to [Denny] Walling. Ground ball to second. Lopes has got it. Over to Garvey. *WE GOT A PLAYOFF!*

It was the only time I can recall Ross resorting to the first person.

> Win or lose tomorrow, you gotta love the Dodgers. They just never give up. They were counted out so many times in recent days and here they are three back, three to play, and they win three *one-run decisions* over Houston, and we're going to have a 163-game schedule, friends, in the National League West.

Not only did they win all three games by one run, but the deciding blows in all three were home runs. In two of the games, they had to come from behind, while in the third, they had to break a tie.

Riding a high, I completed the Big Three sequence with a replay of Cey's eventual game-winning homer as called by Ross—looped, of course, for maximum effect. For once, I had remixed a call not to flog myself in defeat, but to revel in victory. Take it away, Sir Ross-A-Lot . . .

> Garvey goes . . .
> A drive to left-center field and hit deep . . .
> It's gone, I think . . .
> Dodgers lead!
> Dodgers lead!

Dodgers lead!
Dodgers lead!
It's gone, I think
Dodgers lead!
Dodgers lead!
It's gone, I think
Dodgers lead!
Dodgers lead!

5-FOR-5
FIVE GAMES THAT DEFINED THE 1980 DODGERS

#5—"DO OR DIE BREAKER"
Dodger Stadium, October 6, 1980

So what would you do?

You know the question.

Who would you have started: Dave Goltz? Or Fernando Valenzuela?

The case for Goltz:

• Veteran pitcher.

• Had pitched four consecutive quality starts.

• Um . . . that's about it.

The case against Goltz:

• Pretty much stunk the whole year.

• Would be pitching on three days' rest, when his ERA was 4.97.

• Statistically, he was far worse at home than on the road.

The case for Valenzuela:

• A rookie—one whose screwball and artistry baffled unfamiliar batters.

• Had given up no (as in *zero*) earned runs in 15⅔ innings in relief since being called up from the minors in September.

• The Dodgers' hottest pitcher.

The case against Valenzuela:

• A rookie—one who had never started a game before in the majors, let alone one of this magnitude.

• He had pitched two innings the day before, and two innings two games before that.

• Wait, I'm still thinking . . .

We all know that Lasorda handed the ball over to his veteran, Dave Goltz, with the season on the line. At the time, I joined my fellow Dodger fans with howls

Bullpen Session

Worst. Pitcher. Ever.

Frank LaCorte (not to be confused with Frank McCourt) took the loss for the Astros that forced the tiebreaker. There is a school of thought among some sabermetricians that LaCorte's 1977 season was the worst season ever for a pitcher with at least 30 innings. His line from that year: 1–8, 11.68 ERA. In 37 innings, he gave up 67 hits and 48 earned runs. On the bright side, he did pitch another seven seasons in the majors, inspiring future generations of below-average middle relievers to realize their dreams.

of protests. Fernandomania had already taken root amongst the faithful. This kid was something special. His stats spoke for themselves. He had not given up an earned run all year and was averaging a strikeout an inning.

Why not go with the hot hand? Lasorda had his own stat: Fernando had pitched two innings the day before to help preserve the Dodgers' 4–3 victory that had enabled them to get to this point. He had done his job. To ask him to then step in as the starting pitcher would not be fair. At 19, he was still a teenager with acne, for crying out loud. A loss could be a blow to his psyche. As disappointing as Dave Goltz was, he was being paid the big bucks to deliver. He was signed for games like this. End of discussion.

Though I was disappointed that Fernando didn't start, with the benefit of time, I have come to this conclusion: it probably didn't matter who started. They might as well have stuck Vic Davalillo on the mound. The Dodgers scratched out one run and six hits against Joe Niekro, a 20-game winner whose knuckleball handcuffed them all game. Even if Fernando *had* started and put up goose eggs (ironically, he ended up pitching two shutout innings, but only when the game was out of reach), he likely wouldn't have had enough in the tank to go all nine innings. An exhausted Dodger bullpen would have to have been near-perfect to preserve a 1–0 win . . . or, at worst, take a 1–1 tie into extra innings. Not impossible, but it assumes everything would have to go right for the Dodgers' pitching. No, on this day, it was the offense's inability to get anything going against Niekro that lost the game.

The fact that the Astros won by a 7–1 score turned out to be a blessing. I'm sure you've experienced this feeling, too—if you're gonna lose the big game, sometimes it's better to get your butt kicked than to get your heart torn out in a tight, one-run affair. The blowout also cushioned a blow of my own. That morning—a Monday—I found out from my dad that we had scored tickets for the game. Dad announced that he was going to try to wrangle a couple associates at his office to fill out the other seats. For the first and only time in my life, I literally dropped to my knees and begged Dad to let me play hooky from school so I could go to the game with him. Amazingly, he did not say no. He knew I had come this far with the Dodgers. And from the look in his eyes, I could sense that something passed between us, that unspoken bond that happens between men—an understanding that some things are bigger than both of us.

"Ask your mother," he said meekly.

If this were a sitcom, the next scene would be a smash-cut of me sitting glumly at my desk at school, replete with laugh track.

Anyway, that day at school, all anyone could talk about was the upcoming game at 1 PM. News reports likened the entire day to a holiday—businesses closed early, courts took recesses . . . Angelenos everywhere gathered around their radios or TVs (the game was televised nationally on ABC) to watch the Boys in Blue play the first National League tiebreaker since the Dodgers had squared off against the Giants in 1962. Fortunately, my science teacher, Mr. Cudlip, doubled as the school's baseball coach, so he was sympathetic to our pleas to tune in the start of the game when his class started after lunch.

Meanwhile, back at home, I had taken my obsession to document the Dodgers' seasons to sick, new lengths by rigging electric timers to three different radio/tape machines, each designed to click on at separate intervals in order to capture the first 2 hours and 45 minutes without missing a beat. (It was my hope to be at home for the final innings.) Taped to each radio-recorder, I wrote, for Mom's sake: "Don't Touch!!!!" I guess I was still a little peeved.

The Dodgers were without Ron Cey, who couldn't answer the bell after hurting his foot during his epic at-bat the day before. Not that it mattered. In the first inning, the Astros set the tone early. Jerry:

> 1-and-2. Puhl on third, Cabell on second, first inning, one out . . . the pitch. Ground ball to third. Hatcher will come to the plate with it. Aaaaaaand they get him at home—*no*, Ferguson dropped the ball!
>
> Puhl is in safe and the ball got out of Ferguson's glove. He was called out and Fergie couldn't hold on and the run is in. Hatcher's throw was in plenty of time and Puhl came *barreling* into Ferguson. Jarred the ball loose, and he's safe at the plate, the run is in, and it is one to nothing Houston.

It went as an error—the Dodgers' second of the inning. The Astros ended up with two unearned runs in the first. We didn't know it at the time, but that was already enough to win the game. Dad told me later he was still sitting in traffic on the Hollywood Freeway when this all went down.

Goltz was the victim of bad luck, but he was hardly effective himself, giving up eight hits in three innings, including this one to Art Howe in the third:

> 3-and-2 with two away. And the stretch and the pitch . . . high fly ball into left-center field and it is well hit, this ball is gone. Home run, Art Howe. He hit it into the bleachers and the Astros have a four to nothing lead.

Later that inning, Alan Ashby tried to score on a double by Craig Reynolds. He was out at home plate by a mile, but, taking a page from Terry Puhl, the burly catcher aggressively bowled into his counterpart, hoping to jar the ball loose. This time Ferguson held on to the ball. As Ashby got tangled around Fergie's leg, a perturbed Joe kneed him in the shoulder. Alan and the Astros took offense. Both benches emptied, but no punches were thrown. There was no need. The Dodgers were already TKO'd.

In the fourth, the Astros piled on three more runs, thanks to another big hit by Art Howe (3-for-5 with four RBIs on the day). With the Astros now up, 7–0, and the game effectively over, Vin began to write the Dodgers' epitaph. Hearing him wax philosophical about the Dodgers' season and place it in its proper context provided a certain amount of solace as I found myself asking, How *could this* happen? To Vin, the Dodgers were lucky to have made it that far, considering the rash of late-season injuries that had plagued regulars like Bill Russell, Davey Lopes, Ron Cey, and Reggie Smith (who had been out since early August).

> That would certainly sum up the Dodger picture. The line from Milton: "They also serve, who only stand and wait." The Dodgers at the end of the year unfortunately had too many who could *only* stand and wait.

The loss of Bob Welch was a particular blow down the stretch. Losing his services as a starter or spot reliever meant more work for the ineffective Rick Sutcliffe. "The Dodgers needed help from kids they haven't used," Vin said, "and it wasn't there."

In the bottom of the fourth, the Dodgers scored their first and only run—a "murmur of protest," according to Vin. Shortly thereafter, disgruntled Dodger fans began throwing objects at left fielder Jose Cruz—ice cubes, fruit, even toilet paper. Vin, who usually kept his personal feelings close to the vest, didn't mince words:

> And time called for the moment. They are gesturing again out to left field . . .
>
> It is really a shame to *mar* a game of championship caliber—although, come to think of it, it's a shame to mar *any* game—with unsportsmanlike conduct. It is downright *inhuman* to plague a fella who is literally minding his own business. Just doing his job. And of course the Dodgers are

embarrassed for their fans and they understand
how Cruz felt.

> You remember when the Dodgers were in Yan-
> kee Stadium and how the Dodgers were so upset
> over the behavior of the fans in New York. They
> referred to it as the zoo, the animals.

A chorus of boos went up from the Dodger Stadium crowd.

> And *now* the umpires are telling the Houston As-
> tros to come off the field . . . and I don't blame
> 'em! I don't blame 'em . . .

Vin now seemed to be using his pulpit to indirectly admon-
ish the fans in left field responsible for this nonsense. Remember,
these were the days when Vin's voice reverberated throughout the
stadium. I'll let you be the judge:

> There's no shading of this matter. It's *wrong*. It is
> downright *wrong*. And until those fans that have
> been plaguing Jose Cruz come to their senses,
> there is just no reason to continue the game.
>
> Remember, on the road, Reggie Smith walked
> off the field in Chicago . . . they were throwing
> things at him. Remember last year, how badly the
> fans at Yankee Stadium behaved. And it would be a
> *terrible* thing for *Dodger Stadium in Los Angeles*, the
> year of the fans' *enthusiasm*, the year that the fans
> have really showed their *love*, that that same feeling
> would be marred by *downright poor sportsmanship*
> by, I'll grant you, just a few *unthinking* fans.

In the background, John Ramsey issued stern warnings over
the PA system. (When you heard that voice, it was like those old E.
F. Hutton commercials—you listened.) Somehow, both teams got
out of the fourth inning without anyone getting maimed or killed.

I remember getting home from school around the ninth inning, just in time to see the end of the game. Vin called the final Dodger out of the season on TV. Little Jack Perconte, in for Lopes, had the (dis)honors.

> Big chopper, [Dave] Bergman has it, and look out now, as Texas takes over at Dodger Stadium. The Houston Astros beat the Dodgers, 7–1 . . .
>
> So Houston goes on to Philadelphia, and the Dodgers will literally and figuratively lick their wounds, think about what might have been, and we'll make it up and start it in 1981.

Thankfully, the fans ended on a classy note, standing up and giving the team a long, loud ovation. As the Dodgers gathered on the field to congratulate the Astros (would that even happen now?), I remember being surprised to see my dad walk through the door. Like a true casual fan, he had bailed in the seventh inning. His work buddies, bored and riding beer buzzes, had wanted to leave even earlier.

For once, I was *so* glad I hadn't gone. Once again, Mom knew what she was doing all along.

BAGS PACKED

For years, the final televised Dodger games each year always ended with Vin, Jerry, and Ross standing together in a darkened press booth—I always see Jerry in a plaid suit, Ross in a turtleneck/jacket combo, maybe Vin in a mustard-yellow blazer with matching handkerchief—offering post-mortems on the season. I always loved these little impromptu wrap-ups, as it was rare to see all three of them standing together. After the Dodgers and Astros had left the field of this season-ending game, the cameras cut to the threesome, upstairs in their little room. Vin was standing in the middle, holding the microphone like a game-show host and thrusting it in front of whomever he wanted to talk. Jerry was to his right, Ross to his left.

> Vin: Any last thoughts before we bid adieu for '80?
>
> Jerry: It's only five months until spring training and I can hardly wait to get started. I've got my bags packed and ready to go.
>
> Vin: That's right, come to think of it, there are a *lot* of bags packed and ready to go today that won't be going.
>
> Ross: I'd just say that I'm proud of the Dodgers for the way they hung in there with all the injuries. And I'm proud of the fans. Three-and-a-quarter million people came by to see this ballclub. And, I think, a lot to look forward to next year.
>
> Vin: So, like any good marriage, they have weathered the storm . . . maybe a little sadder, but certainly a lot wiser . . . the love has blossomed and continued, and we hope you'll hold hands with us as we pick up again in spring training [of 1981]. And now . . .
>
> Jerry: So long.
>
> Ross: So long to all of you.
>
> Vin: And that will do it for today *and* for the year as Houston wins the National League West and beats the Dodgers, 7 to 1.

7TH INNING
February-May 1981

Me: Hello there, once again, and welcome back to *Homerun Highlights*, this being *Homerun Highlights* number seven. This is the first cassette of the 1981 season, featuring, of course, home runs and highlights of various Dodger games.

  The Dodgers opened up their preseason on a pretty sour note. After winning their first game against the Tokyo Giants, they went on to lose the next few. But the first home run of preseason came from Steve Garvey in the fourth game of preseason play. And it was a second-inning shot against the Houston Astros.

Ross: Garvey thinks Forsch is taking too much time and steps out on him. Now, the 1-2 pitch. Driven to left field and deep! Cruz goes back, to the track, to the wall, and Garvey has homered to tie the game!

Fernando Valenzuela "looking toward the heavens."

For the second year in a row, I fulfilled my quest to capture the Dodgers' first spring-training home run (and, interestingly, my voice seemed to drop another octave—from Peter- to Greg Brady-level). Yep, it had been another long off-season. Since I started following the team at the end of '77, three of their last four seasons had ended in utter heartbreak. I wasn't sure if I could stomach another roller coaster of a season with an inevitable letdown, let alone spare the time and energy to chronicle it. In the back of my mind, I knew that 1981 would be the last year of my *Homerun Highlights* collection. At 15, the innocence of my youth was giving way to acne, sleeping in, hanging out, driver's ed, geometry, trigonometry, AP courses, school newspaper pursuits, pursuits of girls, and everything else that comes with ninth and tenth grades.

You could say my own life reflected that of the Dodgers. We were both getting older. The team's everyday players left over from the 1978 season now averaged 33½ years old, and they were starting to break down. Reggie Smith would never fully recover from shoulder surgery. There was an implicit understanding that this was the last chance to claim a championship for the much-vaunted infield of Garvey-Lopes-Russell-Cey. Many players went on record admitting that their time as a unit was running out.

"We have given you many things, except . . . a world championship," Lopes told a group of fans at a January luncheon. "You shall have it in 1981."

Given this aura of urgency hanging over both our fates, I decided I was going to document this season with a thoroughness like no other.

Thankfully, the Dodgers wrote their own happy ending with a fairy-tale season. But it took the wackiest season in the history of major league baseball to get there . . . one so bizarre, the two teams with the best overall records in the National League's West and East divisions never even made the playoffs.

WELCOME TO SPLITSVILLE

The first major league Division Series of the modern era was not played in 1995, of course, when the current format was instituted, but in 1981, when a one-off divisional series was created to account for the split-season caused by a 50-day players strike starting June 12. If you were born after 1981, or simply forgot why they struck in the first place, the core issue was this: the owners had been pushing for greater compensation when losing players to free agency. The players, behind union head Marvin Miller, felt like their backs were against the wall and were worried (rightly so) that the owners were out to strip away the gains they had made since the advent of free agency in the 1970s.

As a teenage fan who watched what was perhaps the Dodgers' most exciting season ever stripped away from me, I fell in line with most fans: I didn't care *who* was to blame or *what* the reasons were—both sides were at fault. Marvin Miller, with his Boris Badenov mustache, was just as untrustworthy as the owners' chief negotiator, Ray Grebey (whose last name, depending on how you pronounced it, rhymed with either "greedy" or "gravy," both unpleasant connotations).

When play resumed on August 10th, the teams that were in first place when play halted in June were declared the first-half winners. The teams that finished atop the second half of the season would play the first-half winners in a five-game Division Series. If the same team won both halves, it would play the runner-up team of the second season. After that, the postseason would continue apace with a five-game League Championship Series and seven-game World Series.

This was great news for Dodger fans—the Dodgers had won the first half by a mere half game over the Reds—but not so great for Red fans, who saw their team capture the NL's best overall record by a wide margin (four games over the Dodgers), yet failed to make the postseason. That's because Houston, a fellow NL West team that finished under .500 in the first half, finished 1½ games ahead of Cincinnati in the second half. The St. Louis Cardinals, with the best overall record in the NL East, were also victimized by this cockamamie playoff scheme. In an almost mirror-image of the Reds' season, they finished 2½ games behind the Phillies in the first half, and only a half-game behind the Expos in the second half.

But for those teams that did advance to the playoffs, one thing was clear. Whoever was crowned the World Series champion would really have to earn it. They would have to win 10 postseason games—more games than any team in major league history.

THE PLAYERS

The Dodgers' pitching staff was comprised of Fernando Valenzuela and . . . twelve other guys. Actually, to be fair, the corps' success in 1981 was more like that combative, multi-armed Shiva statue from a 1970s Sinbad movie. Their starting rotation was especially lethal, compiling a 3.01 ERA that was second only to Houston's ridiculous 2.66 ERA. While Fernando (13–7, 2.48

Bullpen Session

Best. Yearbook. Ever.

I've collected Dodgers yearbooks over the years, and my hands-down favorite is the one for the 1981 season. The cover features a Norman Rockwellian rendering of a beaming, rippling Steve Garvey being greeted at home plate by Dusty Baker after hitting a home run at Dodger Stadium. At the top of the cover, their hands slap five, framed by a yellow sunburst and the words "High Five!" That's right, the high five had become so popular, it muscled its way onto the cover. Thank goodness they never did a cover in subsequent years that championed "The Wave!"

ERA) was the talk of baseball on his way to earning numerous awards, Jerry Reuss (10–4, 2.30 ERA) and Burt Hooton (11–6, 2.28 ERA) actually had better earned run averages. Bob Welch (9–5, 3.44 ERA) overcame bone spurs in his elbow to put together a solid season. Rick Sutcliffe and Dave Goltz split the fifth spot in a perpetual toss-up of "who's the lesser of two evils?" Out of the pen, Steve Howe and Dave Stewart were a formidable one-two, lefty-righty punch and put up comparable numbers. Newcomers Alejandro Peña and Tom Niedenfuer were also important contributors. Unfortunately, the same could not be said of Terry "Are You Still Here?" Forster (0–1, 4.11 ERA, 0-for-1 in saves), who suffered his third consecutive disappointing year after his lights-out '78 campaign.

Offensively, the Dodgers were hardly a juggernaut. Except for Rick Monday —whose part-time numbers projected to 40-plus homers over a full season—no one on the club put up exceptional numbers, but they got just enough production across the board to once again lead the league in homers (82 in 110 games) while finishing fourth in runs scored. Keep in mind that their final statistics weren't truly indicative of a team giving it all their effort over a full season. Once they knew they were in the playoffs as a result of their first-half finish, you have to figure some players may have eased off the pedal in preparation of the postseason, while others may have rested more so Tom Lasorda could keep them fresh.

The opening day lineup was a little different than what we had come to expect over the last three seasons. Having been burned by the Don Stanhouse and Dave Goltz signings, Al Campanis's only substantive offseason move was to trade for Kenny Landreaux. Otherwise, he wisely opted to give the kids a shot instead of signing another splashy free agent (the Dodgers wouldn't ink another free agent until 1988, the year they signed Kirk Gibson).

- **2B Davey Lopes**—Any way you cut it, 1981 was a disaster for Davey. Marred in a season-long slump, his average did not exceed the Mendoza Line until September 12 (he finished at .206). He made six errors in the World Series—a record for second basemen—but did steal 10 out of 10 bases in the postseason. Injuries forced 21-year-old Steve Sax into the starting lineup for much of August and September. Saxy impressed the Dodger brass enough to make them comfortable bidding goodbye to their captain in the offseason.

- **CF Ken Landreaux**—With Reggie Smith unavailable to play the outfield due to his tender shoulder, the Dodgers acquired Landreaux in a trade with the Twins before the season. Kenny got off to a hot start (three home runs and an .821 OPS in April) then fell into a ditch (just four more homers, and a .229 average in the second half). Still, I'll always think of his poetic left-handed swing—along with Cecil Cooper's and Rod Carew's—as the thing that inspired me, a natural righty, to take up switch-hitting (minus their poetry).

- **LF Dusty Baker**—Dusty came within a point of establishing his career high in batting average (.320), which coincided with a drop in power (a projected 14 over a full season). Still, Baker cleaned up in the hardware department, racking up a Silver Slugger Award, an All-Star berth, and, for his first and only time, a Gold Glove patrolling Bakersfield.

- **1B Steve Garvey**—Blame it on the strike, blame it on his divorce, blame it on age—whatever the reason, Mr. Consistency was anything but. His .283 average and .322 on-base percentage were his lowest since 1972, and his power, like Dusty's, projected to only 14 homers over a full year. On the bright side, he shone in the postseason.

- **3B Ron Cey**—A killer Penguin in '81, and the Dodgers' MVP, really, after Fernando. He established a career high in batting average (.288), finished seventh in the league in OPS, and projected to 24 homers and 95 RBIs. Cey's season ended abruptly on September 9 on a hit by pitch, making him questionable for the playoffs. He returned ahead of schedule, in time for the NLCS and World Series, and played the most inspired baseball of his career.

- **RF Pedro Guerrero**—There was simply no way the Dodgers could continue to keep young Pete's potent bat (.829 OPS in '81, and 32 homers in each of the next two years) out of the lineup—the problem was finding him a position. Reggie Smith's injury made him the de facto right fielder until Cey's injury, at which point Pedro finished out the year at third base, where every ground ball carried more suspense than a Brian De Palma movie.

- **C Mike Scioscia**—1981 began Scioscia's 12-year career as the Dodgers' main catcher, though Yeager got the majority of at-bats against lefties. Mike never did hit for much power, but he had a phenomenal eye at the plate and his plate-blocking and pitch-calling skills were unparalleled—and my sister Monica developed a crush on him. According to the 1981 Dodger Yearbook, sensitive young Mike engaged in "solitary hobbies, such as playing guitar and fiddling around with computer science."

- **SS Bill Russell**—Russell's season looked a lot like Lopes's: injury-plagued and underwhelming. He hit .233 for the year and an atrocious .197 on the road. He had only 11 extra base hits in 262 at-bats. To his credit, he rebounded to form in the postseason.

Who Knew?

In his 13-year career, Mike Scioscia never had one season in which he struck out more than he walked. In 1981, he walked (36) twice as much as he fanned (18). Throughout the '80s he was one of the toughest batters to strike out, and in 1987 he led the majors with only 23 whiffs in 523 plate appearances (one K for every 22.74 PA).

On the reserves front, fans got a glimpse of the future when Mike Marshall and Candy Maldonado got brief call-ups. Sax, as mentioned before, filled in admirably, spelling Lopes for 31 games. Derrel "Spider" Thomas was back in a super-utility role, playing six positions. And though we all remember part-time regular Rick Monday's epic homer in the NLDS, we tend to forget that he had an amazing regular season as well, something I'll touch on later. Of course, everyone took a back seat that year to the kid from Etchohuaquila, Mexico.

"AND A LITTLE CHILD SHALL LEAD THEM . . ."

So said Vin after Fernando blanked the Astros on Opening Day, April 9, 1981. When you think about it, Vin wasn't that far off. Quite simply, Fernando Valenzuela's first full year was epic, starting with his dramatic entrance. In a now-legendary story, the preternaturally composed 20-year-old was given the ball on opening day only because scheduled starter Jerry Reuss had pulled a calf muscle the day before, while potential back-up Burt Hooton had an ingrown toenail.

All Fernando did was hurl a five-hit shutout in front of 50,511 fans at Dodger Stadium. There were hints of his brilliance during the stretch run of 1980, when he pitched 17⅔ innings without allowing an earned run. He carried that streak into the '81 season, extending his total to 34 innings before giving up an earned run to the Giants. Undaunted, he started another streak right after that, this time going 36 straight innings before giving up another earned run.

To me, the biggest casualty of an abbreviated season in which one-third of the games were lost was that it deprived us of seeing Fernando build on his record-setting rookie year. As it was, he led the league in strikeouts (180), complete games (11) and shutouts (8) on his way to becoming the first player in history to win a Cy Young Award and Rookie of the Year in the same season. He also started the All-Star Game, which was the first game played after the players' strike.

Stats and medals, of course, were only a small part of the story. Fernandomania quickly transcended the Hispanic community to become a local, and soon, nationwide phenomenon largely because of Fernando himself. He didn't look like a baseball player. With his round face and pudgy midsection, he was one of us. He carried himself with a boyish enthusiasm, but possessed an old soul's instincts for the game. He was from a dusty village in Mexico, but exuded worldly self-confidence. Entire essays have been written about his windup alone. Just before delivering each pitch, his eyes would momentarily roll skyward—"toward the heavens" was the phrase most often used—clearly an indication that there was a greater power at play here. And then there was his unique pitch that gave batters fits—the screwball.

The *screwball?* The only folks I knew of who threw screwballs were Hall-of-Famer Carl Hubbell and Bugs Bunny.

Adding to his Herculean status, Fernando could hit, too, winning the Silver Slugger Award for his position. He exhibited a kind of freewheeling, free-swinging exuberance at the plate you normally find in Wiffle ball games (he clubbed 10 home runs in his career). Comparisons were made to a young Babe Ruth, and no one blinked. Both were southpaw pitchers with Pillsbury Doughboy bodies; both could swing the bat; both were kids at heart (and loved by kids); and both became bigger than the game

Bullpen Session

Scroogies — An Endangered Species

If a government agency were to create a list of pitches faced with the threat of extinction, screwballs would top the list. Much of that has to do with the stress it creates on the arm. The screwball is basically a reverse-curveball, relying on an unnatural rotation of the forearm that often leads to injuries. You often hear reports that once a screwball pitcher retires, his wrist is permanently skewed outward like Frankenstein's monster (this could just be a myth, but it's a good one).

Fernando and Hubbell were the most well-known screwball specialists, and they were linked by one other stat: both hold the record for striking out five successive batters in an All-Star Game. Other noteworthy scroogie artists included Warren Spahn, Christy Mathewson, Mike Marshall, Tug McGraw, and Mike Norris. But I think what I miss most of all about the pitch is the chance to hear announcers and fans utter it. Like the "knuckle-curve" — another endangered species — "screwball" and "scroogie" are just fun to say.

itself, becoming household names to even the most oblivious non-baseball fan. Sports magazines splashed him onto their covers ("Unreal!" screamed *Sports Illustrated* on May 18).

The one I cherish most is the cover of the June 10 issue of Newsweek Publication's *Inside Sports*. Under the heading "For Fernando, The Sky's The Limit," the pitcher is leaning forward in the dugout in a close-up photo, arms resting on a cement step, his left hand clutching a baseball in what looks like a screwball grip. Beneath a mop of shaggy hair and a Dodger cap, a baby-faced, bemused Fernando casts a wide-eyed gaze off-frame to the upper right, an expression suggesting a future of limitless possibilities, as well as a clever nod to his looking-skyward delivery. Meanwhile, his mouth seems to be in the process of breaking into a grin in that playful, knowing way of his. It's textbook Fernando.

In short order, Fernando would have his likeness sketched by LeRoy Neiman, have two songs written about him by Latin artists Lalo and Mark Guerrero, spawn Fernando dolls, bumper stickers, T-shirts and pennants, be the subject of Johnny Carson monologues on *The Tonight Show*, and meet President Ronald Reagan at a White House luncheon. (Later, his image would grace boxes of Kellogg's Corn Flakes.)

Meeting the president may have been a big deal, but you know you've *really* arrived when you're the target of a kissing fan. During an early season homestand, a female fan wearing a "Valenzuela 34" jersey leaped out of the Dodger Stadium stands, put her hands on his broad shoulders, and planted a big wet one on his cheek. True, this amorous admirer didn't carry the, um, weight of the busty Morganna the Kissing Bandit, but all in all it wasn't a bad start for a kid who didn't speak English and wasn't even old enough to legally consume alcohol.

Fernando would go on to play for the Dodgers until 1990. Along the way, he racked up a no-hitter and a 20-win season, led the league in complete games three times, and set a record for consecutive innings to start a season without allowing an earned run (41 innings in 1985). He also compiled an impressive postseason resume, going 5–1 with an ERA just under 2.00 in 63 innings spanning the '81, '83, and '85 postseasons (he was injured in '88).

After bouncing around for another seven years, enduring his share of setbacks, comebacks, and ugly Padre uniforms, Fernando ended up in the broadcast booth for the Dodgers' Spanish radio station. He never did match the mastery of his rookie year, but who could? I equate Valenzuela with the New Wave band the Cars, my favorite pop-rock group from that era. Their first record is a delicious serving of tasty tunes—catchy, fresh, self-assured—almost every song a classic. Though they too had a decent career, the Cars never came close to reclaiming the mojo of that debut record. But in Fernando's case, it didn't even matter. In a mere two months, he had already captured our hearts and sealed our loyalty for the next 10 years. No matter how much he may have struggled in later years, it was impossible *not* to pull for Fernando.

In honor of his historic season, the next two chapters will implement a "Fernando Watch," much as the entire nation did whenever he took the mound in 1981.

SHADES OF '77

Starting with Fernando's opening-day gem, the Dodgers built up a nice head of steam, winning their first six games. Their pitchers were stingy, not allowing more than four runs in a single contest until the 14th game of the season. This compensated for the slow start by everyday players like Steve Garvey, Bill Russell, and Davey Lopes, who at one point fell into an 0-for-25 funk. Also picking up some of the offensive slack was newcomer Ken Landreaux with his hot April. He hit the Dodgers' first home run in 1981, an eventual game-winner at Dodger Stadium in the third game of the season. It came on a hit-and-run play. Ross Porter:

> Landreaux waiting. Now Ruhle at the belt. And the pitch to Kenny . . . a drive to right field and hit deep. Going back is Leonard . . . to the track . . . to the wall . . . home run!
>
> [Twenty-seven seconds of crowd noise.]
>
> That's what I call a pretty good hit-and-run play. I'll hit it, and when it goes in the seats, you just take your time going around the bases.

The Dodgers enjoyed a 13–3 record—matching their hot start of 1977—and a four-game lead as the Giants rolled into town for their first visit to Dodger Stadium on the last Monday in April. It marked Fernando's second start against San Francisco after shutting them out earlier in the month, and his first start at Dodger Stadium since opening day.

Fernando Watch

Houston, We Have a Problem

April 22. The Houston Astrodome. In a televised game, Fernando squared off against new Astro Don Sutton, looking goofy in his rainbow-hued, disco-striped jersey. Fernando came in with a 3–0 record that included two shutouts won by 2–0 scores. The first batter, Terry Puhl, drove a double to right field. Craig Reynolds attempted to bunt him over to third. Displaying surprising athleticism, Fernando fielded the bunt, saw Puhl trapped off second, and raced after him to tag him out. He then whirled and fired the ball to first base, almost catching Reynolds overrunning the bag. Moments later, he picked Reynolds off, but the runner was safe when Garvey's throw failed to get him at second. Valenzuela struck out Jose Cruz and Mike Ivie to end the threat—two of his 11 strikeouts.

In the fifth inning, he came up with two outs and Guerrero on third base in a scoreless tie and Vin behind the microphone.

The 1-0 pitch . . . Valenzuela hits a *line drive extra base* hit down the left field line. Into the corner to get it is Cruz, and Valenzuela, who was *perfectly* content to stop at first, goes into second base. Is there *anything* this kid can't do?

Fernando's RBI single turned out to be the only run of the game. He pitched his third shutout and the Dodgers won, 1–0. Even Bill Virdon, the Astros' stoic manager, had to admit afterward that there was something "a little bit amazing" about this kid.

5-FOR-5
FIVE GAMES THAT DEFINED THE 1981 DODGERS

#1—FERNANDOMANIA: WILD & UNCUT!
Dodger Stadium, April 27, 1981

Though Valenzuela came into his April 27 home start with a 4–0 record, three of those wins came on the road. You can imagine the pent-up energy going into this game. For most of the month, we had to watch Fernando make history from afar on our TV sets or through the radio. For his homecoming, Fernando lived up to his billing—and then some. I was not fortunate enough to attend this game, but luckily we all had the next best thing—Vin.

The game was scoreless until the bottom of the fourth inning. After getting two quick outs, starter Tom Griffin faced the bottom third of the order. Scioscia singled, and Russell kept the inning alive with a single to right, allowing Mike to go to third. That brought up the Dodgers' best hitter so far on the year. Vin with the call:

> Valenzuela singled in the third inning—the first Dodger hit. So of course now, Griffin has been warned. Valenzuela with five hits in his 13 at-bats. 1-for-1, hitting .385 . . .
>
> So Mike Scioscia at third, Bill Russell at first, with two out in the fourth. No score . . .
>
> Griffin at the belt, ready, delivers . . . Valenzuela *lines it into right field, base hit! Dodgers lead, one-to-nothing!*

As the crowd went into a frenzy, organist Helen Dell trotted out the "Paso Doble" theme you typically hear for the matador at a bullfight—"Tuh DUHHH . . . tuh duh duh duh duh DUH-HH . . . tuh duh duh duh duh . . . DUH!" This would become a signature sound "drop" for the man they would call El Toro whenever he did something amazing.

Forty-one seconds later, Vin came back on:

> And they are going *wiiiiiiild* at Dodger Stadium. There's no *way* this game will continue, not for a while. Valenzuela is told by Manny Mota, "Take your helmet off!" And Valenzuela said, "Okay!" He lifted his helmet high in the air, and the crowd *loves* it.
>
> I swear, Fernando, you are too much in *any* language. Can you imagine, on this night of all nights? He's 2-for-2, he got the first Dodger hit, he just drives in a run, and the Dodgers lead, 1–0 . . . and here's Davey Lopes. 0-and-1.
>
> Griffin ready and delivers, and it's waved at and missed.
>
> *Listen* to this crowd just *talking* to themselves. [Laughs.] What a show!

Valenzuela's hit opened the floodgates. Two singles later, the Dodgers led, 4–0.

Fernando, of course, wasn't done at the plate. In the bottom of the sixth, he singled to left for his third hit of the day. He would close out the month of April with a .438 average. The Dodgers added another run in the seventh, and Fernando took a 5–0 lead into the ninth inning. He was on the verge of pitching his third consecutive shutout, his fourth in five starts.

Leadoff batter Larry Herndon greeted him with a single, but El Toro retired the next two batters on flyouts. This brought the crowd to its feet. And Jim Wohlford in to pinch-hit for the light-hitting Johnnie LeMaster.

Of course, it wasn't just Fernando who was giving us goosebumps. Just as Da Vinci was inspired by the Mona Lisa, Vin was thoroughly relishing Fernando's storybook season, and we were the lucky recipients.

That said, I am going to pause here to bestow my "True Blue Ribbon" Mic Award for the 1981 season.

AND THE 1981 "TRUE BLUE RIBBON" MIC AWARD GOES TO . . .

The maestro, of course! That's right, the single greatest call during the regular season came with one out left in this April 27 game, with Wohlford at the plate, Fernando on the mound, and Vin behind the mic.

There is a common perception that Vin Scully's finest hour as a broadcaster came when he called the final out of Sandy Koufax's perfect game on September 9, 1965—particularly Sandy's final battle with batter Harvey Kuenn. Considering the stakes, it's hard to disagree—the clip is truly a masterpiece. But like Sandy's perfect game, his final call of Fernando's fifth win deserves to go down in the annals of his all-time calls. Vin put on a clinic for how to stage a historic moment, peppering his play-by-play with classic literary devices that add gravity to the moment without feeling stuffy or premeditated. Actually, that's what makes it all the more brilliant—the fact that he did it all live, with no script to fall back on.

Here is Vin Scully calling Jim Wohlford's complete at-bat against Fernando Valenzuela, which lasted 3½ minutes:

> And with two out, Jim Wohlford will come off the bench and bat for Johnnie LeMaster.

Vin paused to let PA announcer John Ramsey set the stage:

> Your attention please.
> For the Giants.
> Batting.
> For LeMaster.
> Number One.

Jim.

Wohlford.

Jim Wohlford is one of those guys who makes you wonder how he ever amassed a 15-year career. As a mostly corner out-fielder, he wasn't blessed with power or any real speed (he stole 17 bases in 1977, but was caught 16 times). The best you can say about him was that he didn't strike out a lot. Coincidentally, my junior varsity baseball coach once told me that was my best asset, too, calling me "plucky"—right before cutting me from his team.

Back to Vin:

> So here is Jim Wohlford, hitting .400. Right-hand batter. And this crowd now, on its feet. Theyyyyyy want to see it.
>
> Valenzuela, out of a stretch, the pitch to Wohl-ford . . . *screwbaaaaaall* for a strike!

The crowd roared, as they would for each strike. Vin used rep-etition—in this case, repeated usage of the word "more"—to build the moment, its emphasis establishing a neat rhythmic meter.

> And every time Valenzuela gets on the rubber, *more* people stand, and *more* people cheer, and *more* people applaud. And the night is coming to the end that they had hoped for.
>
> The strike-one pitch . . . screwball, outside.

The crowd voiced its disapproval with plate umpire Fred Blocklander.

> We had said it earlier, it really *is* too good to be true. A full house came to see him, and he has not dis-appointed a soul. The 1-1 . . . *screwbaaaaaaaaall*, is swung on and missed! 1-and-2.

Vin returned to repetition, using "and" to link all the disparate moments of this at-bat into one unifying story that was building to its inevitable climax. If that wasn't enough, he mixed in some Spanish and assonance.

> And now you can hear it—the English cheers, and the Spanish *"Zurdo! Zurdo!"**
>
> And the applause . . . and there hasn't been *anything* like it, *anywhere, anytime*. And Wohlford, the right-hand batter, waits, Valenzuela ready, the 1-2 . . . fastball missed . . . ball two.

More boos.

> 2-and-2. And the Spanish phrase, they tell me, is "Se quita la gorra"—a tip of the cap. And that's what this crowd wants to give Valenzuela now. The left-hander ready, and the 2-2 pitch . . . fast-ball fouled away.

Wohlford's battle with Valenzuela reached the two-minute mark. Vin used the occasion to speak to not just the length of this game, but baseball's unique ability to suspend us *all* in time.

> It has taken almost three hours to get here. But baseball is the *one sport* that is not measured in time. Nobody *cares* that the run scored at a certain time. And no hitter has to worry that time is running out. Time doesn't mean a *darn* thing here tonight. Here's the 2-2 . . . fastball, hit foul. And Wohlford, a good hitter, still up there 2-and-2.
>
> There is no one in the Giant on-deck circle. It's against the rules. You're supposed to have somebody out there. But the fact that the on-deck circle is empty might sum up the kind of *mastery*

---

* *Zurdo* is Spanish for "southpaw."

> and *spell* that Valenzuela has cast so far tonight.
> He has shut out the Giants . . . he has two out
> in the ninth . . . he has 2-and-2 the count to Jim
> Wohlford . . . and the crowd is *begging* him to
> make *one last pitch* and call it a night.

You can't set it up any better than that. If Fernando couldn't strike him out now, it would almost feel like a betrayal of Vinny.

> The 2-2 pitch . . . fastball, fouled away.

D'oh! But Vin was quick to remind us that the batter had a say in this, too.

> And Wohlford is paid to hit, and *hit* 'em, he is.
> 2-and-2.

Vin then broke the wall, as he sometimes did—veering from his narrative to drop in a little personal aside—then referred to the date for good measure. You always knew it was a historic moment when Vin gave the date or time.

> A new supply of balls brought out up to Fred
> Brocklander. What a memorable night, huh? Just
> one game, April the 27th, but whaaaat a game to
> remember.
> Valenzuela's 2-2 pitch . . . *fastball got him swin-*
> *gin'!*

His voice was drowned out by the crowd—sheer *fan*demonium for 19 seconds.

> It is *incredible*, it is *fantastic*, it is *Fernando Valen-*
> *zuela*. He has done something I can't believe any-
> body has ever done or ever *will* do. *Twenty* years
> old. He makes *five* big league starts. He has *four*
> shutouts. *Five* complete games. He's allowed *one*
> *run*. Unbelievable.

He's going to be our guest, we're gonna sign off as quickly as possible. The final score: Dodgers 5, Giants nothing . . .

Bullpen Session

Jack Attack, Part IV

One weeknight in early April, I called into a sports radio show on 710 KMPC hosted by Steve Somers, the former sports guy for *KNBC Channel 4 News*. I had a few things I wanted to get off my chest: the Lakers' playoff chances, a rumored Angels trade for catcher Ed Ott, a correction concerning a call from another listener, and my predictions for the 1981 baseball season. At one point, Somers made mention of the San Francisco Giants, to which I couldn't help but snort, "Jack Clark thinks they're gonna have a good team this year." Steve Somers then launched into a mock play-by-play that instantly made him my favorite talk show host ever:

Steve: There's a fly ball to right, there's a runner on third. Okay, he's tagging, a fly ball to right . . . *and Jack Clark is throwing the baseball to second base, the run comes in to score, the Giants lose!*

Me: [Laughing] I see you're a Jack Clark hater also.

Steve: I'm not a hater of anybody . . . you see, people who watch him in San Francisco *know* that he is really *not* the superstar that people in other cities might *think* he is.

Okay, so maybe I baited the man. But he took the ball and ran with it, going so far as to say even Giants fans didn't much care for him—a position that may have been totally baseless, for all I know. Either way, to hear a talk show host validate my Clark-bashing was music to my ears.

In the background, the matador cue made another appearance on the stadium's loudspeakers. Fernando's stats after the game: 5–0, 0.20 ERA—five starts, one earned run—and millions of captivated baseball fans.

PAST TIME:
LES EXPOS DE MONTRÉAL

The following is a list of things that used to be "cool" and current, but over time became "uncool" and passé.

- AOL (remember when they *owned* the internet?)

- Sears (for about 100 years, the Sears Roebuck catalog reigned supreme come Christmastime, but by the 2000s, the company was bought by . . . *Kmart*?)

- Charlie Sheen (from *Platoon*, to *Hot Shots!*, to *Two and a Half Men*, to . . . Duh! Winning!)

- The metric system (we were *so* close to joining our European brethren at one point)

- Bowling (I used to live for Chick Hearn's *Bowling for Dollars* game show and ABC's *Pro Bowlers Tour*)*

- Jay Leno (back when he appeared as a recurring guest on *Late Night with David Letterman*, he was acerbic, skinny, and mod; hundreds of millions of dollars later, as host of *The Tonight Show*, he lost his edge—and clearly had no desire to go looking for it again)

- The Montreal Expos/Washington Nationals

---

* Bowling became so uncool that it eventually became cool again once the Gen X-ers, of which I am part, gave it their Stamp of Ironic Approval. And the popularity of *The Big Lebowski* certainly didn't hurt.

Sometimes it's hard to remember that the Expos once wielded a certain cachet before they became such a joke. In my childhood, it began with the city of Montreal hosting the 1976 Summer Olympic Games. The Expos received a residual cool factor by playing in the state-of-the-art Olympic Stadium. They fielded a competitive team, had a fiery manager in Dick Williams, and had that whole French Canadian thing going at a time when such bilingualism (and all things French) was still sort of neat-o. They regularly drew over two million fans. They almost outbid the Yankees to sign Reggie Jackson for the '77 season. Not even a lame mascot named "Youppi!" could bring them down. Heck, even Pete Rose eventually donned an Expos uniform. Try to imagine Derek Jeter playing for the Washington Nationals now, and you get a sense of just how far the franchise's stature has fallen.

Then came 1994. In the history of major league baseball, the two longest work stoppages were the 1981 and 1994 players' strikes. It is well-accepted that the '94 strike was the death knell for the franchise in Montreal. The Expos had the best record in baseball—74–40—when the players packed it in on August 12, wiping out the postseason. With a talented young corps that included Moises Alou, Marquis Grissom, Larry Walker, Pedro Martinez (you're welcome, Montreal), and John Wetteland (you're welcome again), '94 was the Expos' one true shot at winning the World Series. The team never recovered from the monetary hit and the fans never came back. Even Olympic Stadium, so *au courant*, as the French might say, when it first opened, had become a great white elephant by the early '90s. I can still recall watching games where puddles of water dripped through the leaky Kevlar roof, accumulating between the folds of ripped-up artificial turf. In 1991, the Expos faced the indignity of having to play their final 13 home games in their opponents' parks after a 55-ton concrete beam fell onto a walkway. After threats of being contracted out of the league, the franchise moved to Washington, DC in 2005.

But where 1994's strike crippled the Expos, 1981's greatly benefited them. The team squeaked into the Division Series only because they—like the Dodgers in the first half of the season—won their division by a half-game in the second half. It would turn out to be the only postseason appearance in Montreal's 36-year history. Of course, the whole experience was tainted by Rick Monday in a game still known as "Blue Monday" to old-time fans, but at least they got in, which is more than any other Expos squad could say.

The team had already been very good for the previous couple of years, having won at least 90 games in '79 and '80. Even though they won more games than any other NL team during those two years, they had only two second-place finishes to show for it. They featured two Hall of Famers in Gary Carter at catcher and Andre Dawson in center field, two young sluggers in Larry Parrish and Tim Wallach, a .300-hitting Warren Cromartie at first base, and an exciting rookie in Tim Raines. Veteran Steve Rogers led a strong starting trio rounded out by young arms Bill Gullickson and Scott

Bullpen Session

Stolen Stats

From an individual achievements standpoint, Fernando Valenzuela wasn't the only rookie robbed of padding his record-setting numbers in 1981 due to the strike. Tim Raines, who finished runner-up to Valenzuela for Rookie of the Year, established the single-season stolen base record for rookies with 71 in a mere 88 games (he broke his hand in mid-September). Had the Expos played a full slate and he stayed healthy, his projected stolen bases would have totaled 130. Four years later, rookie Vince Coleman of the Cardinals stole 110 over a regular 162-game season, second highest single-season mark to that point in the NL's history.

Sanderson. "Spaceman" Bill Lee had his last effective season in the majors, spot-starter Charlie Lea pitched a no-hitter in May, and Jeff Reardon owned the bullpen. So it was hardly surprising that whenever the Dodgers played the Expos, they had their hands full. Never mind the postseason; the teams' *regular* season games were tough, classic affairs, harbingers of things to come. That was apparent in the very first match-up between them on May 1st.

Playing at the "Big O," the Dodgers clawed back from a 5–0 deficit to tie it in the fifth inning, only to see the Expos pull ahead again, 8–5, in the sixth. In the top of the eighth and the bases empty, Rick Monday, making only his third start of the season, got a hold of a 2-1 pitch by Steve Ratzer. Ross Porter:

> A high drive to center. Dawson turns and goes back. He's at the track, he's at the wall . . . it's gone! A home run for Monday.
>
> Rick Monday hit it to the deepest part of Olympic Stadium—404 feet to the center field wall, and Dawson was up against the wall, at the sign. As he looked up, it cleared his head and out of the ballpark.
>
> So Monday's home run pulls the Dodgers within two here in the eighth inning. For Rick, his first home run of the season.

How fitting that Monday's first home run was at Olympic Stadium. Do you think any of the 28,000 fans on hand that day had a clue that this innocuous, aging slugger would come to represent the Expos' face of evil for all eternity?

That same inning, the Dodgers tied the game at 8 thanks to a two-run single by Ken Landreaux, their second comeback from three runs or more. It was games like this one that led to the Dodgers' nickname for the '81 season—"Team Comeback."

The game entered extra innings, during which the Dodgers

blew their biggest chance to win in the 12th inning. Reliever Bobby Castillo, of all people, doubled over Dawson's head to lead off ("Fernando Valenzuela, look out," Ross said), only to get picked off second base on a snap throw by Gary Carter. Baker would single later in the inning.

In the bottom of the 13th, Castillo started his fourth inning of relief. The clock was about to strike midnight on what would end up being the Dodgers' longest game of the year. Tim Raines was the second batter. Ross:

> Castillo into his windup and the 2-2 pitch . . . is a drive into right field and hit deep, Monday going back, at the track, at the wall . . . it's gone!

The Big O was awash in celebratory sound effects: an air-raid siren, laser beams, and then, curiously, a piano playing what sounded like a soft French waltz.

> Tim Raines, with his first major-league home run, wins it for Montreal in the 13th inning. So this town that's been buzzing about this 21-year-old outfielder all season long gets another chance to rave about him as Raines pounds a home run off Bobby Castillo to win it for Montreal.

C'est la vie.

5-FOR-5
FIVE GAMES THAT DEFINED THE 1981 DODGERS

#2—RALLY OF THE YEAR
Dodger Stadium, May 13, 1981

The Dodgers' May Day spectacle in Montreal turned out to be a mere prelude to an even more unbelievable game on May 13 between these two teams. This time, it was the Dodgers' turn to play host. I was fortunate enough to be in attendance, once again lugging my boombox with me to Chavez Ravine in order to capture the radio play-by-play. What I witnessed just may have been the most exciting regular season game I've ever experienced in person. And once again, the teams gave us a taste of the kind of drama we

Fernando Watch

Escape from New York

After winning the final game of the series in Montreal (May 3)—nine innings and one earned run—the next stop on the Valenzuela Victory Tour was Shea Stadium in New York (May 8). About 40,000 fans—three times their average—were on hand to watch Fernando strike out 11, throw another complete game, lower his ERA to 0.29, and improve to 7–0. Jerry Doggett called the last out:

> Valenzuela is within one out now of his fifth shutout of the year. 3–0 pitch to [Lee] Mazzilli . . .
>
> Popped up, on the first base side, foul, Garvey has a play. He's there, he *got* it! And he *did* it again! He *did* it again! Fernando Valenzuela, on a 3-and-0 count, Mazzilli fouls out to first, and the Dodgers are all *over* him out there on the mound. Five shutouts for Valenzuela!
>
> And I'm telling you one thing . . . this is really some kind of a story. He puts the *Big Apple* on its *ear*, and they're still doing *high fives* out there on the diamond for the Dodgers.
>
> And Valenzuela [laughs], he goes walking off with a big grin on his face!

It was official: New York had been warned. If Fernando could make it there, he could make it anywhere.

could expect come October.

To paraphrase an old hockey joke, I went to a pitchers' duel and a slugfest broke out. Really, this was two games in one. Through seven innings, the Dodgers and Jerry Reuss were breezing along, nursing a 1–0 lead. The first batter in the top of the eighth was the Hawk—Andre Dawson. Vin was behind the mic for the call, as well as for the rest of the game's action:

> One run, five hits for the Dodgers. No runs, seven hits for the Expos, and here we are in the eighth.
>
> Reuss ready and delivers, and there's a high drive into deep left field . . . that has a chance . . . back goes Baker to the wall . . . iiiit's gone . . . and with one swing, the Expos get even.
>
> For Jerry Reuss, the *first* home run that he has allowed this year. And it's enough to tie him. And for Andre Dawson, his seventh home run and his 14th run batted in.

The Expos did not score again in the inning. Meanwhile, on *Homerun Highlights* tape seven, I announced that we are going to cut to a "live" report from Dodger Stadium.

> Studio Paul: Okay, with the score 1–1, we are now going to turn to some guy named Paul Haddad—he's out there live at Dodger Stadium—well, not actually live right now, it is tape-delayed—but he will be telling us what is going on out there, and I'll be asking him a few questions. So let's go now to Dodger Stadium for a report.

That's right, I was essentially interviewing *me*. If Bugs Bunny could play all nine positions in a baseball game, I didn't see any reason why I couldn't be in the "studio" and at the stadium at the same time. I had meticulously planned this audio sleight of hand for some time, figuring I could work in gaps during my live report from the stadium so I could drop in questions (from Studio Paul) later, when I got home.

Confused? How do you think I felt trying to pull this thing off?

As the Dodgers prepared to bat against Scott Sanderson in the bottom of the eighth, I switched from my boombox's radio mode to live mic—just as I had done the year before to capture the Seventh Inning Stretch. Reporter Paul set the stage from his Aisle 14 seat. David, naturally, was also present, as were my brother and his friend, Jack.

> Reporter Paul: Okay, we're here at Dodger Stadium live, it's 9:34, and, well, it is tied, 1–1. Andre Dawson has just hit a home run to tie up the game. Oh, and uh, I have here, David . . .
>
> David: Hi, I'm David.
>
> Reporter Paul: Yeah, we know, yes, David . . . and, uh, I guess it's *rally* time right now. Yes! Reuss is hitting . . . all right, let's get some runs here.

Sorry, I just have to point out something you would *never* see in a game now. Jerry Reuss had just given up the tying run (his ninth hit allowed), and in a 1–1 ballgame, his spot is the first one up. Seems like a good time to pinch-hit, does it not? But Tommy Lasorda elects to have Jerry Reuss (6-for-68, a .088 average, the previous season) hit. In 1981, this was just part of baseball culture; starters, if they were going well, finished what they started. Today, a manager would get crucified for not pinch-hitting in this situation.

Back to my exchange. This is what it sounds like on *Homerun Highlights*:

Studio Paul:	Is it a good game?
Reporter Paul:	What was that?
Studio Paul:	I said, was it a good game?
Reporter Paul:	Yeah, uh-huh . . . yes, it is.
Studio Paul:	Do you have the attendance there?
Reporter Paul:	Yeah, the attendance was 42,712, something like that.
Studio Paul:	That's pretty good!
Reporter Paul:	Uh-huh.

This stunt was going nowhere. Luckily, Reuss bailed me out with a surprising base hit.

Reporter Paul:	And uh . . . whoa hooo . . . hey heyyyyy! Yes, base hit! There has just been a base hit by Reuss, the Dodgers' sixth hit of the game, to go with one run and one error, and here comes Lopes and it looks like the Dodgers might have something going in the bottom of the eighth.
Jack:	[Audible in the background, uttering his nickname for Lopes] "Frozen *Rope*," Davey Lopes!
Reporter Paul:	So uh—right now on the message board they are putting up the word "Charge!" However, in the background they have a picture of some elephants. Don't ask me to explain, 'cause I don't understand. Lopes, he might sacrifice, they've got the big bats coming up . . .
Jack:	Lopes *never* sacrifices.
Reporter Paul:	Yeah, right . . . well, we're gonna

	be signing off right now because it is really getting exciting here, and uh, there's a 1–1 tie . . . we're gonna leave you here . . .
Studio Paul:	Okay.
Reporter Paul:	We'll catch you later. So long.
Studio Paul:	Okay, you heard it all right there from Dodger Stadium! And as it did turn out, the Dodgers *did* have a rally in that inning. Therefore it's time for . . . [cue theme music] Another Dodger Rally!

So Lopes did attempt a sacrifice, but Gary Carter muffed it for an error. After a wild pitch put runners at second and third, Landreaux worked a full-count. Back to Vin Scully:

> 3–2 pitch to Kenny Landreaux is a line driiiiiive . . . *fair* down the right field line! *Iiiiiiiinnn* comes Reuss . . . *iiiiiiiinnn* comes Lopes on a double by Kenny Landreaux!

3–1 Dodgers. A Baker single put runners at first and third, then Garvey stepped up.

> Sanderson, hands at his sides, reading Carter, and the 2-2 pitch to Garvey is *lined* into left field . . . that'll be a base hit and get Landreaux home, Baker stops at second, and the Dodgers lead 4–1. And here comes Dick Williams, and that will be all for Scott Sanderson.

The Dodgers took that 4–1 lead into the ninth inning. With Jerry Reuss and his 1.03 ERA on the mound, a win seemed automatic. But Big Bird gave up three consecutive singles and was relieved by Bobby Castillo, who was no better. After three batters, *he* was replaced by Steve Howe. Seven of the first eight batters reached for the Expos, who scored five runs before the inning mercifully ended. The Dodgers were now trailing, 6–4.

Woodie Fryman was on in relief. Steve Yeager, pinch-hitting for Howe, led off the bottom of the ninth and flew out to center. After Lopes got hit by a pitch, Landreaux drove a ball deep to right-center, but it was caught on the warning track. Two outs.

At that point in the game, my party and I had moved down to the first row of seats on the field level. Much of the crowd took off when the Dodgers went ahead, 4–1, in the eighth, and many others were filing for the exits. We sat next to two spirited, white-haired women in their sixties wearing Expos caps and jackets. They had the loudest voices in the whole section, willing Woodie on to close out the game. God bless 'em, but as grumpy Dodger fans at our home park, we were annoyed.

"Old hags," David muttered.

Reggie Smith, making only his ninth appearance all year, hit a limp ground ball to shortstop on a 1-2 pitch. I stood up and grabbed my radio. Game over. Or was it? Vin:

> There's a ground ball to short. Speier juggles, picks it up, can't throw to second, throws to first—too late!

Here we were on May 13, and that was Chris Speier's 13th error of the season. The day before against the Dodgers, he had made four errors. That is not a typo. I said, "four."

Now there were runners at first and second and still two outs. Steve Garvey came up. The count again went to 1-and-2.

> Fryman checking . . . Lopes on a *double-steal*, and it's a fly ball to right field. Wallach coming in a huuurryyyy, and the ball is *off* the glove of Rodney Scott! *Iiiiiiinnn* comes one run, *iiiiiiiinnn* comes Reggie, and it's *all even!*

The play was ruled a single, but it was definitely catchable by either Wallach or second baseman Scott. Regardless, the Dodgers had tied a game that should have been over—twice. David was showing particular animus toward the two Expo fans, who had put their hands over their mouths in disbelief. He was screaming, "In your face! In your face!"

The next batter was Ron Cey.

> 2-and-0 pitch to Cey is a high fly ball into *deep* left field . . . back goes White . . . a-*waaaaaaaaaaay* back . . . it's *goooooooooooooooone!*

Dodger Stadium exploded—the "10th Man" was what we came to be called that year. David went hoarse screaming, "&^%#* you, you old hags!!!" I was too excited to feel bad for them or anybody. The Dodgers had won 8–6 with four unearned runs in the bottom of the ninth. The line from the game read:

> Expos   0 0 0 0 0 0 0 1 5—**6 14 2**
> Dodgers 1 0 0 0 0 0 0 3 4—**8 11 2**

Vin Scully came back on the air after 47 deafening seconds:

> Ho-hum, just another Dodger ball game. Can you *believe* it? Can you *possibly* imagine as wacky a game as *this one?* Holy *mackerel,* there were 13 runs scored in the last two innings. So the game they had won . . . was the game that they lost . . . is the game that they finally win.

In 1980, when the Dodgers lost the season by a mere game, it was easy to pinpoint backbreaking losses that could've made a difference in the standings. On the flip side, this come-from-behind victory defined Team Comeback, and would prove to be a key difference-maker when the Dodgers won the first half by half a game.

Who Knew?

There is a perception among some longtime baseball fans (myself included) that the 1970s and 1980s were a golden age for shortstops. Players like Mark Belanger, Dave Concepcion, Frank Taveras, and, of course, Ozzie Smith stand out in our heads as players who weren't great hitters, but were superb defenders. We tend to think the 1990s brought us shortstops who could hit for average and power, but whose defense couldn't quite match up to their predecessors'.

Sabermetrics aside, a quick check of simple stats and videotape reveals that not only are today's shortstops better hitters, they're largely better defensively, too—more athletic *and* more fundamentally sound. Bill Russell (who refused to dive for balls) and Chris Speier weren't the only shortstops coughing up their share of errors every year. Frank Taveras won a championship with the Pirates in '79 but never went an entire full season without committing at least 24 miscues, and he played 10 years. Even Gold Glovers were given a pass. The Reds' Dave Concepcion won the award five times, including two years in which he committed 27 errors ('76 and '79) and one in which he committed *30* ('74).

Gone are the days when shortstops could regularly make 30 errors a season and still have a job. In fact, one of the highest fielding percentages among National League shortstops with at least 1,000 games is held by Jimmy Rollins, a former 30-homer guy who immediately makes you think, "Offense first." As of 2011, Jimmy's never had over 14 errors in one season. Even slugger Miguel Tejada has a fielding percentage equal to that of Concepcion's. The good ole days were good, all right. Good and sloppy.

8TH INNING
May–October 1981

One of the joys of Fernandomania was that it amplified the communal feeling among fans at Dodger Stadium. You know that sudden urge you get to slap fives with a total stranger when the Dodgers hit a dramatic home run? Fernando brought out the high fives in all of us. It wasn't just the Chicano community that beamed with pride; like Hideo Nomo among Japanese Americans, Jackie Robinson among African Americans, Chan Ho Park among Korean Americans, or Sandy Koufax among Jews, Fernando made us proud to be Dodger fans partly because he was so quintessentially a Dodger. He represented what so many of us love about the organization—a history of breaking taboos, embracing players of all colors and creeds, a team perfectly in sync with its melting-pot fan base.

Of course, that's not to say it's been a walk in the ballpark, either. The Al Campanis/*Nightline* debacle in 1987, in which the GM had to retire due to racially insensitive remarks, was obviously a low point for the franchise. But there were also some disquieting comments made by unnamed Dodger brass in 1981 with regard to the thousands of extra fans who filled Dodger Stadium whenever Fernando pitched. According to the June 30, 1981 edition of *Inside Sports*, "a member of the Dodger family . . . wondered if more brown faces in the bleachers . . . would result in more

Rick Monday, semi-removed from it all, except when it mattered most.

rowdyism in the stands. It is not clear that the polite, cool, white Dodger fans want to sit next to great clumps of Latinos."

Ultimately, I'm sure, any private concerns by one or two skittish employees were put to rest by the general goodwill and extra revenue that the carefree pitcher brought to the organization. As Vin Scully said himself—referring to the fact that Fernando relied on friends like scout Mike Brito to drive him to and from the stadium each day—"The way he's been going, he ought to be delivered in a Brink's truck."

5-FOR-5
FIVE GAMES THAT DEFINED THE 1981 DODGERS

#3—"IT'S GONE, FERNANDO, IT'S GONE!"
Dodger Stadium, May 14, 1981

Team Comeback followed up their improbable May 13 win against the Expos with yet another game for the ages the following night. The largest crowd of the season turned out to catch Fernando fever. It was a game that marked the apex of his regular season, and is remembered as much for Vin's classic call that sealed the victory for Fernando—and the Dodgers.

We were living on borrowed time. We knew that, on any given day, Fernando would prove his mortality and fall to earth. He had won the first nine decisions of his young career, going back to his relief appearances at the end of 1980. But there was a part of me that believed, that *really wanted to believe*, that this guy could go undefeated for the year. Prone to bouts of wildness, he had shown signs he was not invincible, but like Harry Houdini, Fernando was always at his greatest when wriggling out of a jam.

Tonight against the Expos, he got his first test of what it felt like to give up his first big-league home run. It happened in the top of the third. Ross Porter was behind the mic:

> Valenzuela, an above-average fastball. Good curve, and the screwball . . .
>
> There's the scroogie, driven to left and deep . . . going to the corner is Baker, he's at the pole, it's aaaaaaaaaaaaa home run for Chris Speier, just fair inside the left-field foul pole. And Speier can also say now, "I'm the only man to have a home run off Fernando Valenzuela in the National League."

It was fun to listen to Ross pronounce Valenzuela's name in his rookie year. While most of us were saying, "VAL-en-ZWAY-luh," with four syllables, Ross broke it into five syllables, with an accent on the second and fourth: "Val-EN-zoo-EH-luh."

Meanwhile, El Toro was unfazed by the homer; he didn't give up another run through eight innings. Expos starter Bill Gullickson was almost equal to the task. He was shutting out the Dodgers through 5⅓ innings. With runners at second and third, Steve Garvey came up. Vin with the call:

> Garvey trying to muscle one out of the infield and at least get Lopes home. Gullickson will pitch out of a stretch . . . Ron Cey on deck. The right-hander ready . . . and the pitch . . .

At this point during my recording of the radiocast, my audio drops out for a few seconds for unknown reasons. Perhaps my dog, Ginger, stepped on a button, or the tape got wrinkled. Whatever happened in this Watergate-type gap, the action picks up again after a few seconds, and I am able to decipher that Garvey had singled home Lopes and Baker, the second run scoring on a bang-bang play at the plate:

> . . . Baker having to be restrained! And I think, he

felt that Bill Gullickson had thrown a *shoulder* at him as he was trying to score!

The crowd was booing, but their hearts were not into it. The Dodgers led, 2–1, and Fernando was in line to go 8–0. Once again, he was living up to expectations, not just on the mound, but at the plate. After singling in the third, he did it again in the seventh, raising his average to .360. Back to Ross:

> The windup and the first one to Fernando is driven to center fiiiiieeeeeld . . . base hit!

Helen Dell played the matador cue.

> Valenzuela gets his ninth hit of the year—his third two-hit game. He's also got a three-hit game!

In the eighth inning, leading 2–1, El Toro got the first two batters, but then walked Chris Speier. Vin Scully struck an ominous tone by pointing out that meant that Andre Dawson, the Expos' best hitter, would get a chance to bat in the ninth inning. But first Valenzuela had to get out of the eighth. The speedy Tim Raines, pinch-running for Speier, stole second base, putting the tying run in scoring position. Fernando had to face pinch hitter Chris Smith, a rookie. It was his first-ever major league at-bat. What do you say to someone like that? "He's pretty much unhittable, kid, but uh . . . try not to embarrass yourself up there." Fernando got two quick strikes. As he did so often with hitters who were worried about diving for a screwball, he came back with a heater. Vin:

> Fernando, reading Scioscia, now set at the belt, and the strike two—*fastball*, got him looking!

Welcome to the bigs, Chris.

Reliever Steve Ratzer retired the Dodgers in order in the bottom of the eighth. Now the stage was set for the ninth inning.

Fernando had to get through the Expos' top of the order—Jerry White, Rodney Scott, and Andre Dawson. If he could go 8–0, he'd tie a record for most consecutive games won by a major leaguer to start a season, and the Dodgers would possess a 5½ game lead.

Valenzuela got White on a groundout and Scott on a flyout. The crowd was giddy with anticipation. Vin set the stage for his confrontation with Andre Dawson:

> So you have *two* out in the ninth inning, and Andre Dawson, actually the *last cannon* unless Carter gets a chance. And Dawson has grounded to third and popped up twice. Andre, 0-for-3. Came into the game hitting .292. He has seven home runs, tops on the Expo team, 15 RBI . . .
>
> And *listen* to this crowd with two out in the ninth. A lot of people are *standing* now. You would think it's the last out of the [World] Series.

But then . . .

> And a *screwball* is hit to *deep* left field. Back goes Baker, a-waaaaaaaay back . . . it's *gone* in the bull- pen, and it's aaaaaaaaaall tiiiiied up. He hit the screwball *out*. So that *walk* in the eighth inning that allowed Dawson to come up in the ninth has made it a tied-up game.

Vin worked in an symbolic side-story—in this case, the Dodgers' foiled attempts to fly Fernando's parents up from Mexico to make it to Dodger Stadium in time to see their son pitch.

> And what was it we were saying tongue-in-cheek earlier, remember? About how Fernando Valenzuela's parents had *missed connections*. They were not *on* the plane from Phoenix. And they would not *get* here to see him pitch "*unless*"—and the

> "*unless*" was, the game went into *extra innings*.
>   Can you believe this? Here's Gary Carter . . .
>   And all those red lights disappearing out of
> the parking lot, I'm *so* sorry.

It always amazes me that people would be driving off in a moment like this. Then again, the second-most famous image of the Kirk Gibson homer—after Gibby pumping his fists while rounding the bases—is that of a car's brake lights in the parking lot, visible beyond the right field pavilion, its driver no doubt hearing the call on the radio and blurting, "Oh &#%@!"

Back at home, I, like the fans in attendance, was shellshocked. Was this the point in Fernando's career where miracles actually ceased?

The first batter up in the bottom of the ninth was Pedro Guerrero. Vin:

> 1-and-1 to Guerrero.
>   Ratcher comes back to his hitter, and there's a
> drive into *deep left field*, back goes White . . . it's
> *GOOOOOONE, FERNANDO, IT'S GONE!*

Are you *kidding* me? In the heat of the moment, Vin *personalized* the home run—not to be cute, but to buoy Fernando. It had been such a dispiriting moment when the kid gave up the homer to Andre Dawson, Vin spoke for all of us in his dedication. This spontaneous moment remains one of the top calls in Vinny's storied career. After 47 seconds of delirious noise, he came back on:

> There are no *words* to express what's going on
> here. The sound of a cheering crowd tells it all.
> The Fernando Valenzuela magic is *alive* and *well*,
> and so are the spirits of 55,000 at Dodger Stadium as Pedro Guerrero homers, and the Dodgers
> win it, 3–2.

Valenzuela has now tied the major league record of 8 and 0, and who's to *say* when it will end? Fernando's going to be our guest on the post-game show with Jaime Jarrin and Jerry, so stay with us . . .

Jaime Jarrin, of course, was the Dodgers' Spanish play-by-play announcer thrust into the role of Fernando's interpreter. Signing off, Vinny played with the name of the post-game show to reflect the fact that Fernando had been the guest virtually every time he pitched.

Now, for Jerry Doggett and Ross Porter, this is Vin Scully inviting you to stay tuned for the Fernando Valenzuela Show, coming right up.

Who Knew?

Fernando's nickname, "El Toro," stuck after the *Los Angeles Herald Examiner* polled fans to come up with a good moniker. El Toro was already being tossed around by the media and even the Dodgers' marketing department. Other nicknames considered included Señor Cero (Mr. Zero), El Incredible, Titan del Pitcheo, and—one I heard more than once by snickering sportstalk hosts—El Pauncho. Personally, I've always thought El Matador was a more fitting nickname than El Toro. A bull may be strong but is ultimately duped by the bull*fighter*. That was Fernando, messing with batters' minds, tantalizing them into chasing the dancing red cape that was his screwball before pulling the string.

Fernando's season line: 8–0, 0.50 ERA, seven complete games, five shutouts. Who *was* to say when it would end?

KING PEDRO

I always rooted extra hard for Pedro Guerrero. Although he was acquired in a trade with the Cleveland Indians while he was still in the minors, he was essentially a home-grown product. The Dodgers, of course, already had lots of them, but folks like Garvey, Yeager and Cey came along before I was following the team. Pedro was someone whose career arc I could actually track, starting with his first plate appearance in the bigs.

It came on September 22, 1978, at Dodger Stadium. He singled. He played in four more games that year, all at first base, and finished 5-for-8, a cool .625 average. I remember getting lots of chances to check him out in the season-ending series in San Diego, which was televised. For some reason, he reminded me of a grasshopper. He was incredibly skinny and had a wide-open stance at the plate. When he hit the ball, he seemed not to roll his wrists like most players do when they make contact with the ball. Instead, he derived his power by dropping his forearms and sweeping them across his torso, much like a golfer, but without the wrist bend to finish the swing. Consequently, his straight-arm uppercuts often seemed incomplete on their follow-throughs, but somehow the ball flew off of his bat anyway. It's like the whole thing was an optical illusion.

While Fernandomania was reaching a fever pitch in May of '81, Pedro Guerrero was doing his best to distract us. For the month, he put up impressive numbers, which probably propelled him into the All-Star Game as a reserve:

Pedro Guerrero—May 1981 (26 games)

AB	AVG.	HR	RBI	OBP	SLG.	OPS
103	.361	7	23	.388	.649	1.038

Pedro was particularly clutch at home. On May 15, just one night after belting the game-winning "it's gone, Fernando, it's gone!" homer, he hit *another* late-game home run to key a come-from-behind victory . . . and spur another great call out of Vin.

The Mets were on top, 5–4, going into the bottom of the eighth. Pedro was leading off against reliever Neil Allen, who sported a "13" on his jersey. Vin pointed out that you don't see players wear bad-luck Number 13 much anymore (I guess A-Rod sort of ended that superstition). But Allen, not a superstitious sort himself, liked the number anyway and wore it all through high school. Vin picked it up from here:

> When Allen came to the Mets, he asked to wear 13 and they told him no. They said the number would *bother* you, it might be a *jinx*. They wouldn't let him wear it.
>
> The 1-0 pitch is high.
>
> But then *last* year, when he saved 22 games and became one of the premier relief pitchers in baseball, they said, okay, if you want to wear Number 13 you can . . .
>
> [Audible crack of a bat.]
>
> And he's *wearing* it . . . and *there* goes the ball . . . into the bleachers!

Besides the obvious irony at play here, Vin literally shouts the word "wearing" like no other call I've heard; even he seems caught off-guard in a sort of "whoa!" moment.

> Well, who said lightning doesn't strike twice? Lightning has struck three times. Neil Allen has allowed only *two* home runs this year, both of them to Guerrero, and each one *tied* the game. And, of course, Guerrero last night hit the home run to *win* the game.

The Dodgers won the game in the bottom of the ninth— their third in a row in their last at-bat.

Guerrero finished out the season batting .300—exactly his career average over 15 years. In fact, many sabermetricians have put forth compelling arguments that Pedro Guerrero was the second-best hitter in the National League in the 1980s with a minimum of 3,000 plate appearances after Mike Schmidt. The numbers would certainly seem to back it up. He was second in batting average and third in slugging, and he finished in the top four in MVP voting four different years.

What I find even more impressive are the stats he put up as a Dodger, from 1978 to 1988, when he was traded to the Cardinals midway through the year for pitcher John Tudor. I mean, I always knew he was great, but didn't realize how much so until comparing Guerrero's offensive lines to every Dodger slugger

Dodger Sluggers—1958 to 2011 (7 Years Minimum)

Dodger Players	Years	Era	AVG.
Mike Piazza	7	'92–'98	.331
Pedro Guerrero	**11**	**'78–'88**	**.309**
Raul Mondesi	7	'93–'99	.288
Ron Cey	12	'71–'82	.261
Rick Monday	8	'77–'84	.254
Steve Garvey	14	'69–'82	.301
Adrian Beltre	7	'98–'04	.274
Eric Karros	12	'91–'02	.268
Dusty Baker	8	'76–'83	.281
Joe Ferguson	11	'70–'76 '78–'81	.245
Mike Marshall	9	'81–'89	.271
Wes Parker	9	'64–'72	.267

who had put on a uniform since the team moved to Los Angeles. Below is a sampling of the top offensive players from 1958 to 2011, with on-base percentage, slugging and OPS as the telling numbers.

Caveat: I only included those with at least seven years in L.A. I wanted players who played long enough that you think of them as *Dodgers*, rather than mercenaries like Gary Sheffield or Manny Ramirez, who put up superior numbers but in four years or fewer. This chart also doesn't include Matt Kemp and Andre Ethier, who ranked #3 and #4 in OPS after their first six years in Blue.

If this list tells us anything, it's that Raul Mondesi was even better than we thought, Joe Ferguson really liked to walk, and the 1960s truly were a wasteland for power hitters. Of course, numbers will skew up or down depending on the era, but even taking that into consideration, Pedro Guerrero was easily the L.A. Dodgers' second greatest offensive player among those with at least seven years' service—and certainly the most versatile. Depending on the circumstances, Pedro was the team's starting left fielder, center fielder, right fielder, third baseman, first baseman, even second baseman in Tommy's short-lived experiment in 1980. Pedro was never a threat to win a Gold Glove. He often got

OBP	SLG.	OPS
.394	.572	.966
.381	**.512**	**.893**
.334	.504	.838
.359	.445	.804
.355	.443	.798
.337	.459	.796
.332	.463	.796
.325	.457	.782
.343	.437	.780
.359	.419	.777
.325	.449	.774
.351	.375	.716

the wrong jump on fly balls and did not have soft hands at third, but we tend to overexaggerate his defensive deficiencies when it comes to making the routine plays. Statistics bear out that he was about as good as anyone in the majors at getting to the ball. And if you compare Pedro's 15-year career fielding percentage with the 15-year career of Derrel Thomas—a man known for being a late-inning defensive specialist who played eight positions in his career—you may be surprised to find that Pedro has him beat: .977 to .965. Granted, Derrel played more games at harder positions like shortstop and second base and had far greater range. But the point is that, given his bat and versatility, Guerrero's defense was sufficiently adequate, with his offense making up for any liabilities.

Pete lost a step after 1986, when he ruptured a tendon in spring training and missed most of the season, but there was even a time when he brought speed to his game. In 1982, he was the first Dodger to amass 30 home runs and 20 bases in a season, a feat he repeated in '83 (Raul Mondesi became the team's first 30/30 player in 1997). He peaked as a Dodger in 1985, when he led the league in OBP, SLG., and OPS and tied Garvey's single-season home run record of 33. In June of that year, it didn't just seem like he hit a home run in every other game—he basically did, whacking 15 homers to tie a major league record for the month of June. During one stretch, he reached base 14 straight times.

And while he may not have played much in 1986 because of his injury, nobody—and I mean, *nobody*—gave a more memorable performance in the endlessly mocked Dodger music video equivalent of your high school yearbook—the Baseball Boogie Bunch doing "The Baseball Boogie." If you haven't seen the video yet on YouTube, no amount of warnings can prepare you for the sight of your favorite '80s Dodgers—Reuss, Welch, Hershiser, Duncan, Scioscia, et al—losing their dignity on the dance floor as they shimmy and shake in satin warm-up jackets to a bad '80s beat while taking turns "singing." It's like a bad dream, only it's real. In the center of it all stands Pedro Guerrero, clad in pink satin and positively blinding us with his gold bling—two large necklaces with medallions, two chunky bracelets (one on each arm), and five fat (or is that phat?) rings. But I will say this about Pedro—he *owns* it, and the producers entrusted him with delivering an important verse that tells us: "In Español and English too, we're gonna get down a little just for you!"

Things get a little creepy toward the end of the video when the "Official Ball Girls" enter the studio in their white hot pants to bump and grind it out with the players. Like a pimp in a bordello, Pedro points to a brunette and says "Get that one!" then turns to two blondes and repeats "Get that one!" Eighties music videos were nothing if not misogynistic—hey, girls just wanna have fun too, right?—but it's hard to look at the Good-Times Pete in this video without thinking of his sad life after baseball. In an infamous recording from a 911 call, OJ Simpson called the cops in 1999 to complain that his woman friend had been "doing drugs for two days with Pedro Guerrero!" You know you've hit rock bottom when you're running the same circles as

Bullpen Session

Cey Hey

Pedro Guerrero wasn't the only position player on fire in May. Ron Cey clubbed nine home runs during the month and came within inches of two more. After a two-run homer off the Mets' Pat Zachry on May 17 to give him five for the week, Vin made reference to Cey's reputation for putting the team on his shoulders from time to time:

> Is he *ever* hot! Ron Cey, the one guy who can carry the ballclub all by himself. He's gotten a lot of help, but he could sure have been carrying them all *this* week. He has *always* been that way. When he gets hot, he can burn the house down!

OJ. The 911 clip became a staple on sports talk shows like Jim Rome's. That same year, Pedro was arrested on cocaine trafficking charges, but was acquitted in 2000 when his lawyer argued that Pedro's IQ was too low for him to be held responsible for his own behavior. (Insert your own joke here.)

Fernando Watch

The Philadelphia Story

May 18, Dodger Stadium. The good news: Fernando Valenzuela's parents finally got a chance to see him pitch in person, courtesy of the Dodgers. The bad news: the Phillies were the defending World Champions, and they weren't intimidated by anyone. League MVP Mike Schmidt made that clear in the first inning. Vinny:

> Fernando into the windup, and it's a fastball lifted to right field and deep. Back goes Guerrero, to the track ... it's gone—a home run. Mike Schmidt hit a fastball the other way, over the right-center field wall. And just as he did in his last game, Fernando finds himself behind on a home run.

The Dodgers appeared poised to take the lead in the bottom of the first. With a runner on second, Garvey belted one to right off Marty Bystrom:

> The pitch is a breaking ball, and a high drive into right field ... but going back is Lonnie Smith and *makes the catch at the wall* at the 370 sign.

Leading off the second, Ron Cey reaffirmed that the breaks just weren't going to go the Dodgers' way that night.

> Cey hits a high fly ball into deep center field, back goes

Pete may not have been a model citizen after his playing days, but during his career, he exceeded my hopes to become an even better homegrown Dodger than any player who came before him . . . yes, even Steve Garvey.

Maddox, *at the wall, leaps in the air and makes the catch for the out!*
So the Gold Glove of Garry Maddox is very much on display as he leaps *high* in the air at the 395 sign to take a home run away from Ron Cey.

By the seventh inning, Fernando was losing 4–0, and the magic spell was broken on the next play, as called by Ross:

All right, Valenzuela's 3-2 pitch with the runner going . . . a ground ball to Valenzuela—he looked to second, he *can't get the ball out of his glove*, and he throws *wide*, and everybody's safe.

It was his first error of the inning. The Phillies handed him his first big-league loss, and afterwards crowed in the papers that the key to beating Fernando was to be patient with his screwball, which often landed out of the strike zone. Big words for a team that only managed three hits off him the entire game.
Fernando's line was now 8–1 with a 0.91 ERA. He would still put up some big games for the remainder of 1981, but his record after this game was about break-even (5–6). Not coincidentally, the Dodgers would play .500 ball (37–37) for the remainder of the year as well.

5-FOR-5
FIVE GAMES THAT DEFINED THE 1981 DODGERS

#4—DODGER/PHILLY-BUSTER
Dodger Stadium, May 20, 1981

May 12–20 was a fun time to be a Dodger fan. Team Blue played a nine-game homestand that would have to rank among the greatest homestands the team has ever played. I've already hit on most of the highlights this chapter and last:

- The 8–6 comeback win against the Expos, when the teams combined for 13 runs in the last two innings.

- Guerrero's game-winning homer to secure Fernando's 8th win to start the season and put him in the record books.

- Three games in a row won in the bottom of the ninth inning.

- Five home runs by Ron Cey.

- While not a success, it also included Fernando's first major-league loss.

Which brings us to the final game of the homestand, another classic affair that perfectly encapsulates the Dodgers' formula for success in 1981: great starting pitching, some timely hitting . . . and no shortage of drama.

The Philadelphia Phillies had already taken the first two games of the series. Game 1 was their victory over Fernando, and Game 2 was a tight contest in which Dick Ruthven outpitched Bob Welch. The Dodgers were looking to avoid a sweep, but they'd have to beat future Hall of Famer Steve Carlton. Burt Hooton went for L.A.

The Phillies took a 1–0 lead into the bottom of the second inning. Steve Garvey got aboard on a Mike Schmidt error. That brought up the scorching Ron Cey. Vinny:

> Carlton ready, and the 1-2 pitch to Ron Cey . . .
> is a high drive into *deep* right field . . . back goes
> Lonnie Smith to the waaaaaaaall, it's *off* his glove
> . . . I believe off the *wall* . . . Garvey goes back to
> first, and let's see . . .
>
> They're gonna rule it a catch. Lonnie Smith
> went high up against the wall, and John Kibler
> is explaining that the ball didn't *hit* the wall—it
> went into Lonnie Smith's mitt and came up in the
> air again, and he caught it a second time. Manny
> Mota and Ron Cey arguing with John Kibler, and
> Tommy Lasorda's going to go out.

Vin, lip-reading:

> And Lasorda said, "No, it hit the *wall*." Lasorda is
> still jabbering and pointing, saying it hit the wall.
> And Kibler is saying, "No." On instant replay, Lon-
> nie Smith went back to the track, ran parallel to the
> wall, finally got to the wall, leaped high in the air,
> and it hit his glove. Then he seemed to pinch his
> glove and the ball went up in the air. But whether it
> grazed the wall while it went up in the air, we won't
> know for sure, even with instant replay.

The crowd was letting Kibler have it, no doubt spurred by Lasorda's shenanigans. Kibler, by the way, would be the first-base umpire when Bill Buckner made that key error in Game 6 of the 1986 World Series.

> But Lasorda and Kibler are jawing and jawing.

"Go *ask* somebody," Lasorda said. In other words, I think Tommy wants a second opinion from another angle. "You bet your. . . ," Tommy is saying. "It hit the dash wall," Lasorda said. And, of course, Lasorda is seeing his club lose the last two. He is *ticked* off.

And Kibler has thrown him out!

And Lasorda, who was furious . . . and we could read most of it . . . and now . . . *noooow* Lasorda is all over him . . . he's letting it *aaaaaaall* out now.

The crowd loved it. Vin gave us an edited version of Tommy's cuss words, letting our imaginations fill in the rest.

You talk about dangling participles and split infinitives . . . he is hurling semicolons and colons . . . he's just hurled an exclamation point! There's some hyphens . . .

And now Manny Mota . . . and now Lasorda's saying, "Get out of here" to *Mota!* He just told Mota, *"Get out of here!"* And he's talking to Kibler, if you want to call that talking. He is venting his *spleen*, as the poet would say.

And he has finished what he had to say, but he is also gone.

Once order was restored, Pedro Guerrero dug in. You know what happened next.

The Dodgers trying to battle back now. The 3-2 pitch to Guerrero . . .

[Audible crack of a bat.]

Swung on, and a *high drive* into center . . . back goes Maddox, a-*waaaaaaaaaay* back, to the wall . . . it's gone!

The fans were so loud, Vin's "it's gone" was barely discernable. Pedro's homer put them ahead, 2–1.

The Phillies came back to tie it in the third. Then, in the fifth inning, first baseman Pete Rose stepped up. It was a historic at-bat. It made him the all-time leader for most at-bats in the National League. But Garvey ruined the moment. Vin:

> Hooton at the belt. A look back at Lonnie. Double-checking him. Now the 1-0 pitch to Rose . . . line-drive . . . a *great catch by Garvey*, they *double-up Lonnie Smith!*
>
> What a *magnificent* leaping catch by Garvey on the all-time at-bat leader in National League history. And Rose was going to make the most of it. It looked like a *cinch* double and an RBI, and instead Garvey turned it into a double play.

It would remain tied into the bottom of the ninth. Tug McGraw was on in relief. With two outs, Guerrero raked a single, his fourth hit of the day, and Steve Yeager worked a walk. Spectator/pinch hitter Reggie Smith came up to bat for second baseman Derrel Thomas. Vin again:

> The 2-0 pitch to Reggie Smith—McGraw delivers, and there's a fly ball down the right field line . . . Lonnie Smith on the dead run . . . diiiiives . . . he *caught* it! Oh what a catch! A *fantastic* catch by Lonnie Smith in right field, and we're gonna be here a while!
>
> It didn't appear he had a chance, but of course he is a rabbit, and he needed all his speed to save the Phillies' bacon.

After Steve Howe got out of a jam in the top of the 10th, left-hander Tug McGraw started his second inning for the Phillies. The Dodgers needed to pinch-hit for Howe, but Ross Porter pointed out that they were out of right-handed bench players, so that left Rick Monday, a lefty. In a part-time role, Rick had gotten off to a slow start in 1981, but he'd shown signs of warming up, with three hits in his last four at-bats to raise his average from .136 to .231.

> The 3-1 pitch to Monday . . . a drive to right field
> . . . back goes Smith, to the track, to the wall . . .
> Monday's hit it out and the Dodgers win!

Back in the clubhouse, Tommy was hurling all exclamation points.

MANIC MONDAY

Make no mistake, 1981 was the year of redemption for Rick Monday. Since coming over from the Cubs in 1977, he was largely a disappointment for the Dodgers—often injured and never quite living up to expectations (especially for someone picked #1 in baseball's first ever amateur draft).

By the start of the 1981 season, what had Rick Monday really *done* for the Dodgers? With all the other players, you at least knew what you were getting or what they stood for. Who was Rick Monday anyway? My impressions of him at the start of the season were shaped by two images:

1. The now-classic photo of Rick saving the American flag from being burned on the outfield grass of Dodger Stadium by two protestors, back when he was a Chicago Cub.

2. A 1978 Topps baseball card I had of "Mo," in which—I kid you not—he is standing in a warm-up jacket, arms crossed, using his thumb to either scratch his sneering lip or wipe some spittle off. This seemed to sum Rick

up to me—just sort of hanging around, removed from it all, straddling that netherworld between player and coach, full-time and part-time, and perhaps amusing himself with some silent commentary as he contemplates his future in broadcasting.

But then a funny thing happened on the way to the stadium. In a reversal of past years, it was now *other* players getting hurt, with Monday, cast aside to start the season, suddenly playing the role of the spot starter who made the most of his opportunities.

The other funny thing that happened was that he slowly became my favorite player, sneaking up on me like a rash. Steve Garvey? He was *so* predictable. Guerrero? His future was already written. Cey, Baker, Lopes—been there, done that. I needed a new hero, someone who could surprise when least expected. What better role model than a broken-down, 35-year-old, part-time outfielder who resembled Lurch from *The Addams Family*?

Monday was no false idol. Ever since he got hot in that mid-May homestand, he had only gotten hotter. Even Vin started to notice something afoot in a June 1 home game:

> 1-and-1 the count . . . Monday hits a high drive into center . . . back goes Murphy, a-way back, to the track, to the wall . . . it's gone!
> [Thirty seconds of crowd noise.]
> Boy, Rick Monday seems to be getting *stronger* the more he plays. His *last* home run he hit back into the Dodger bullpen in left field, and he hit what looked like a *marble* over the center field fence, it was hit so high. His fifth home run, he has eight runs batted in.

Wisely, Tommy Lasorda resisted the temptation to run him out there every day, keeping him fresh for the rest of the year and the postseason. As a result, Rick's second-half stats (.348 average,

.477 OBP, six homers in 69 ABs) told the story of someone whose trajectory couldn't have been on a better course for the postseason. In fact, his final average (.315) and OPS (1.031) were his high-water marks for the season. To put his entire year in perspective, Mike Schmidt led all National Leaguers with one home run for every 11.4 at-bats. Monday was right behind him at one in

Fernando Watch

The Brave One

Here's a sobering stat: After going 8–0, Fernando Valenzuela's ERA for the rest of the first half (six starts) was 6.16. On May 23, he followed up his first loss with a no-decision in Cincinnati, where he drew 40,000 curious spectators (20,000 above their average). It was the second straight start in which he gave up four earned runs.

Then, on May 28, the roof caved in: seven earned runs in 3⅔ innings in Atlanta, where 26,597 jeering fans (15,000 above *their* average) came out, though in fairness, he was victimized by some very shaky Dodger defense.

His next start was a rematch with the Braves on June 1, this time at Dodger Stadium. Rick Monday got the Dodgers out in front with his two-run homer in the first inning, and Fernando returned to form with a complete-game 5–2 win that included 11 strikeouts, including this one, as called by Vin to close out the fourth inning:

All right, one ball and two strikes to Dale Murphy. Fernando into the windup and the pitch is a screwball— got him swinging! He *struck* out the side—*olé*!

Nothing like a little home-cooking to get your head on straight. Fernando's year-to-date stats after this game: 9–2, 1.90 ERA, eight complete games.

11.8 at-bats, though Schmidt did have three times as many plate appearances as an everyday player.

When Rick hit his pennant-clinching homer in Montreal during the Championship Series, I remember casual fans registering shock. *Rick Monday? Does that guy even still play for the team?* Of course, the home run was unbelievable, but the guy who hit it shouldn't have been. Quietly and methodically, everything he had been doing had been building toward that moment. Against all odds, the man mostly known for saving a flag at Dodger Stadium became known for saving an even bigger one—the National League pennant.

STEEEEE-RIIIIIKE! WE'RE OUT!

We have just received news that on this June 11th, 1981, the players of the major leagues have called a strike. Yes, that is right, a strike.

[Roll in booing and hissing from another tape.]

Yeah, yeah . . . We know . . . Fans very unhappy. And, well, we don't know how long this thing could last, but this just might be the final day of the season. If it is [snarky laugh], that means the Dodgers come in first place by half a game over the Reds! Woo-hoo!

It was the night of June 11, a Thursday. The void, the betrayal, the emptiness in the pit of my stomach—none of it had hit me yet, and so I was flippant while announcing the news on *Homerun Highlights* tape eight. This labor stuff was all beyond my comprehension, and I was in a sort of denial. Or was it relief? The threat of a strike had been looming for weeks. Since the beginning of June, it had seemed like an inevitability. Coincidentally, that was just about the time the Dodgers hit their first slump, while the Reds got red-hot.

On May 31, the Dodgers whipped the Reds, 16–4, to go up 5½ games. From June 1 to June 11 (the final game of the first half), L.A. went 3–6, including their first four-game losing streak. Cincinnati went 8–1, finishing out the "first season" with a seven-game winning streak. As the clock ticked down, I watched in horror as the Dodgers' lead shriveled from 5½ to one-half in the final eight games. The strike may have ruined baseball for a while, but to me, it saved the Dodgers from themselves. I was convinced that one more game would've swung the standings and put the Reds in first place. The Dodgers narrowly averted a collapse that would have rivaled Gene Mauch's '64 Phillies, who lost 6½ games with 12 games remaining.

Rudderless and confused, I looked for guidance from the one voice who could offer some perspective—Johnny Carson. Like many Americans, I made a point of watching his *Tonight Show* monologues every night before bed (and suffering the sleep-deprived consequences the next day). This was still in the days when the late-night host was the sole dispenser of cultural bons mots. Sure enough, the baseball strike was the hot topic of the night. I preserved his monologue on my *Homerun Highlights* collection:

> There's good news and bad news. The bad news is there may be a baseball strike tomorrow. The good news is Reggie Jackson just offered Fernando Valenzuela a job as a gardener.

On the tape, the audience laughs and applauds. Did Johnny really just crack a gardener joke about Valenzuela?

> Valenzuela said, "I can't believe the ballplayers are going on strike." He said, "What more can a player ask for?" He said, "I'm already getting three pesos a day from the Dodgers."

Uh, okay . . . so the early '80s were not the most PC of times.

> When he learns to speak English, salaries are gon-
> na go up!

Johnny then turns his barbs on some other baseball targets, including these zingers:

> I'll tell you, the strike is really a disappointment
> for the Cubs. They were on a streak—two rain-
> outs in a row!

> Have you heard the latest demands by the ball-
> players? While on camera for televised matches,
> they want to be paid by the itch.

> Billy Martin could use the rest. Really. The other
> night, he got carried away, and he threw a piece
> of artificial turf at one of the umpires, and then
> [Howard] Cosell asked for his toupee back.
>   Good ol' Howard! I'm glad Howard's around.
> We wouldn't have any material without Howard.

If any good came out of the strike, it was that it forced me outside a little more that summer. It also made me more jaded about baseball, seeing it more like a business than a birthright. This created a healthier distance between the sport and myself at an age when I probably needed to open up my worldview, anyway.

HERE WE GO AGAIN

On August 10, the so-called second season began. There were lots of questions among Dodger fans. Since the Dodgers had been de-clared the winners of the first half, how much incentive would they have to play hard in the second half? Would Fernando shake his slump and regain his glory from April and May? Would people even care anymore after a bitter labor stoppage in which fans and low-wage stadium employees were (as always) the ultimate losers?

Bullpen Session

A Tip of the Sombrero

Vin Scully's most famous Fernando call was no doubt this one:

If you have a sombrero, throw it to the sky!

He actually didn't utter this line until nine years later. It was the capper to Valenzuela's first and only no-hitter, on June 29, 1990 — his last year with the Dodgers.

That same day, *Sports Illustrated* heralded the season by doing an odd thing on its cover. Under the heading "Here We Go Again!" they showed a photo of George Brett and Mike Schmidt, the MVPs from the previous year. It was the *exact* same cover they had used for their April 13, 1981 baseball special issue, only that one had a different headline—"Hot Shots at the Hot Corner."

Whoever approved the duplicate cover must've been going for a déjà vu vibe to reflect the headline, but to me it achieved the exact opposite. I found it confusing and lacking in creativity, especially from a magazine known for its great covers. And here it was, August 1981, and they were still leaving in the fact that Brett and Schmidt were the MVPs from 1980? Wasn't that really *old* news? Or were they saying that *SI* picked them as the MVPs for the first half of '81? (Which couldn't be, since Brett was having—for him—a mediocre year.)

But before the second season officially began, the All-Star Game—originally slated for mid-July—had to be played. There were rumors that disgruntled fans would boycott the August 9 game in Cleveland, raising the prospect of the game being played in the midst of a sea of empty seats. Not quite. Municipal Stadium was crammed with 72,086 fans—the largest crowd ever to see a Midsummer Classic. It turned out to be a thrilling, come-from-behind 5–4 win for the National League, and offered proof that, at the end of the day, we as baseball fans are nothing more than powerless, quivering invertebrates when it comes to controlling our baseball fixes. I was particularly invested in the game since the Dodgers were represented by six players—the most of any NL team. Fernando was the starter, pitching one uneventful inning. Burt Hooton pitched a less-than-effective two innings in relief. Steve Garvey, Dusty Baker, and Pedro Guerrero were chosen as position-player reserves. Ironically, the only Dodger to be voted in by fans was the one having the worst year—Davey Lopes. Davey carried a .169 average into the game, with three home runs, seven RBIs, 13 stolen bases and 25 runs. It was a testament to his popularity among Dodger fans that they thought enough of him to overlook his anemic offense and nagging injuries.

After the break, however, the fans' unconditional acceptance of Davey quickly ended, as he suffered one of the swiftest falls from grace to ever hit a ballplayer.

5-FOR-5
FIVE GAMES THAT DEFINED THE 1981 DODGERS

#5—LOPES'S KISS-OFF
Dodger Stadium, August 12, 1981

During the baseball strike, Davey Lopes was very vocal as a player representative. At one point, he annoyed some of the player reps from other teams by questioning their qualifications, then appeared to backtrack on some comments under pressure from Marvin Miller. He certainly didn't endear himself to Dodger fans. Letters to the *L.A. Times* castigated Davey Lopes for his perceived insensitivities. He appeared to *really* cross the line when he went on record to criticize the Dodgers' sacred cow—Steve Garvey— for allegedly getting paid during the strike when most other players did not. He said there might be a stigma against Garvey by other players when play resumed.

When the second season started at Dodger Stadium, Lopes was viciously booed by a large faction of fans, much as one-time darling Brett Butler would be after his comments about "scabs" after the 1994 strike. No doubt some of the boos were related to Davey's horrible year, but fans often look for scapegoats to take out their frustrations, and Lopes was an easy target. Things got so bad that, by the third game of the homestand, even the Dodger announcers couldn't ignore the problem.

Going into this August 12 game, Davey's second-half looked a lot like his first. He was in a 1-for-9 skid coming into the rubber game against the Cincinnati Reds. The jeers only got louder after he grounded out to the pitcher to lead off the first, then fouled out in the second. But he singled in the fourth, drawing a smattering of applause. In the seventh, he came up with a runner on and the Dodgers leading, 6–4. Jerry Doggett:

> Here's Lopes coming on now . . . Lopes winning back a lot of fans, who were booing him soundly. We haven't been able to figure out just exactly why they were on Lopes . . .

Jerry seemed unaware of the strike controversy, unless he was choosing to overlook it.

> . . . Because, when you figure out, Lopes was voted to the All-Star Game. And most of those votes that carried him to the All-Star Game came from *right here*. All these folks booing Davey were no doubt those who voted to get him into the All-Star Game. So why they've been booing him since the second season began, we don't know.
>
> Oh, he's been not hitting as much, but a lot of guys slump. Davey's been an outstanding player here for a long, long time.
>
> Here's a curve, down low, one ball and no strikes.

> All players will go into slumps from time to time, but Davey, boy, he's been a crowd-pleaser for many years in this ballpark . . .
>
> [Audible crack of a bat.]
>
> Fly ball to left-center field, he hit it deep! Back goes Mejias, this ball is gone! Hello, Davey! Welcome back.

The crowd began to cheer.

> So Davey Lopes hits one out of here, and that *really* turns the boo-birds off . . . and he's going to get a standing ovation going to the dugout. Well, that's more like it. Takes his cap off, salutes the crowd. And a hug from Tommy Lasorda, and the Dodgers lead, 8 to 4.
>
> And Lopes, really getting a royal greeting down in the dugout, he's a very popular player with his teammates. A standing ovation! That's a way to turn those boos around.
>
> Here's Landreaux at bat. Here's the pitch . . . swing and a foul.
>
> And the fans, as if to apologize, *won't stop*. They want Davey to come back for an encore. The fans are saying, "Davey, we're sorry, we had you all wrong, come on out!" Time called . . . he's gonna be called back. Here he comes—thatta boy!

Another huge cheer.

> Okay, I guess everybody's kissed and made up now.

Not really. Just two nights later, against the Braves at home, Lopes was still roundly booed whenever John Ramsey announced his name. The dissenters seemed to be more concerned about his slump, really letting him have it in the fourth inning. Vin:

> Davey hitting .181. Lopes has struck out, hit into a double play. And here he is now, with Guerrero at third, Scioscia at second and Goltz at first. And the pitch to Lopes is *popped up*. And it'll be the second baseman, Hubbard, waiting and waiting, backs up now and makes the catch.

And the boos came out, even though the Dodgers held a 3–0 lead.

Two weeks later, Lopes left the lineup due to a groin injury, returning in early September to hit a respectable .274 for the rest of the year. Call me a Lopes apologist, but it truly saddened me to see Davey's final days as a Dodger (even though we didn't know it yet) marred by such a torrent of bad will after everything he had given to the fans. It wasn't the send-off he deserved. Happily, he was finally able to win a World Series ring before the Dodgers traded him to Oakland in the off-season. And proving that time heals all wounds, probably the highlight of the 2010 off-season amongst longtime followers was the news that Davey would be returning to the Dodger family as a first-base coach—a nice coda for player and fans alike.

GEARING UP

Although it was comforting to know that the Blue Crew had an automatic playoff berth, I spent the last several weeks of the second season praying that none of the players would suffer a season-ending injury that would knock them out of the postseason.

On September 9th, my worst fears were realized in a game against the San Francisco Giants. It was the first of three noteworthy moments in September and October that would directly affect the Dodgers' postseason.

Fernando Watch

The Kid Stays in the Picture

As expected, attendance dropped off at Dodger Stadium after the strike, but fans continued to come out in droves to see Fernando pitch. Despite perceptions that he was mostly ineffective in the second half, his ERA was virtually the same as the first half, and he still pitched three more shutouts. While his pre-strike days were marked by a brilliant April and May but a horrible June, Valenzuela was more consistent to finish out the year. In 11 starts, only once did he give up more than four earned runs. His record would've been better than 13–7 if the Dodgers had given him more run support in his final three starts, when they totaled only three runs. The real killer was his last start of the season, which came at Dodger Stadium.

The Dodgers were losing 1–0 when they started a rally in the eighth inning. They loaded the bases with only one out. Lefty Ken Landreaux was due up against southpaw Fred Kuhaulua. Tom Lasorda pinch-hit for Landreaux with Jerry Grote, a 38-year-old journeyman catcher recently re-acquired from the Royals. Granted, Landreaux was having a lousy second half. But he hit higher against lefty starters (.333) than righties (.241), and brought speed. Jerry Grote was making his first appearance as a Dodger, in a new league, and ran like, well, a catcher.

Jerry promptly hit into a double play, and the Dodgers and Fernando fell, 1–0.

Fernando Valenzuela's Final Line for 1981

W	L	ERA	SHO	CG	SO	BB	IP	Gms start
13	7	2.48	8	11	180	61	192.1	25

"Fernie" would lead the National League in games started, complete games, innings pitched, shutouts, and strikeouts.

1. The Penguin's Fractured Wing (September 9)

It was the final game against the Giants in a three-game set at home. The Dodgers had won the first two games, thanks in large part to Ron Cey, who was 3-for-6 with two home runs and four RBIs. The Giants jumped out to a 2–0 lead in Game 3. After a Steve Garvey single in the fourth, starter Tom Griffin sent what might be termed a purpose pitch . . . if the purpose was to knock Cey out for the rest of the year. Vin with the call:

> Ron back up, Griffin right foot on the rubber. Now delivers, and the pitch inside and it *hit* Cey. And he's going to be awarded first base. But Cey is acting like a man who's hurt. He slammed his helmet down and bat, and walked away as if he was not only angry, but he knew he needed some help.

Diagnosis: a fractured left forearm, just above the wrist. Early accounts were that Cey might be lost through the World Series, if the Dodgers got that far. Upside: Guerrero would move to third base, creating more playing time for Rick Monday in the outfield. Still, the loss of Cey stung, and his absence was a big blow for a starting infield already weakened by injuries to Lopes and Russell, who limped into the division series with a stress fracture in his left foot.

2. Sutton's Fractured Kneecap (October 2)

In his first start at Dodger Stadium as a visiting player earlier in the year, Don Sutton decked his nemesis, Steve Garvey, prompting a round of boos from the home crowd. The Dodgers knocked him out of the game, and seemed to be on a mission to exact revenge on Sutton the rest of the season. In one game, they asked the umpires to check Don's person to see if he was scuffing the ball (perhaps they knew something about their former teammate?). Then, in a season-ending series with the Astros, Jerry Reuss shattered Sutton's kneecap with a fastball when Don squared around to bunt. The Astros would clinch the second season later in the series, assuring a first-round appearance against L.A. in the Division Series. But they'd be doing it without their best pitcher in the second half (7–2, 1.75 ERA). Advantage: Dodgers.

3. Sutcliffe's Fractured Ego (October 4)

"I'm going to have a good year. I know it. It's going to be . . . lots of fun." So said Rick Sutcliffe in the Dodgers Yearbook for 1981. But for the second year in a row, 1979's Rookie of the Year struggled, and his frustration boiled over when Tom Lasorda told his big right-hander on the last day of the season that he would not be including him on the postseason roster.

In an incident that lives on in Dodger lore, Sutcliffe took the news about as well as Jack Nicholson handles the waitress's admonition of "no substitutions" when he orders toast in *Five Easy Pieces*. Sutcliffe swept everything off of Tommy's desk, threw a chair, and called his manager a liar. And he didn't deny any of it. Besides his anger about being passed over, Sutcliffe, like his fellow future broadcaster, Sutton, seemed to resent the Hollywood culture that permeated Lasorda and the Dodgers.

"I can't play for the man," Sutcliffe told the Associated Press. "I was brought up in the Midwest. I'm conservative."

The Dodgers accommodated Sutcliffe's request for a trade after the season, and Rick went on to have a pretty decent career, winning the Cy Young Award only three years later. But, to this day, whenever I see Rick Sutcliffe on TV, my first thought is always: *Trashed Lasorda's office.*

And for some reason, there's always a bowl of pasta being upended in that mental picture too.

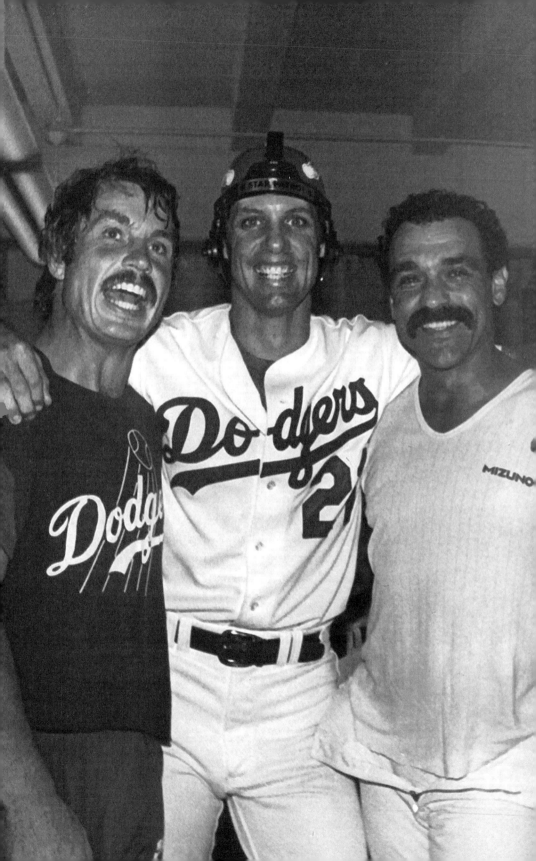

9TH INNING
October 1981

THE 3RD SEASON

For the 1981 season, the Dodgers held an 8–4 record against the Houston Astros, but—to borrow a page from Vin—"What have you done for me lately?" In the last two months of '81, while the Dodgers were going through the motions, the Astros cruised to a 31–18 record to clinch the second season and set up a showdown against the Dodgers in the divisional series. The 'Stros gained a key psychological edge when Nolan Ryan no-hit the Dodgers at the Astrodome on September 26—the fifth of Ryan's career, to break the record he held with Sandy Koufax.

Nolan's no-hitter spoke to the challenges the Dodgers would be facing in their Best of Five series. At 34, Ryan led the league with a 1.69 ERA, but Houston's other four starters were also better than average. Bob Knepper, Joe Niekro, Vern Ruhle, and Don Sutton (out with his knee injury) all compiled ERAs under three runs. In the cavernous Astrodome, the Astros' starting staff had a wispy 1.77 ERA. Not fair!

Compounding matters for the Dodgers was the fact that Ron Cey was still out with a broken arm, and the hobbled Lopes was still a shadow of his former self. As clichéd as its sounds, it was clear that this was a series in which the winning team would be

Ron Cey, Jay Johnstone, and Davey Lopes soaking in the 1981 World Championship.

the one that made its pitches when it mattered most. There would be little margin for error—one mistake could cost the game, and the series.

The following are my thumbnail impressions of baseball's first Division Series in the modern era (thank you, strike!). The first two games would be played in Houston, and the final three in the City of Angels.

NLDS—GAME 1 (HOUSTON ASTRODOME)
Astros 3, Dodgers 1

Fernando Valenzuela went up against Nolan Ryan, whose last start against the Dodgers was his no-no. The Dodgers didn't waste any time getting a hit off him—a single by Landreaux in the first inning—then proceeded to go hitless through the next five innings. The Astros won on a two-out, two-run homer in the bottom of the ninth that broke a 1–1 tie.

High Fives:
- Steve Garvey hit a 406-foot home run off Nolan Ryan to tie the score, 1–1, in the seventh inning.
- Fernando pitched eight innings of one-run ball.

Heartbreaks:
- The Dodgers managed only two hits off Ryan the entire game.
- Alan Ashby hit a walk-off homer in the bottom of the ninth.

Monday Morning Managing:
- Where was Steve Howe in the bottom of the ninth? After getting the first two outs, Dave Stewart, relieving Fernando, gave up a single and was allowed to face the switch-hitting Alan Ashby. True, Ashby was not much of a power threat, but the lefty Howe would've turned

him around to his weaker side. The previous season, Ashby hit .167 with no homers as a righty. In his career, his splits were pretty substantial:

Alan Ashby—Career (4,123 at-bats)

	Batting Avg.	Slugging Pct.
Right-handed batter	.215	.302
Left-handed batter	.256	.383

He was also hitless in his career against Howe. Moreover, Stewart had a propensity for giving up ninth-inning home runs, most recently just two weeks earlier against the Reds. So instead of Howe likely retiring Ashby to send the game into extra innings against the Astros' bullpen, Stewart gave up a gopher ball, negating a gutsy performance by Fernando and losing the first game against the league's hottest pitcher—one they would have to face again if the series went all five games.

Mental State:
• Cloudy, with a chance of self-flagellation.

NLDS—GAME 2 (HOUSTON ASTRODOME)
Astros 1, Dodgers 0 (11 innings)

Just when I thought the Dodgers couldn't lose in a more gut-wrenching fashion than in Game 1, they continued to shock and surprise. In a repeat of the game the day before, this one featured two starters at the top of their game (Jerry Reuss vs. Joe Niekro), leaving the outcome to the bullpen. The end result was exactly the same—only, this time, the Dodgers prolonged the agony in an extra-inning contest that lasted almost four hours. They left Houston down, 0–2, having scored one measly run in 20 innings.

High Five:
- Nine innings of shutout ball by Jerry Reuss.

Heartbreaks:
- Check out these numbers for L.A.:
  Left on base: 13.
  Runners in scoring position: 0-for-9.
- For the second game in a row, Dave Stewart lost in the late innings. This time, he gave up singles to Phil Garner

Bullpen Session

Going to Bat for Joey

The Astros' last season in the Houston Astrodome, baseball's first domed stadium, was 1999. This seemed appropriate, given that the idea of artificial-turfed, non-retractable roofed, multi-purpose stadiums was *so* 20th century. I'll never forget attending my one and only game in the space-age monolith. It came on July 7, 1989, in the middle of a cross-country road trip with my college buddy, Don, who hated baseball but agreed to tag along with the promise of lots of cold beer and my insistence that the Dome was the "eighth wonder of the world."

It was a . . . curious experience, much like my first visit to the Mall of America. The first thing that struck me was how *green* the Astroturf was, like a plasma TV with the color cranked to 100. Everything seemed too bright, too big, too echoey, too sterile. Before the game started, the giant bald head of Art Howe (by then the Astros' manager) materialized on the scoreboard in a prerecorded message welcoming fans and coaching them in the ways of ballpark etiquette. It was very Big Brother, made even more so by Art's stiff, Max Headroom-like delivery, and the fact that the producers of this little clip didn't give much consideration to Art's eye line. Instead of having him look

and Tony Scott to lead off the 11th. Tommy Lasorda replaced him with Terry Forster, then Tom Niedenfuer, to
stop the bleeding. With two outs and the bases loaded,
Niedenfuer faced Denny Walling. Jerry Doggett with
the call:

> I tell you one thing, it's an emotional ballgame.
> 1-and-1 to Walling. Here's the stretch. Here's the
> look. And here's the pitch. Fly ball to right-center

down at the fans, who were seated *below* the scoreboard, Art's gaze was fixed straight ahead at the opposite wall of the arena just below the steel girders, creating a cold, detached vibe very much in line with the Dome itself.

As for the actual game, I couldn't even take it seriously. It seemed like a practice game for a real one that would be played outside. But the people were friendly and Don appreciated the roving beer ushers—something you don't get at Dodger Stadium. Also, it just so happened to be Bat Day. I thought the bats would be baby ones like Dodger Stadium used to give out, but they were regulation-size wooden bats! (They do everything bigger in Texas.) Unfortunately, when I stuck my hand out for one, the usher said, "Sorry, just for 14 and under."

I hadn't driven 1,500 miles to be denied a bat!

"It's for my sick 10-year-old brother, Joey!" I cried. Despite my ridiculous sob story, the usher smiled crookedly and hand-ed me the bat, giving me my first taste of Southern hospitality. Don later told me I was going straight to hell for that stunt. Un-til then, I still have the bat, which coincidentally came already painted Dodger blue.

field. Thomas on the run . . . can't get it. The game is over.

For the second time in two days the Astros got a walk-off hit with two outs. In order to advance, the Dodgers would need to sweep the Astros at Dodger Stadium, à la their season-ending series the year before (minus the one-game playoff, of course).

Monday Morning Managing:
- In the top of the 11th in a scoreless tie, the Dodgers had their best chance to take a 1–0 lead. With one out, Steve Yeager delivered a pinch hit double, and Bill Russell was walked. Reggie Smith struck out, bringing up Davey Lopes—the only Dodger in the game with two hits. But Tommy sent in Mike Marshall to pinch-hit for Lopes, even though Steve Sax, a contact hitter, was available. Mike was a prodigious minor-league hitter, but he was batting .200, had only 25 at-bats in the bigs, and was facing a strikeout pitcher in Joe Sambito. Sambito struck him out. In the bottom of the 11th inning, Lopes was replaced defensively by . . . Steve Sax.

Mental State:
- Someone shoot me if I have to witness one more Astrodome game that ends with animated, rip-snorting bulls and rootin'-tootin' gunslingers on the scoreboard. What is this, a baseball game or a rodeo?

NLDS—GAME 3 (DODGER STADIUM)
Dodgers 6, Astros 1

There was a distinct feeling of déjà vu as the Dodgers returned home for a Friday-Saturday-Sunday series with the Astros in October, needing a sweep. While this game—and the following two—would largely lack the nail-biting suspense that accompanied the finale of the 1980 season, the Dodgers' success against the Astros in those three games can now be viewed as a sort of primer for *this* series. Plus, the Dodgers had won 11 of their last 13 contests against the Astros at Dodger Stadium. A side of me couldn't help but think, "We got 'em right where we want 'em."

High Fives:

• After their offensive drought in Texas, the Dodgers wasted no time getting on the board in the first inning. Baker hit an RBI double, then Garvey made it 3–0 on a two-run homer, called by Jerry:

> [Bob] Knepper up with the arms, and the pitch on the way. Line drive to left field, waaaaay back. Going, going—goodbye, she's gone.
>
> Steve Garvey belts one into the bleachers, half-way up. And the Dodgers just like that lead, 3–0. And the Dodgers trying to start off with a blast of a few skyrockets here. Baker hit the left field fence, Garvey hit the left field seats.

• Burt Hooton, after faltering in the '77 and '78 postseasons, looked like he might turn it around big time in 1981, starting with this game. He allowed only three hits through seven innings, his first of five quality starts in five October games.

Heartbreak:

• None!

Monday Morning Managing:

• Gotta give it up for Tommy in this one. Bob Welch was next in line to start this game, but the manager opted to bump Welch to the bullpen and start the veteran Hooton, a move seemingly motivated by the heavy toll on his pen in the 11-inning game, and the fact that Welch had experience in relief. Happy pitched a gem and Welch closed out the game in the ninth inning.

Mental State:

• Hopeful. Fernando was going the next day but wouldn't have to face Nolan Ryan, whom manager Bill Virdon was saving for a Game 5.

NLDS—GAME 4 (DODGER STADIUM)
Dodgers 2, Astros 1

Pitching on three days' rest, Fernando hurled his second gutsy game in a row, giving up one run and four hits in a complete game win. Once again, the Dodgers were stifled by the Astros' pitching. Discounting Game 3, they had now scored three runs in 28 innings. But their two runs on this day were just enough to make a difference, tying the series up with a chance to avenge the previous year.

High Fives:

• Fernando, on three days' rest, was perfect through four innings (but so was Vern Ruhle).

• Pedro Guerrero broke a scoreless tie with two outs in the fifth inning. Porter:

> There's a drive by Guerrero, left field and deep . . . it's gone!
>
> The first Dodger base runner of the evening touches 'em all. Pedro Guerrero shoots one to the bleachers in left. The Dodgers lead, 1–0, and the crowd . . . on its feet, they want Guerrero to make an encore appearance . . . and here he comes!

Heartbreak:

• None again—though, to be fair, the Houston fans

deserve a special mention. In the fifth inning, Cesar Cedeno broke up Fernando's perfect game with a single, then broke the hearts of Astro fans. Ross:

> Cedeno not doing, so far, a very effective job of reading Valenzuela's move . . . here's the stretch by Valenzuela. He's got him picked off! The throw to Garvey, down to Russeeeeeell . . . they got him!
>
> Cedeno is on his stomach, not getting up at second base . . . and they are feeling the back of his right leg. And it might be that hamstring muscle that has bothered Cesar the last couple of weeks.

This play represented the turning point not just of the game, but the entire mini-series. You sensed a momentum shift as the speedy Cedeno writhed on the ground in pain and the fans went nuts over Fernando's sleight-of-hand. Guerrero would homer to break up *Ruhle's* perfect game in the bottom of the inning, and put the Dodgers up to stay.

Monday Morning Managing:
• It was the bottom of the seventh inning, the Dodgers clinging to a 1–0 lead and needing insurance. Steve Garvey singled to lead off. That brought up Rick Monday. *You did not sacrifice with Rick Monday.* His last sac bunt had been when Jimmy Carter was president. Rick Monday was the Dodgers' hottest hitter; he was clearly up there to swing away. But in a series where two runs could win a game, Tommy surprised everyone and ordered Monday to bunt. Even more amazing, Monday got it down, pushing Garvey into scoring position. Three batters later, Bill Russell drove Garvey home with a single. It proved to be the eventual game-winner.

Mental State:
- Guarded optimism. I had tickets to the game the following afternoon, but was petrified of the Ryan Express.

NLDS—GAME 5 (DODGER STADIUM)
Dodgers 4, Astros 0

It's impossible to overstate just how formidable Nolan Ryan was at this point of his career. I remember, when he was with the California Angels, that he was known as a sporadically brilliant strikeout specialist with bad control and a .500 record. When the Angels let him enter free agency, GM Buzzie Bavasi famously quipped that he would essentially replace Ryan with two .500 pitchers. But Ryan matured as he got older, becoming more of a pitcher than a thrower. I wasn't even a year old when Sandy Koufax retired, but I imagine that Ryan's dominance was the closest thing a fan from my era could see that would compare. He was opposed in the finale by Jerry Reuss.

High Fives:
- Dusty Baker. In the sixth inning of a scoreless tie, he worked a tough at-bat against Ryan, fouling off several pitches, including a pop-up that first baseman Denny Walling lost in the sun. Baker eventually drew a walk. After a perfectly executed hit-and-run single by Steve Garvey, that brought up . . .

- Rick Monday, who immediately got behind on the count. From my perch at the stadium, there was a palpable tension in the hushed crowd. Then, something improbable happened. Ross:

  > The count 1-and-2. Now the stretch, and the pitch to Monday . . . line-drive, base hit, right field! Baker scores. Dodgers lead, 1-0!

Monday's breakthrough sent a message: *We can beat this guy!* The Dodgers broke through with three runs in the inning.

• Jerry Reuss's complete game shutout, adding up to 18 scoreless innings in the series. The final out, as called by Ross on both TV and radio, featured a confusing ending. It wasn't clear whether the batter fouled off the pitch, or if Scioscia merely missed the third strike and had to throw him out at first.

> Dave Roberts—the last obstacle standing in front of Jerry Reuss and the Dodgers. A year ago, the Dodgers couldn't win the game they had to win against the Astros in the playoffs. Now they're so close. [Pause.] A strike . . .
>
> Reuss has struck out three, he's walked three. He's scattered five singles. He was in trouble in the middle innings, he's finishing like a thoroughbred. [Pause.] Strike two!
>
> He had three days' rest. You'd never know it, the way he pitched. [Pause.] Foul, away from Scioscia. [Roberts is] walking away, he doesn't know he fouled it. Scioscia might have to throw to first base . . . to Garveeeeeey . . . Dodgers win the West! They're going to Montreal!

Heartbreak:

• On the way to the ballpark with my brother, Michael, and friends, I sat in the back of our family's Buick station wagon, making a sign out of a large piece of cardboard. It read: "Dodgers & Rick Monday #1!" In the bottom corner, I recreated the NBC logo, right down to the proper colors (the game was nationally televised). I was excited to declare my bold worship of an unhip hero to all of America. But when I tried to enter the stadium with it, security guards told me to either take the sign back to my car or throw it away, citing Dodger Stadium's "no signs or banners" rule. Crushed, I dumped it in a trash can outside the field level.

Monday Morning Managing:

• Whose bright idea was it to send Tony Scott? In the top of the sixth in a 0–0 game, Scott drew a walk against Jerry Reuss, then got gunned down by Mike Scioscia in an attempted steal of second. Art Howe and Jose Cruz followed up with a single and a walk, thus thwarting a possible bases-loaded, no-out situation. Instead, the Astros didn't score, and the Dodgers broke the game open in the bottom of the inning.

Mental State:

• I was in blue heaven.

MANIFESTING DESTINY

As referenced earlier, the Dodgers' toughest opponent in 1981 was the Montreal Expos, and it seemed to be a *fait accompli* that they would be facing them in the postseason.

There was another thing that seemed preordained, and that was their chance of finally winning it all. I'm always intrigued by teams whose success seems to be in the cards, when everything just seems to go their way. Starting with Fernandomania, L.A.'s season was unfolding in the type of storybook fashion that seems to define Teams of Destiny. We know them when we see them: the 1997 and 2003 Marlins; the 2002 Angels; the 2004 Red Sox.

Sometimes, though, destiny pulls a head-fake. The 2001 Yankees, on the heels of 9/11, seemed like a lock for the title after winning two dramatic come-from-behind games at Yankee

Stadium, only to see the Diamondbacks come back in games six and seven for their first franchise championship. And the Rockies of 2007 were unstoppable after winning 21 of their last 22 games, including the postseason, until they ran into a tough opponent—the American League. The Red Sox swept them in four games. It remained to be seen if the '81 Dodgers were merely flirting with destiny or truly committed to it, but things were starting to line up in their favor with so many ready-made storylines—Fernando's infectious magic, the Team Comeback reputation, a shot at redemption against the Yankees, and the record-setting infield's last chance at a title after three previous failures in the Series.

In the papers, the theme among the players was "This Is the Year."

"This team is destined to win it all," Reuss told the *Herald Examiner*. "I can just feel it."

Perhaps they were merely echoing Tommy's motivational speeches, but either way, one could only hope that their prophecy would become a self-fulfilling one.

To lay claim to their entitlement, the Dodgers would have to overcome a scheduling quirk. The National League Championship Series was still a Best of Five affair in 1981 (they wouldn't expand to seven games until 1985), with home-field advantage alternating between West and East divisions each year, regardless of team records. The 1981 Dodgers had a better overall record than the Expos—63–47 versus 60–48—and held a 5–2 series edge in the regular season. But because the East had home-field this year, the final three games would be held in frigid Montreal. This disadvantage was even more glaring when you considered that the Boys in Blue had won 18 of their last 19 games against the Expos at Dodger Stadium. In typical fashion, the Dodgers would have to rise above the challenges if they were to manifest their own destiny.

NLCS—GAMES 1 AND 2
(DODGER STADIUM);
GAMES 3 AND 4
(OLYMPIC STADIUM)

The Dodgers got off on the right foot when Burt Hooton led them to a 5–1 victory in Game 1. Ron Cey made an early return from his broken arm and immediately reminded the Dodgers what they had been missing by doubling in the first run. He even scored the second run on a squeeze play by Bill Russell. With Fernando opposing journeyman Ray Burris in Game 2, it seemed likely that the Dodgers would take a 2–0 lead into Montreal. But Burris flummoxed them with his junk pitches and the Expos shocked the Dodgers, 3–0.

The Dodgers were greeted with near-freezing temperatures in Game 3, and their bats were equally cold against Steve Rogers, who went the distance in a 4–1 win. Once again, the Dodgers were in the position of being eliminated, just as they had been three games in a row against the Astros. Fortunately, they righted the ship in Game 4, 7–1, thanks to another heroic outing by Burt Hooton and 12 hits against four pitchers.

Game 5 was scheduled for Sunday, but the game was called off due to rain. This meant the make-up would be played on a Monday—just one day before the World Series was set to begin. Worse yet, it would start at 10 AM Pacific time, while I was in school. Today, it's hard to fathom *any* decisive postseason game being played during a workday. I guess, with the World Series starting the next day, a night game was out of the question. For the second year in a row, I would be imprisoned in a classroom when the Dodger season came down to a one-game showdown.

TRUE-BLUE MONDAY
NLCS-Game 5 (Olympic Stadium)

This make-it-or-break-it game featured a rematch between Fernando and Ray Burris. Any hopes that Burris would revert back to the mediocrity that had defined his career were dashed when he allowed only one hit through the first three innings—a one-out triple by Russell, who was stranded at third. Fernando, meanwhile, was rudely greeted by Tim Raines, who doubled to lead off the bottom of the first, was sacrificed to third, and scored on a double play ball. It remained 1–0 Expos until the fifth inning, when Fernando, Mr. Silver Slugger himself, scored Rick Monday on a groundout to make it 1–1.

Unfortunately, I never heard those plays, since I was in my classes. The year before, my sympathetic science teacher had let us openly listen to a portion of the one-game playoff against the Astros. No such luck this year. Like a kid sneaking cigarettes, I found myself ducking into the restroom between periods with David and some other Dodger fans to dial in KABC on my transistor radio and get caught up on the action. Clearly, this was a game that could go right down to the wire.

Although I had set up my timers at home to record the game, I *had* to hear it in real time. This was killing me! For a brief moment, I thought of ditching school for the rest of the afternoon, but, considering that it would lead to suspension or even expulsion, I quickly banished the thought. The Dodgers were important, but they weren't worth jeopardizing my prospects for college.

It was time to resort to Plan B—Operation: T.R. (Transistor Radio). The mission was simple: Set radio volume to its lowest setting. Smuggle radio into backpack. Lay backpack on desk. Press ear against backpack.

It would be like those nights of listening to games under my pillow. Only, in this situation, it would be done in broad daylight, in a small classroom, under the prying eyes of a teacher.

The risk of getting caught lay somewhere between "definite" and "what're you—crazy?" But it had to be done.

It remained 1–1 through seven innings, with Fernando retiring 19 out of 20 at one point. The final innings just happened to coincide with the start of my geometry class, taught by a humorless ramrod named—and I'm not making this up—Mr. Bland.

I would've felt a little guilty about my ruse if it was against a teacher I liked. But Mr. Bland did not endear himself to anybody with his condescending attitude. Just a week before, a student in the front row seeking some untold payback purposely spilled some blue pen ink on a desk Mr. Bland sometimes sat on to get off his feet for a while. Predictably, Mr. Bland hoisted his posterior onto the puddle of fresh ink, then got up to write on the chalkboard. We spent the next half hour biting our lower lips and turning purple, trying to stifle laughs as we gazed at the blue blob hitching a ride on the cheeks of his khakis.

There were three rows of desks in our classroom, and I strategically positioned myself in the back row, behind the tallest kid in class. Two desks to my left sat my friend, Andrew, whose Dodger devotion rivaled mine. Andrew had also brought a transistor radio to class and stashed it in his backpack. Redundancy would be essential. If one of us got busted, the other could still relay signals.

As usual, Mr. Bland spent much of the period with his back to the class, jotting mind-numbing formulas on the board, giving us ample windows to bend our heads toward backpacks. I was having a hard time tuning in to KABC, but Andrew wasn't. He updated me on every at-bat by passing notes to me through a complicit student who sat between us. In the top of the eighth, I received Andrew's first missive:

LOPES, 1B.

I immediately wrote back:

HOW MANY OUT?

Andrew flashed one finger. I nodded, and Andrew pressed his ear against his backpack again. After a few moments he grinned and jotted another note through our intermediary:

LOPES SB!!!

My heart, already racing due to our crazy stunt, beat even faster against my chest. I tried to get a read on the next play off of Andrew's expressions. Why was he taking so long to write his next note? Maybe Bill Russell singled him in! It felt like we were two prisoners exchanging intelligence, although in hindsight the fragmentary way in which I was receiving reports for each at-bat was kind of like a primeval version of those auto-updates you get online at ESPN.com or MLB Live.

Mr. Bland briefly addressed the class again, then turned toward the board. Andrew scribbled a hurried message:

RUSSELL GROUND BALL.
LOPES OUT, RUNDOWN.
#@$%^%!

I replied with my own expletive. Baker grounded out to end the inning and the Dodgers blew their chance to go ahead. Other students turned in their seats to mouth, "What's the score?" or "What's going on?" A low murmur spread throughout the class.

I sensed that Mr. Bland may have been catching on. He refused to turn toward the board for the next five minutes and seemed to be casting a suspicious eye on the back row, though it may have just been my paranoia. The entire bottom of the eighth inning passed without Andrew or me knowing that Fernando was dispensing of the Expos in order.

As the top of the ninth inning got underway, with the score still 1–1, Mr. Bland returned to the chalkboard to jot out a new sequence of formulas, and I renewed my efforts to tune in to the game. Through a bunch of static, I was just able to catch Jerry

Doggett's familiar baritone. Steve Rogers had come in to replace Ray Burris and had just gotten Garvey to pop out to start the inning. One out and Cey at the plate.

The next couple of minutes were incredibly nerve-wracking. My right ear, pressed against my backpack, followed each pitch of Cey's at-bat, while my left ear was on the "look-out" for any changes in Mr. Bland's voice amidst his droning geometric equations, the two stimuli comingling uncomfortably in my head like a talk-radio station trying to drown out another one playing music:

> "Here we have alternate interior angles . . . "
> 1-and-1 to Cey . . .
> "Which creates a null set . . . "
> Two balls and one strike . . .
> "Triangle ABC . . . "
> 3-and-1 now . . .
> "Triangle DEF . . . "
> Fly ball to left field . . .
> "Hypotenuse . . . "
> Two outs . . .
> "The result would be incongruent . . . much like someone putting their head against a backpack to listen to the radio."

I lifted my head. Mr. Bland was staring daggers at me.

Oops.

"Gentlemen," he said evenly, looking at Andrew and me, "this is a classroom, not a ballpark. Turn the radios off."

I had to give him credit for the "ballpark" reference, no doubt a nod to the uniquely L.A. phenomenon of fans bringing radios to Dodger Stadium to hear Vin Scully.

Off our radios went. I waited for the next shoe to drop. But it never did.

Mr. Bland turned his back to the class and resumed his lecture.

Andrew and I exchanged hopeful looks, each of us thinking the same thing: *Maybe the game will go extra innings. If it does, lunch hour is next and we could listen to the rest of the game uninterrupted down by the bleachers.*

Moments later, the stale air of the classroom was pierced by the muffled cry of students:

> "YEEEEEEEEEEAAAAAAAAAAAAAAHHHH-
> HHHHHHHHH!!!!"

It crashed through the walls. It penetrated the windows. It came from all around us, a tidal wave of exuberance descending into hoots and hollers. Mr. Bland's chalk froze on the board. A sick, sinking feeling overcame me, knowing something heroic—no, *historic*—had just happened. Clearly the other classrooms were all tuned into the game.

Mr. Bland put down the chalk, wiped the dust on his khakis, and momentarily left the room. I turned up my radio so the rest of the class could hear and caught Jerry Doggett's follow-up to the most momentous home run in Los Angeles Dodgers history:

> . . . Monday hits one over the *center field fence*, and the Dodgers lead by a score of 2–1, and they're *killing* him as he comes off the field after circling the bases!

Mr. Bland reappeared a few seconds later. "Home run, Monday," he announced, blandly.

Duh.

At home that afternoon, I heard the home run in its entirety on my tape recording, but it wasn't the same as hearing it live. Nonetheless, here is how it sounded when Steve Rogers delivered that eventful pitch:

> A 1–1 tie. A dandy ballgame to settle the championship. These two clubs have put on a great

series—win, lose, or draw. Here's the 3-1 pitch to Monday. And he hits a high fly ball to left-center field, back for it goes Dawson, a-way back, this ball has a chance, it is *gooooooooooooone!*

Home run for Monday! Over the center field fence. And the Dodgers lead 2–1, and they're out of the dugout all *over* him!

Taking a 2–1 lead into the bottom of the ninth inning, Fernando got the first two outs, then walked Gary Carter and Larry Parrish. Tommy Lasorda brought in Bob Welch to pitch to Jerry White with the tying run in scoring position. On the first pitch, White grounded out to second.

Game. Series. Pennant. Hello, New York.

The next day in the *L.A. Times*, a series of photos captured Monday's epic shot, along with an odd caption declaring the Dodgers the first team in major league history "to win a pennant on foreign soil." Columnist Jim Murray called Monday a "'has-been" who "is again."

I couldn't help but feel vindicated. From the bemused looks of my friends, to the security guard who made me throw away my Monday sign, my single-minded stance to get behind the Dodgers' affable has-been had exceeded my wildest expectations. In Montreal, the game instantly became known as "Blue Monday," a reference to Mo and the day of the week on which it occurred (for musicphiles, it's also the title of Fats Domino and New Order songs). The closest the Montreal franchise would come to sniffing the postseason again would be in 1994—the year they were in first place before the next baseball strike wiped out the remainder of the season and the World Series. Three decades later, on www.baseball-reference.com, a reader sponsoring the Expos' page wrote: "In fond memories of the MONTREAL Expos. May 'Blue Monday' not be the last playoff appearance of a Montreal MLB team."

I harbored my own sentiments when it came to the Yankees, who had beaten Milwaukee and Oakland in their respective play-offs to get back into the Fall Classic. If I had one wish, it was that the team I loved so much would leave a legacy that could eclipse the debacles of the '77 and '78 Series. Rarely does one get a second chance in life, let alone a *third* one. Would the third time be a charm . . . or a complete strike-out? There were just 24 hours to go before I'd begin to find out.

I wanted to throw up.

THE WORLD SERIES

When I was a kid, I could never measure up to my older brother. For one thing, I had your classic pencil-neck geek physique, while Michael was blessed with muscular arms and calves and broad shoulders framing a thin waist, not unlike the V-shaped trunk of Claudell Washington of the Atlanta Braves. It just so happened that Michael and I liked a lot of the same activities, so whatever it was—basketball, baseball, skateboarding, dirt-bike jumping, even bowling—Michael regularly dominated me in humiliating fashion, the way a cat toys with a mouse.

I imagine this is how the Dodgers felt whenever they played the Yankees. The teams had met a record 10 times in the Fall Classic, with the Yankees holding an 8–2 edge and the Dodgers often losing in agonizing fashion. The tone was set in their very first meeting, when Dodger catcher Mickey Owen infamously dropped a third strike that cost them a victory in Game 4 of the 1941 Series. The Dodgers lost the next four matchups in 1947, 1949, 1952, and 1953 before finally prevailing in 1955, the first and only championship for the team in Brooklyn. The following year, Don Larsen pitched his perfect game, and the Yankees trounced them again.

After the Dodgers moved west, the teams met three more times. Thanks to Sandy Koufax and a lights-out pitching staff, the

Dodgers steamrolled the Yankees in 1963, holding them to four runs and a team batting average of .171 in a four-game sweep. Alas, it was a rare flower in the field of burrs that has canvassed the Dodgers' sorry history against the Bronx Bombers, as their next two meetings resulted in the crushing defeats of '77 and '78. Frankly, the last thing I wanted was to face our tormentors again. So while Tom Lasorda was publicly declaring that he couldn't wait to play the Yankees again, I was privately thinking, *Why couldn't it be the Brewers?*

There was one dose of good news before the series began. Reggie Jackson injured his calf muscle in the ALCS and would be unavailable for at least the first couple of games. But this was tempered by the fact that *our* Reggie was still not healthy enough to play the field, and the fact that Dusty Baker sprained his wrist by allegedly getting in a fight with some soused Expos fans in the Olympic Stadium parking lot following the Dodgers' pennant-clincher in Montreal. According to *The Montreal Gazette*, after the fans threatened Dusty and a couple reserve players, the left fielder responded by, in his words, "throwing uppercuts." (If the fans were truly pissed, shouldn't they have gone after Monday instead?) Dusty downplayed his wrist injury, but it's probably not a coincidence that he hit only .167 in the World Series, with one RBI and no extra-base hits in 26 plate appearances.

Meanwhile, the Dodger and Yankee lineups underscored the contrasts in organizational philosophies. Talk about continuity: L.A.'s starting eight in Game 1 of the '81 series was virtually identical to the '78 version—the only difference was that Guerrero took the place of the injured Smith. (The DH was used in '78, but pitchers batted in '81. Back then, they alternated years.)

The Yankees, on the other hand, fielded only four '78 alums —Lou Piniella, Graig Nettles, Reggie Jackson, and Bucky Dent, though Mr. October was sidelined and Dent was out for the year with a torn ligament in his hand.

Dodgers World Series Lineup

1978	1981
Lopes	Lopes
Russell	Russell
Smith	Baker
Garvey	Garvey
Cey	Cey
Baker	Guerrero
Monday	Monday
Lacy (DH)	Yeager
Yeager	(Pitcher's spot)

Yankees World Series Lineup

1978	1981
Rivers	Randolph
White	Mumphrey
Munson	Winfield
Jackson (DH)	Piniella
Piniella	Watson
Nettles	Nettles
Chambliss	Cerone
Stanley	Milbourne
Dent	(Pitcher's spot)

Dave Winfield and, to a lesser degree, Bob Watson epitomized the increasingly "win at all costs" agenda of owner George Steinbrenner. The Boss had signed free-agent Watson to a three-year, $1.7-million contract before the 1980 season, but that was a pittance compared to the reported 10-year, $25-million contract he doled out to Dave Winfield before the 1981 season. The ballyhooed transaction landed Winfield on the cover of *Sports Illustrated* under the headline "The Man Who Hit the Jackpot." By the end of the '81 season, however, that jackpot weighed on him like an anvil, subjecting him to hyper-scrutiny among the New York media, fans, and, famously, Steinbrenner himself, who had it out for Winfield for the entire subsequent decade, even though the future Hall of Famer put up consistently great numbers every year.

On the mound, the Yankees had the AL's oldest pitching staff—and its best. Its 2.90 ERA and 13 shutouts were tops in the league. Their three best starters were all southpaws—Ron Guidry, Tommy John, and rookie Dave Righetti—and manager Bob Lemon lined them up for the first three games. With their preponderance of right-handed batters, the Dodgers matched up pretty well, although it did mean less of Mike Scioscia and more of Steve Yeager catching. Fu-Manchu-ed Goose Gossage, another carryover from '78, was more dominant than ever. The year 1981 marked the best of his Hall of Fame career: 3–2, 0.77 ERA, 20 saves, 48 strikeouts in 46 innings in the strike-shortened season. Set-up man Ron Davis had an even better strikeout ratio—83 in 73 innings. If there was one point to be taken away by the Dodgers, it was this: get the lead before the seventh inning, or this was going to be a short series.

As I got home from school on Tuesday, October 20th, I had about an hour and a half to get all my recording equipment set up before the start of Game 1. ABC would be handling the TV broadcast that year, with Vin Scully and Sparky Anderson teaming up on CBS Radio. If I had spoken Spanish, you bet I would've recorded the Spanish play-by-play, too. This was the *World Series*.

Nothing less than a full sound and vision assault would do.
    Play ball!

NOTES ON A SCORECARD

For all you old-time Dodger fans, I am presenting my collection
of thoughts and images of the 1981 World Series in a piecemeal
fashion that channels Allan Malamud. For 22 years, his popular
"Notes on a Scorecard" column on page two was a wonderfully
addictive fixture of the *L.A. Herald Examiner* and, later, the *L.A.
Times*.

WORLD SERIES—GAME 1 (YANKEE STADIUM)
October 20, 1981

Due to the alternating schedule that was in place then, it is the
AL's turn to host the World Series, giving the Yankees home-field
advantage. Next to cancer, nothing is less appealing to me than the
prospect of having to play a Game 6 and 7 in the Bronx . . .

    Since this Series is being broadcast by ABC, it means we are
treated to their dated disco opening graphics . . . and lots of col-
or man Howard Cosell. Howard never fails to entertain, but the
Brooklyn-bred announcer's famous New York-bias threatens to
cast a pall over the entire series . . .

    In an odd maneuver, ABC is implementing two different play-
by-play men. Keith Jackson is calling the games in New York,
and Al Michaels will take over when the series shifts to L.A. for
the middle three games. Couldn't they do the same with Howie,
maybe drop him off at Pete's Tavern on the flight out to L.A. and
pick him up again upon returning to the Big Apple? . . .

    Highlight of the on-field introductions: Reggie Smith's awe-
some 'fro. Ahem . . . Reg, this is 1981. Maybe you didn't get the
memo, but massive Afros that make your hair look like Mickey

Mouse ears when your cap is on went out of style about the same time as mood rings and L-shaped sideburns. Check out Oscar Gamble across the diamond. When your hair is half the size of the former Afro king, you know something's out of whack . . .

Davey Lopes leads off, and hits a hot smash down third-base line. Craig Nettles is up to his old tricks again. He dives on the ball, gets up in the dirt, and nips the speedy Davey at first. It's as if 1978 never ended. Must. Resist. Urge. To. Turn. Off. TV . . .

Other shades of '78: Starter Ron Guidry is sharp as ever, blanking the Dodgers through four innings. Jerry Reuss looks like 1979's model, the one who went 7–14. He's replaced by Bobby Castillo in the third. The Dodgers are already losing 5–0 after four innings. I hate to see what the score would be if Mr. October were playing . . .

You know things are going bad as a Dodger fan when the highlight of the game is a sighting of the Rainbow Man! You remember the guy . . . that ubiquitous hippie dude with the giant rainbow Afro-style wig who used to always find the camera at major televised sporting events in the 1970s and '80s. (I once dressed as him for Halloween, right down to writing "John 3:16" on my T-shirt, which he adopted later on.) This time around, he's got a placard that says, "Uncle Willy Sez the 80s' are for The Ladies, Yankees and ABC." I'm not sure who Uncle Willy is, but if he sez so . . .

My only beef is, where's the justice in a world where any crackpot can get free airtime for a nonsensical sign, but when I make one extolling the virtues of Rick Monday, I'm forced to throw it away? . . .

Oh yeah . . . the game . . . Craig Nettles makes some more amazing plays, including a leaping stop of a wicked Steve Garvey frozen rope in the eighth inning. Keith Jackson on the broadcast:

> Garvey . . . a . . . whoa! What a play by Nettles at
> third base. I've never seen such a burglar!

Who Knew?

For years, we wondered about the true identity of the Rainbow Man—also known as "Rock 'n' Rollen."

His real name is Rollen Stewart. After fading from the scene and our TV screens in the late '80s, he re-emerged in the early '90s when an L.A. news station ran a live story in which the Wigged One had wigged out at a hotel near LAX. I remember being glued to the hours-long standoff as cameras pointed to his hotel window, which was plastered with signs displaying "John 3:16" and other scripture to the outside world. Stewart had tried to kidnap a couple of day laborers, threatened to shoot down planes taking off from the airport, and barricaded himself in a hotel room along with an unsuspecting maid. Police finally grabbed him when he sat down to smoke a joint. The end of the Rainbow Man will likely come behind bars. He is currently serving three consecutive life sentences.

Goose Gossage comes in to slam the door. The crowd is chanting "Goooooose!" He throws up goose eggs over two innings. The Dodgers' goose is cooked . . .

Game 1	R	H	E
Dodgers	3	5	0
Yankees	5	6	0

WORLD SERIES—GAME 2 (YANKEE STADIUM)
October 21, 1981

The less said about this one, the better . . .

Burt Hooton starts for the Dodgers. Aside from being a little wild, he keeps them in the game . . .

The real storyline tonight is former Dodger Tommy John, better than ever at 38 years old with a bionic arm. Since joining the Yankees as a free agent in 1979, John is 52–26, with a 3.07 ERA . . .

He allows no runs, three hits, and no walks in seven innings, his sinker inducing 13 ground ball outs. *Siiiiiiggghhh* . . .

Where's Morganna the Kissing Bandit when you need her? . . .

Once again Goose shuts L.A. down for the final two innings, hitting 98 on the gun. If the Dodgers can't figure out how to grab a lead before the latter innings, this series is not going more than four games . . .

The Dodgers are down 2–0 again in a postseason series. And Reggie Jackson still hasn't played yet. Time to manifest some more destiny . . .

Game 2	R	H	E
Dodgers	0	4	2
Yankees	3	6	1

WORLD SERIES—GAME 3 (DODGER STADIUM)
October 23, 1981

Back at home for a raucous Friday night with Fernando on the mound, facing Dave Righetti—two rookies squaring off in the World Series for the first time since 1950 . . .

The stakes don't get much higher. No team up to this point has ever come back from a 3–0 deficit to win a Best of Seven series . . .

Sorry to Revel in Others' Misfortune Dept.: Reggie Jackson is still not back, and now Graig Nettles is joining him on the shelf. He jammed his left thumb diving for a Bill Russell hit in the sixth inning of Game 2. Take that, burglar! He'll be replaced by the lesser Aurelio Rodriguez (hey, it's the Yankees' original A-Rod!). If the

Dodgers don't win this game, they don't deserve to win anything . . .

Ron Cey begins a stretch of the most inspired baseball of his career. In the first inning, with two on and two out, he immediately diffuses the tension among Dodger fans. Vin on CBS Radio:

> Righetti at the belt, checking the runners, delivers
> to Cey . . . *fastball* . . . a high drive into left field,
> back goes Winfield, a-waaaaaaay back . . . it's *gone!*

The Penguin looks fresh and strong. He uncoiled from his stance like a snake, sending Righetti's eighth pitch halfway up the left-field bleachers for a 3–0 lead . . .

Fernando can't capitalize. He quickly gives up two runs in the second. Typically, Fernando's catcher is Mike Scioscia. Tonight, with a lefty going, Yeager is making a rare start as his receiver. Could that have something to do with it? . . .

The Yankees take the lead, 4–3, in the third on their second home run. After the top of the fifth, Fernando has walked six batters and is on thin ice. "This might be the worst game I've ever seen Valenzuela pitch," Vinny says.

The Dodgers string together a rally in the bottom of the fifth, thanks to a couple of lucky breaks. Garvey leads off the inning by beating out a bouncer to third. Later in the inning, Guerrero scores him with a bouncing-ball double down the left-field line. Both balls take tricky, high hops off the hard Dodger Stadium infield. A-Rod couldn't handle them. Nettles probably could . . .

In the booth, Howard Cosell is incensed. "You think luck isn't important!" he huffs, drawing silence from the rest of his team. Then, pouting, he mutters, "A *lot* of luck." Maybe, Howie, but I prefer to think of it as the scales of karmic justice being rebalanced to make up for the '77 and '78 Series . . .

The Dodgers score the go-ahead run two batters later when Mike Scioscia, batting for Yeager (and Reggie Smith on deck to hit for Fernando), hits a run-scoring double play ball. With L.A. now holding a 5–4 lead, Tommy Lasorda calls Reggie back and allows Fernando to hit. The ABC announcers are shocked to see Fernando still in there. But Tommy knows Fernando better than anyone. File this one under the apt truism: Sometimes the Best Moves Are the Ones a Manager Doesn't Make. Fernando makes out, but has regained the lead, 5–4, after five . . .

Seventh inning: Roving correspondent Bob Uecker is interviewing Lee Majors in the stands about his new ABC series—*The Fall Guy!* Lee's got his brown-tinted shades on at nighttime. He's married to Farrah Fawcett. He's better than you . . .

Turning point of the series: In the eighth inning and the Dodgers clinging to a 5–4 lead, the Yankees get the first two men on with no outs. This is a pivotal moment. If the Yankees go ahead and Gossage enters the game, it's lights out on the Dodgers' season . . .

But Tommy puts his faith in El Toro, who has thrown well over 100 pitches. "A high wire act in a windstorm" is how Vin Scully is describing his performance . . .

Bobby Murcer pinch-hits for pitcher Rudy May. Manager Bob Lemon orders him to sacrifice. Al Michaels:

> Mercer tries to lay one down and Cey makes a *diving* catch in foul ground, throws to first—*double play!*

The replay shows it all—Cey gets completely airborne. His giant torso barrels onto the ground as his glove, extending in front of him, cradles the falling baseball. He snaps to his feet and fires a bullet to Garvey for the second out. It's the greatest play—on the biggest stage—he's ever made . . .

A fan in the loge level unfurls a banner saying "WHO NEEDS NETTLES, WE GOT CEY." Uncle Paul sez: How did that fan get that banner past security? Someone arrest that guy! . . .

Thanks to Cey, Fernando gets out of the eighth inning unscathed, then gets the first two Yankees in the ninth. The last batter is Lou Piniella. Dodgers still up, 5–4. Vinny on the radio:

And now, everybody up. The entire ballpark.
56,000 people on their feet and cheering. And
Fernando trying to rub a wrinkle in the new
baseball, standing behind the rubber. 2-and-2 to
Piniella.

Fernando, ready, delivers . . . fastball got him
swinging!

Fernandomania lives. Somehow Valenzuela made it across the
high wire without falling. But he is not beaming. He's got his
game face on. The smile of youthful exuberance has been replaced
by the glare of a hardened veteran . . .

Al Michaels informs us that Fernando threw 149 pitches tonight. If that happened today, you know the player's agent would
be sending a nasty text to the front office. . .

Tommy Lasorda explains his decision afterwards with a simple "This is the year of Fernando," likening his ace to a poker
player who had best bluff going . . .

On TV, Al Michaels sums up Fernando's performance
nicely . . .

It wasn't one for the art museum, but it was ef-
ficient, and he got the job done!

. . . while on the radio, Vin utters another line for the ages
that is similar in structure to Al's, but even better . . .

Somehow, this was not the best Fernando game.
It was his finest.

Once again telling us what we think, but in words we could
never think of . . .

By the way, once Scioscia, Fernando's regular catcher, entered
the game in the fifth inning, the pitcher did not allow another run
for the remainder of the game. Coincidence? Discuss amongst
yourselves . . .

Game 3	R	H	E
Yankees	4	9	0
Dodgers	5	11	1

WORLD SERIES—GAME 4 (DODGER STADIUM)
October 24, 1981

A beautiful Saturday afternoon at Dodger Stadium, and yours truly has tickets to his first-ever World Series game. Rick Reuschel, who looks like my Uncle Jack, will oppose Bob Welch . . .

While A-Rod is still playing for Nettles, this game marks the first appearance for Reggie Jackson. Privately, I'm glad Mr. October is back in there. After all, he's the man who broke my heart in 1977 . . . and made me a Dodger fan for life. I couldn't imagine seeing my first World Series game and not having my childhood nemesis in there . . .

In the first inning, he digs in against *his* former nemesis, Bob Welch. Howard Cosell remarks, "It remains to be seen how much he's rusted at the plate." Answer: Not very much. Reggie slaps a single to left field. Bobby looks terrible. He has not gotten any of the first four batters out and has already given up a run.

Tommy makes it clear that Welch will not be given the luxury of bluffing his way out of trouble like Fernando. After only 16 pitches, he brings a quick hook. Lasorda is bringing in . . . Dave Goltz?! Gasoline, meet fire. Two and a half innings later, the Dodgers find themselves in a 4–0 hole and I can't figure out if my indigestion is from the Dodger Dog I just ate or the game itself . . .

Fortunately, Reuschel, who enjoyed a long career despite resembling a beer leaguer, chooses this day to pitch like one. The Dodgers send him to the showers with two runs in the bottom of the third. One of their hits comes on a high-hopper by Garvey hit off the hard clay around home plate. After witnessing similar plays the day before, Howard calls it a "patented" play by the Dodgers . . .

The game is turned over to the Yankees' middle relief, their weakest link. The Dodgers score one more run in the fifth to close the gap, 4–3, going into the sixth . . .

Hold everything! The ABC cameras are cutting to a glum Tom Bosley sitting in the stands. "From *Happy Days!*" Howard chirps, and isn't that convenient, another actor from another ABC prime time show. "Not looking too happy there," analyst Jim Palmer points out. "Must be for the Dodgers" . . .

In the sixth, Howard Cunningham has even more reason to be unhappy when the Yankees score two unearned runs off Tom Niedenfuer, thanks to an error by Bill Russell. It is 6–3 Yankees going into the bottom of the sixth . . .

In front of us sits an older couple with season tickets. For three years, I have seen them speak nary a word to each other. The husband spends much of the games flipping through stacks of newspapers. Between innings of this one, I hear him lean over and say to his wife, "Wanna go so we can beat traffic?" She convinces him to stay one more inning, not because it's, like, the World Series or anything, but because she expects the overdue Carnation Malt guy to come around . . .

Thanks to a tardy vendor, the older couple get to witness one of the most memorable half-innings in L.A. Dodger history. Ron Davis is on to pitch. He gets Guerrero for the first out, then walks Scioscia. Resident flake Jay Johnstone, who was on the Yankees' '78 roster, pinch-hits for Tom Niedenfuer. Vin on the radio:

> The 1-2 pitch to Jay . . . swung on, a high drive
> into deep right-center field, back goes Brown . . .
> it's gone!
>
> Jay Johnstone, who had three pinch-hit home
> runs during the regular season, hits a two-run shot
> over the right-center field wall, and it brings the
> Dodgers back to life. They looked *dead* until that

happened. Now it's Yankees 6, Dodgers 5, and the crowd wants Johnstone to come out and take a bow . . . Here he comes!

From my vantage point down the right field line, the ball didn't seem to be hit that hard. But it kept carrying and carrying, perhaps aided by the heat and the lack of a marine layer. We've also seen how the sun can affect the defense during day games. Cue the next play . . .

Davey Lopes lofts a high fly ball into shallow right field. Reggie Jackson, shades down, takes a serpentine route under it. It's obvious he's having a hard time picking it up. I am screaming at the top of my lungs along with thousands of others, hoping to add to his disorientation. On TV:

Al Michaels:	Jackson is coming on, Reggieeee has it drop and can't make the catch.
Howard Cosell:	[Horrified] Ohhhhhhhh!
Al Michaels:	Watson picks it up and Lopes is at second . . . Reggie played that ball as if he never saw it.

Tears of joy well up in my eyes. This cannot be happening. All around me, people are pointing at Reggie and laughing. They are serenading him with sarcastic chants of "Reeee-ggieeeee . . . Reeee-ggieeeee." In the *Lord of the Flies* that is the World Series, Reggie has turned into Piggy . . .

A strange tingling envelops me. Maybe this really *is* the year . . .

Lopes takes advantage of the shaken opponent and steals third—uncontested. "Unbelievable!" snorts Howard. Bill Russell then atones for his error by singling in Davey to make it 6–6. Napkins rain down from the upper decks, and Dodger Stadium looks like a ticker-tape parade . . .

After burning through four pitchers in the first six innings, Lasorda sends in Steve Howe in the seventh. Lemon, wary of *his* bullpen, brings in starter Tommy John to relieve George Frazier in the bottom of the inning. Steve Yeager drives in the go-ahead run with a sacrifice fly. 7–6! . . .

Then, with two outs and a runner on third, Lopes swings on a 3-0 pitch and whacks the ball into the hard clay around home plate. By the time A-Rod fields the ball, Lopes is safe at first with a base hit—and driven in the Dodgers' eighth run. Howard is apoplectic:

> The whole thing has become absurd! The most patented attack I've ever seen! I talked about Seaver and geology . . . hit the ball straight down on that clay around home plate, you've got a base hit!

Watching the replay, Jim Palmer defends Lopes: "Here, you see a sinker. . . " he calmly states, as if to say, uh, yeah, hitters tend to pound sinkers into the ground whether they intend to or not. But in Howard's world, it's a preconceived, underhanded conspiracy, no doubt dreamed up by the Dodgers' coaching staff . . . and some geologists . . .

Howard, catching his blatant Yankee homerism (or perhaps getting an earful from his producer), follows up his earlier comment with

Who Knew?

Howard Cosell's oddly-timed "Seaver and geology" statement was a reference to the fact that pitcher Tom Seaver once spent his off-seasons testing the infield soils of National League stadiums as part of a field course toward earning a bachelor's degree from USC. I think it's safe to say he was the only SC student to graduate with honors in multiple All-Star Games and a Cy Young.

a forced: "It's . . . *funny*. Heh heh heh . . . "

In the eighth, Reggie Jackson hits a solo shot off Howe. It's the fifth homer of his career at Dodger Stadium, and his fifth time on base in the game . . . all overshadowed by his defensive blunder if they lose . . .

In the ninth, Howe makes an error and the Yankees get two on with two outs. Willie Randolph hits a long fly ball to center field. Like Johnstone's homer, it keeps carrying and carrying . . . and (tell me when to open my eyes) . . .

. . . Finally lands in Derrel Thomas's glove about 380 feet away . . .

The Dodgers, once down 4–0, squeak out an 8–7 victory and have evened the series at two games apiece . . .

Somewhere, Tom Bosley is very happy.

Game 4	R	H	E
Yankees	7	13	1
Dodgers	8	14	2

Bullpen Session

Mr. Octob-err

The next day, the *L.A. Times* sports section tooted: "Jackson Gets Something Off His Chest . . . It's the Ballgame," accompanied by a photo of Reggie's game-changing error. We saw Reggie wincing under the sun as the ball (circled by the *Times*' editors) slammed off his chest. Under that a cheeky caption read: "Reggie Jackson, who didn't even major in anatomy at Arizona State, beat the Dodgers once upon a time with his hip. Saturday he made up for it, helping them win one with his chest."

I couldn't resist jumping on the *schadenfreude* bandwagon,

WORLD SERIES—GAME 5 (DODGER STADIUM)
October 25, 1981

A rematch of Game 1, Reuss vs. Guidry, in another afternoon game . . .

This game breezes along, the opposite of yesterday's "slog-fest." Pitching on four days' rest—as opposed to three—for the first time in four starts, Reuss is performing with an efficiency we've come to expect . . .

The Yankees look surprisingly flat out there, not hustling to first on routine grounders. This isn't the same fiery Yankee team we saw in New York. I think they really miss Nettles too . . .

What's this? In the fifth inning, Dave Winfield has just gotten his first base hit—a blooper to left field—and he's asking for the ball? They lob it into the Yankee dugout. Don't know if he's serious or just having fun, but either way I'm actually embarrassed for the guy. I'm sure the Boss has something to say about it . . .

Through six innings, Reuss is holding New York to one run; if not for a Lopes error, he might have a shutout. Guidry is just

drawing a comic book-y dialogue bubble in which Reggie uttered: "Duhhh . . . "

To the right was another photo of the slugger, this one a close-up of him gnashing his teeth. The caption read: "Jackson grimaces after taking a cut and failing to make contact." Despite the fact he reached base all five times, the *Times* chose to focus on a single swing-and-miss! Naturally, I had to graffiti this photo, too, making the words "Damn it!" come out of Reggie's mouth.

Juvenile? You bet!

as good, allowing two harmless hits through the same stretch . . .

The Yanks are clinging to a 1–0 lead. For the third game in a row, the Comeback Kids will have to work some magic . . .

In the bottom of the seventh, after racking up Dusty Baker for his ninth K, Guidry faces Pedro Guerrero. Pete is actually having a poor series up to this point. Vin on the radio:

> And the strike one pitch to Pedro Guerrero . . . breaking ball, a high fly ball to left, back goes Piniella . . . it's gone!
>
> Boy, it's something, a great effort suddenly explodes on one pitch.

The crowd is still buzzing when the next batter, Steve Yeager, steps up. Yeager homered off Guidry in Game 1 and quickly falls behind, 1–2:

> Now the 1-2 pitch to Yeager, swung on, *another* high drive, back goes Piniella . . . it's gone!
>
> Well, they call him "Louisiana Lightning," and Guidry's been hit by it!

It truly was like lightning. In a five minute span, those two homers would represent half the Dodgers' hit total for the entire game . . .

Now all Reuss needs to do is get six more outs . . . and pray Davey Lopes doesn't make any more errors (he now has three in the game, part of his record-setting six in the series) . . .

File under: Brush with Big Dodger in the Sky. Goose Gossage comes on in the eighth. He's facing Ron Cey with two outs. He unloads a 94-mph fastball that nails the Penguin on the side of the head.

"Look out!" Al Michaels cries on TV. "Right off the helmet!" . . .

Cey's helmet explodes off his head and lands clear out of the batter's circle. The ball ricochets past the Yankee dugout and into the first base box . . .

Cey crumples to the ground, holding his noggin. He got clocked right above the left ear. Utter silence descends on the stadium, breaths held . . .

"I thought he was dead," said future Yankee Jason Giambi years later. Ten-year-old Jason was among those in the stands witnessing the horror . . .

Cey is assisted off the field, replaced by Ken Landreaux at the plate. The Dodgers don't score, and Goose is bombarded with boos when the inning is over . . .

The next day's papers show Cey's head wrapped in a giant Ace bandage, "swami-style," per the *L.A. Herald Examiner*. The diagnosis is a mild concussion. Ron declares that nothing will stop him from playing in Game 6 . . .

In the ninth, Reuss gives up his first hit since the fifth inning, but Tommy sticks with him. Finally, on his 108th pitch of the game, he strikes out A-Rod. Game over. The crowd goes insane . . .

Reuss has beaten Nolan Ryan and Ron Guidry in the postseason. Not too shabby . . .

The ABC cameras cut to a disgusted George Steinbrenner in the press box. He makes a dismissive "get outta here" motion with his hands. The Dodgers lead the series, three games to two, winning three come-from-behind, one-run games in a row . . .

The camera cuts one last time to Steinbrenner in the booth. Napkins are raining down all around him. He looks like he wants to punch something. Before the night is over, he will . . .

Game 5	R	H	E
Yankees	1	5	0
Dodgers	2	4	3

WORLD SERIES—GAME 6 (YANKEE STADIUM)
October 28, 1981

Due to lousy weather in New York, Game 6 is pushed from Tuesday to Wednesday, allowing an extra day for Cey to recover from his concussion. Unfortunately, it also gives Graig Nettles another day to heal his thumb. They're both in the lineup to start the game . . .

Burt Hooton is facing Tommy John. With the exception of Guerrero in the outfield, Lasorda is trotting out his veterans. As expected, Steve Yeager is in there to counter the southpaw John, but so is lefty Rick Monday, whose game-winning RBIs in the decisive games of the previous two playoff series were no doubt not lost on Lasorda . . .

The Dodgers' first four batters are Lopes, Russell, Garvey,

Bullpen Session

Wanted: Blue Man Group

It's one of those stories that instantly entered Dodger-Yankee lore when it happened. The morning after the Dodgers beat the Yankees, George Steinbrenner went public with a bandaged hand. He claimed he hurt it in the elevator of a Los Angeles hotel while decking two drunk Dodger fans who were saying bad things about the Yankees. The local media, to put it kindly, was skeptical, saying he made the whole thing up to fire up the team.

Steinbrenner's phantom punch became a punch line. If the Boss *did* punch something that night, it was something that wouldn't punch him back, like a wall or a bedpost. To this day, we've been led to believe that no victims or witnesses ever surfaced.

and Cey—the four members of baseball's longest-running infield. As a fan, you're always on the lookout for omens. This feels like a good one . . .

Still, now that the series has shifted to Yankee Stadium, a feeling of dread has returned. The Dodgers have lost seven of their last eight here. What weird plays will turn this series around? Will it be Graig Nettles's glove again? Lou Piniella's mouth? Another part of Reggie Jackson's anatomy? . . .

I have settled into our family room with Michael and my dad. I consider taking in the game from our shopworn loveseat, but recall that that's where I was when Reggie Jackson had his three-homer game in the 1977 Series. I move to the floor with a bunch of throw pillows . . .

On TV, Keith Jackson is back in the broadcast booth, bouncing Al Michaels as play-by-play. Howard Cosell is back in his

Or did they?

While researching this story, I came across an article that appeared in the *Montreal Gazette*, of all places. Within 24 hours of this incident, a 22-year-old man named John called a Los Angeles sports radio talk show and outed himself as one of the men who had confronted Steinbrenner in the elevator.

By John's account, they razzed George, who took a swing at John's friend. His friend ducked, and George hit his hand on the elevator door. The friend retaliated and landed a glancing blow on George's lip. The Boss beat a hasty retreat when the elevator doors opened.

Still—much of this caller's story didn't hold water.

D. B. Cooper. Biggie Smalls. George Steinbrenner. Seems like some cases just weren't meant to be solved.

element. Like his beloved Yankees, he is home now, which seems to embolden him even more. His blowhard statements through-out the game are his blowhardiest yet. More on that later . . .

The Yankees draw first blood—a home run by Willie Ran-dolph off Burt Hooton in the third inning. 1–0 Yanks. That fa-miliar, gnawing pit in my stomach has returned, full-fledged . . .

During the commercial break, my dad gets up to get some-thing to eat. "Oh well," he says, "they gave it a good shot." It's only the third inning and he's already throwing in the towel. I wish he'd just stay in the kitchen. Any time the other team scores first, Dad always writes the Dodgers off. Now I don't just want the Dodgers to win, I want them to prove my father wrong . . .

The Dodgers tie the game in the top of the fourth. In the bottom of the inning, Tom Lasorda, as he would explain it later, makes a move meant to get Tommy John out of the game. With two outs and a runner on second, rather than pitch to eighth hit-ter Larry Milbourne, Lasorda elects to have Hooton intentionally walk him, bringing up the pitcher's spot . . .

The camera cuts to the Yankee dugout, where Lemon is speak-ing with Tommy John. Howard Cosell attempts to enlighten us as to their conversation . . .

> Lemon is asking Tommy John how he feels. Lem-
> on is *not* disposed to take out one of his aces early.

Maybe Howie is projecting some wishful thinking, because the next thing we know, Lemon is sending Bobby Murcer up to pinch-hit for Tommy John. Jim Palmer:

> I think he's done for the night.

John is *pissed*. He's thrown only 49 pitches and given up only one run. The ABC cameras do an excellent job of showing the drama unfold. We see John storm to the other end of the dugout, away from Lemon, and slouch against the opposite wall, refusing to sit down. He removes his batting helmet, shakes his head, and clearly mouths the words, "I can't believe that" . . .

Lasorda has been outmanaging Lemon all series long, and the ploy works as planned. Murcer flies out to right field. The game is now turned over to the combustible Yankee bullpen . . .

The pitching change pays immediate dividends for the Dodgers. George Frazier, who has already lost twice in the Series, comes in and gives up three runs and four hits, though only one of the hits—a triple by Guerrero—is hit hard. Howard Cosell is screaming foul on TV. The Dodgers are winning ugly—*how dare they!* It's 4–1 going into the bottom of the fifth . . .

Things get even better in the bottom of the inning. With two outs and Reggie Jackson at the plate, Hooton knocks Reggie flat on his back like a boxer hitting the mat . . .

"Take *that!*" I snarl at the TV, hovering mere inches from Reggie's face. I'm loving Happy right now. He hasn't just reclaimed his cool; he's sending a clear message. "We will *not* be intimidated. This time, it's *our* turn." Reggie grounds out meekly to end the inning . . .

In the top of the sixth, the Dodgers nibble away at two more Yankee relievers, who issue four walks. Even Graig Nettles proves he's human by making an error. I decide the baseball gods have issued their final decree: the Yankees are done. I'm too amped to sit down and pretty much stand for the rest of the game. With the score 6–1, Pedro Guerrero steps up with the bases loaded. Vin on the radio:

> Pedro Guerrero is trying to come up and apply the knockout punch . . .
>
> Here's the 1-2 pitch to Guerrero, swung on and hit toward left-center field, sinking, and it's a base hit. Iiiiiiinnn comes Garvey, iiiiiiinnn comes Thomas, Baker to third, Guerrero to second. It is 8–1 Dodgers, and Yankee Stadium is in *shock.*

Not just Yankee Stadium, but Howard. Now that it's apparent

the Yankees don't stand a chance, Cosell is really letting his Yankee freak flag fly. He cannot get himself to praise the Dodgers. He can only see the Yankees as beating themselves. My brother and I have started our own little side-game to count the number of times Howard rears his blatant bias. We lose track after 10. The other announcers are pretty much ignoring him. He's like your myopic family relative in the back of the room, working on his next beer, muttering conspiratorial comments to no one in particular . . .

In honor of Howard's "hot air," here is a chronological list of my favorite Blatant Howard Homerisms from Game 6, measured in hot air balloons, of course (1 to 5, 5 being best) . . .

After Dusty Baker bloops a hit into center field just out of the reach of Willie Randolph, the Dodgers' third hit of the fifth inning:

> It's *agonizing!* [Quickly catches himself.] Must be,
> for the Yankees. They haven't had a well-hit ball
> this inning!

Clearly, dying quails were another patented play of the Dodgers' attack, to go along with their hard choppers on the Dodger Stadium infield from Game 4 (remember "geology"?). The Dodgers would score three runs in the inning.

After left fielder Dave Winfield, fielding a base hit, throws a six-hopper to home plate in the sixth inning, allowing the sloth-like Burt Hooton to score the fifth run from second base while standing up and wearing his warm-up jacket:

> *Everything* is coming apart! A *very* poor throw!

Winfield's "hurls like a girl" throw is replayed more times than the Zapruder film. It cements Winfield's "Mr. May" nickname (coined by Steinbrenner), along with his 1-for-22 performance in this series.

After Hooton scores on the above play, Lopes and Russell execute a double-steal with a 5–1 lead:

> This Yankee performance tonight has become an *embarrassment* to the owner who wants *everything* for the fans of the Yankees.

Sort of like Veruca Salt's father.

Later, with the Dodgers building an insurmountable lead, Keith Jackson is giving props to the Dodgers. Howard can only grumble:

> This game is an *embarrassment* to the Yankee *tradition.*

Y'know, the same tradition that Billy Martin, George Steinbrenner, and the entire Bronx Zoo upheld so proudly.

As the Dodgers go up, 8–1, in the sixth inning, Howard waxes reflective as Rick Reuschel issues an intentional walk and the cameras pan to the Yankee manager:

> One has to feel sympathy for Bob Lemon, who's a beautiful man, who's weathered the vicissitudes of life and great personal tragedy very well . . . as the intentional walk is now effectuated.

Huh? First of all, just as there is no crying in baseball, no-where is there room in the sport for words like "vicissitudes" and "effectuated," let alone in the same sentence. (And yet, the best he could do to describe Lemon was "beautiful"? What was wrong with "pulchritudinous"?) Howard's statement is so over-the-top and verbose, it's an instant classic—and earns a full five hot air balloons . . .

Back to the game. Guerrero puts the capper on a five-RBI day with a home run that makes it 9–2 in the eighth. He would finish the game a double short of the cycle . . .

Earlier, Keith Jackson and company predicted that Cey would win the MVP award, but now they're not so sure . . .

"Will there be some call for a second ballot here?" Keith ruminates . . .

Meanwhile, ABC flashes a graphic that tells the tale of the series. It says: "Yankees relievers in Series: 0–2, 9.75 ERA vs. Gossage, 0.00 ERA" . . .

As the camera scans the Dodgers' giddy faces in the dugout, I can't resist a good-natured dig at my father the pessimist . . .

"What do you think, Dad?" I ask. "Did they give it their best shot?" . . .

It remains 9–2 going into the bottom of the ninth inning. Steve Howe is beginning his *fourth* inning of relief. I'm experiencing something akin to levitation. I've never known this feeling before . . .

After walking Randolph, Howe gets the next two batters out, setting up the perfect ending: the Dodgers versus Reggie Jackson. Howe goes full-count to Reggie, who then hits a routine, game-ending ground ball to Davey Lopes . . .

. . . Who boots it. It's his sixth error of the Series. Somehow this seems appropriate, too. It sums up his disappointing year and presages his departure a few months later . . .

That brings up veteran Bob Watson, quietly having a great Series. Vin:

Watson 0-for-4. Howe out of the stretch. A check of the runners, and the 1-0 pitch. Watson hits a high fly ball to Landreaux, this is it! Landreaux waiting and waiting—he's got it.

The Los Angeles Dodgers have just about done the *impossible*. Lasorda throws his hat away, runs out with his hands and arms held high in the air to grab Steve Garvey, and the Dodgers, who were down two games to none and beat Houston, they were down one game to two and beat Montreal, they were down two games to none to the Yankees and beat them four straight.

The Dodgers spill onto the field. The whole thing is too surreal. My brain can't process it yet. Michael and I high-five, but instead of cutting loose, I lose myself in the details of the celebration, noticing odd things like: What is all that lumpy stuff Lasorda is carrying in his right rear pocket? It looks like he has a rock collection stuffed in there. Or the fact that Steve Howe, swinging his arm to thrust it in the air,

Bullpen Session

Worst. World Series Pitcher. Ever.

Burt Hooton was the winning pitcher in the clinching game, the culmination of a redemptive postseason that saw him go 4–1 with a 0.82 ERA in five starts, including two wins in Dodger-elimination games. But Yankees reliever George Frazier made history. As the losing pitcher, he was tagged with three of the Yankees' four losses (his ERA was 17.18). His three losses tied the previous World Series record set by Lefty Williams of the 1919 Chicago White Sox. Yes, *those* White Sox, who threw the World Series that year. So does that even count?

totally pops Steve Garvey in the mouth . . .

Speaking of Garvey, there's something unsettling about the way he's celebrating. It looks—dare I say it—kind of fake. Like he's doing what you're *supposed* to be doing, instead of just doing it like the other players . . .

I shake myself from my fog and soak in the post-game celebration. The magnitude of what is happening is sinking in. And then I feel it—the waterworks are building up. Oh no. This can't be happening again. I get closer to the screen to shield my eyes from Michael . . .

"Hey, I can't see!" he says . . .

Four years ago, I was an eleven-year-old, budding True Blue fan experiencing his first major heartbreak, which took place on this same field of play. Now I'm trying to hide my tears of joy. Same reaction, different results. The circle is complete. What is it about this game—about this *team*—that has such a hold on me? . . .

Who cares? The time for self-reflection is over. The Dodgers are the *World Freakin' Champions*. *Homerun Highlights* is complete. Let others analyze the results. Me, I'm going to enjoy just being a fan . . .

Game 6	R	H	E
Dodgers	9	13	1
Yankees	2	7	2

LEGACY

From opening day onward, the story of the 1981 season was Fernandomania. But as the postseason got underway and different players, from starters to role players, stepped up to contribute, the Dodgers proved the axiom that a team's sum is greater than its parts. The Dodgers would go on to be the only team to win two World Series in the 1980s, making them, by definition, the Team of the Decade.

And yet, when baseball fans compare the two teams, the '81 squad often gets short shrift. I think that's because the 1988 team is so wrapped up in legend—Gibson's home run, Orel's consecutive game streak, the fact that they were such underdogs against the mighty A's and their Bash Brothers—and perhaps because our memories of '81 are tainted by the strike. But baseball's work stoppage also created a unique oppor-

Bullpen Session

Start Spreading the Sorry

Mere moments after the Dodgers clinched the championship, George Steinbrenner issued an eye-rolling statement that said, in part: "I want to sincerely apologize to the people of New York and to fans of the New York Yankees everywhere for the performance of the Yankee team in the World Series. I also want to assure you we will be at work immediately to prepare for 1982." *Finally*, something for Cosell to smile about.

tunity that made the Dodgers' accomplishments that much more special. They became the first team to have to win three postseason series—a total of 10 games—to win the World Series. And the way they did it was unprecedented.

They were the first team in history to come back from an 0–2 deficit to capture a Best of Five postseason series. They came from behind, two games to one versus Montreal, to win the NLCS. They became the only National League team in World Series history to lose the first two games on the road, then sweep the next four. They came from behind in all four of their World Series victories. Five times they faced elimination in the playoffs. They won all five. The selection of tri-MVPs (Cey, Yeager, Guerrero) was also the first time more than one World Series MVP player was named.

Where the '88 team featured perennial *non*-All-Star Players like Jeff Hamilton, Dave Anderson, Franklin Stubbs, and John Shelby in the lineup, the '81 Dodgers boasted a dream team of once and future All-Stars: seven pitchers, six outfielders, five infielders, and two catchers, to be exact. It also featured three Rookies of the Year and three Cy Young Award winners.

Let's face it—if the Dodgers didn't win the 1981 World Series, the team of my youth would be labeled perennial underachievers when it mattered most, chokers against a franchise that had their number going back to their Brooklyn days. The 1981 championship represented one of expectations finally realized, more a sense of relief than surprise. This brought its own sense of triumph, one augmented by their suspenseful postseason run that was marked by a zombie-like determination (hard to kill, always coming back from the dead). It may not have been their most improbable season. But it remains their most indelible.

AFTERWORD
Extra Innings

The great thing about your favorite team winning a World Series is that you have an entire offseason to bask in the afterglow and claim bragging rights to chumps like Jered the Giant Fan up the street. Just as the Dodgers' agonies of defeat were *my* agonies from 1977 to 1980, I felt that the fruits of victory were my justifiable reward for my undying devotion and obsessive record-keeping. From elementary school to the start of high school, I happily chose the Dodgers over normal kids stuff in order to preserve on magnetic tape the Dodgers' final glory years that were the late '70s and early '80s.

But where do you go once you've finally reached the top? Second place, as it turns out. In 1982, the team finished one agonizing game behind the Atlanta Braves. Aside from casting off Davey Lopes, Al Campanis mostly kept his core intact, which meant declining veterans were now a year older. Even the most casual fan could see that they were probably not going to repeat as champions. And so, I decided to quit while I was ahead. During that '82 season, I started doing things that normal 16-year-olds were doing—cruising around in my ratty Toyota, hitting the beach and movies, and going on my first date (a blind one, of course, since no girl in her right mind would knowingly go out with me). I still followed the Dodgers religiously, of course, but with my new extracurricular activities and AP classes devouring my life, I didn't really miss producing my *Homerun Highlights* tapes at all. And so I packed away my 10 tapes for almost 30 years, occasionally pulling them out so my Dodger friends and I could travel down memory lane, but for the most part keeping them safely stored in a K-Swiss shoebox.

Along the way, like any long-term relationship, my unconditional love for the Dodgers was tested. In the late '90s, with Fox ownership taking over and Mike Piazza being shipped off in the dead of night, I grew into something of an anti-fan—someone who still pledged allegiance to the franchise but secretly wanted them to falter so that Fox would be forced to sell the team. An unsatisfaction in my own life made me more cynical about everything. I started to disdain things about Dodger Stadium itself: the proliferation of ads; the fact that organ music was replaced by AC/DC; and even the outfield pavilions, whose corrugated roofs looked less like a charming early '60s holdover and more like cheap aluminum siding bought by the yard at a home improvement store. But through this love/hate period, Vin Scully was the one constant that kept me connected to the team.

In the 2000s, Fox finally relinquished the team, and by the end of the decade—*pre*-McCourt divorce proceedings—the franchise was experiencing its first real glory years since the late '70s/early '80s squad. My fanaticism was reignited. I was now happily married with two kids, and while it saddens me that my children are too young to grow up truly appreciating Vin Scully, at least they can sample his greatness on Dad's dorky *Homerun Highlights* tapes.

Then, during spring training in 2010, about to enter his 61st year with the Dodgers, Vin suffered a fainting spell at home and was hospitalized. The news made the front page of the *L.A. Times*. Even my mom called me that morning to tell me about it. Thankfully, Vin recovered quickly and, in typical fashion, was apologetic about all the fuss when he announced his first game of the year, a March 21 contest against the Cleveland Indians at Camelback Ranch in Arizona:

> Hi everybody and a very pleasant Sunday to you, wherever you may be. Hope you don't mind if I take a moment out. First of all, I'm sorry to have caused the accident that caused so much stress. I apologize for that. I'd also like to salute the general heroes of 911 in Calabasas, and the doctors and nurses at West Hills Hospital for taking care of me so very, very well.
>
> However, now that I've done that, let's get to the more important things, and that is the game.

Coincidentally, around that time I had already begun cataloging all my old tapes, spurred by two things: pre-emptive mourning of Vin's imminent retirement, and, with my children discovering their own Dodger heroes like Andre Ethier and Casey Blake (my son was convinced he was *the* Casey from *Casey at the Bat*), a desire to re-experience the players from *my* youth. Listening to my recordings of these old Dodger games, I got sucked in all over again at the excitement generated by the last great Dodger nucleus. I also realized that *Homerun Highlights* was more than just about the Dodgers. The best baseball bloggers, like Jon Weisman of *Dodger Thoughts* or Josh Wilker from *Cardboard Gods*, know this better than anybody. Baseball ultimately holds a mirror up to our own lives, and my aural history of the team was at its core an audio diary, a vehicle for me to work out my *stuff* while learning how to adhere to disciplined, self-imposed deadlines. I also learned a thing or two about editing and producing, sowing the seeds for a future career in television and film.

Finally, I realized that the Dodgers of my formative years had a profound influence on my life. Whether we're aware of it or not, most of us try to emulate our role models as kids. Here are just a few life lessons I took away from the Blue Crew of 1977 to 1981.

If some of these seem clichéd, I apologize. But even clichés can speak truth!

NEVER LET THEM SEE YOU SWEAT.

One reason the Dodgers were so successful is that their core was, by and large, cool under fire. Ron Cey, Davey Lopes, Dusty Baker, Steve Garvey, Bill Russell, Manny Mota, Rick Monday, Jerry Reuss . . . the list goes on of different players who stepped up to be the hero. Even poor Bill Hooton finally figured out how to pitch under pressure in 1981. Another true sign of the Dodgers' grace: years later we learned just how dysfunctional and fractious their clubhouse really was. Yet on the field, the players had a single purpose: to win. It's very easy to succumb to life's distractions, which provides a ready excuse for failure. But if you keep your head, you just may succeed.

PLAY WITHIN YOURSELF.

In baseball, controlled aggression is a key component of success. I always marveled at Reggie Smith's ability to combine power with plate discipline, Davey Lopes' aggressive—but smart— base-running, or Steve Garvey's knack of making diving stops in the dirt while never mussing up his hair. Okay, so this latter example is an extreme one, but the lesson I took away is to always give my best effort, but stay within my limits. Lack of control equals a scattershot approach and weakens your cause.

IT'S OKAY TO BE A LITTLE COCKY.

Or, as my dad used to say, "When you got it, you got it." Steve Howe, Davey Lopes, Don Sutton—they all got it and weren't afraid to flaunt it. Both swaggered in their own ways, not necessarily to show off, but to build themselves up, intimidate opponents, and give them that edge as competitors. Some players, like Shawn Green in later years, thrived by going about their business in as unassuming a manner as possible. But what I learned from select Dodgers is that if you project self-confidence, you start believing in yourself.

FIND ONE THING AND BE REALLY GOOD AT IT.

I cannot claim to be really good at anything in my life, which is a constant source of frustration. But that hasn't stopped me from trying. Manny Mota demonstrated the value of being highly specialized at one thing—pinch-hitting—and making a career out of it. I have tried to apply that principle in my television career—focusing on that one special quality that may separate me from others in a competitive market. Which brings us to . . .

WHAT WOULD STEVE GARVEY DO?

Work hard every day. Be a role model to others. Be respectful of authority figures. Keep a stiff upper lip. Eat your Wheaties. Even though many labeled Steve Garvey a phony, whether he was or not was almost immaterial to me growing up. It was my *perception* of Steve's perfection that appealed to my larger ambitions. For example, in high school, I never really rebelled in the classic sense. I was an eager student and found a nerdy nobility in always trying to put my best foot forward, culminating in my being chosen school prefect (it's like a president, only more fancy-sounding) and delivering the commencement speech at senior graduation. Like Garvey, I'm no model human being . . . not by a long shot. But is there anything wrong with aspiring to greatness? To the same tenets we all learned as Boy or Girl Scouts? In fact, this section of my book is partly inspired by Steve Garvey's fine book *My Bat Boy Days: Lessons I Learned from the Boys of Summer*. (It retails in stores for $21, but my wife picked up a copy for me at a 99¢ Only store in Hollywood. That's a 95 percent markdown. Can this man get *any* respect?)

OPPORTUNITY IS JUST AN OPEN DOOR AWAY.

On the eve of the 1981 season, Jerry Reuss got injured. As Dodger fans, we were dispirited to hear the news, but his injury opened the door for Fernando Valenzuela, who was a fixture in the Dodger rotation for the next 10 years. Reuss himself was the lucky recipient of someone else's injury in 1980 when he stepped into the starting rotation on May 16 en route to winning Comeback Player of the Year. I am a firm believer that when one door closes, another usually opens. The key is to be ready when it happens. Throughout my career, I have been discouraged when turned down for a job, only to be rewarded with an even better one later . . . sometimes even finding out that the first job wasn't all it was cracked up to be. Life is a series of blessings often disguised as setbacks. They only reveal themselves in hindsight.

PLAY TO THE LAST OUT.

The Dodgers of 1980—and 1981 in particular—refused to roll over when the odds were heavily against them. They taught me the value of never giving up. Tell me something is impossible, and it fuels my drive to find a way to prove you wrong. Even in my darkest hours, I have somehow always found it comforting to tell myself, "I'm only in the third inning here," with a lot of baseball left to be played and plenty of time to rally.

'STACHES ARE COOL . . . ON THE RIGHT PERSON.

As a child of the '70s, mustaches (and hairy chests) weren't just acceptable accessories for men, they exuded manliness. Actors like Burt Reynolds, Tom Selleck, and Sam Elliott prove the power of the 'stache and in fact look weaker without one, as if their upper lips are too thin. (While we're at it, I am on a *Jeopardy!* strike. I will not watch it again until Alex Trebek regains his mustache. He just looks too weird without it.) Joe Ferguson is the poster child for Dodgers who look better with a mustache. Without it, he looks like his name should be Doug. Bobby Castillo and Davey Lopes had great, bushy whiskers and seemed as if they went to the same mustache stylist (do such people exist?). On the other hand, Jerry Reuss's mustache always looked like he just drank buttermilk from the bottle, only because he's so blond. It's the same problem that has plagued Larry Bird. You can't help but squint and wonder, "Do they have a mustache, or am I just imagining one?" Then there are those who never seemed to figure out what they wanted for their face. Rick Sutcliffe, I'm looking at you. Thankfully, Steve Garvey never joined the Mustache Brigade. Superman doesn't do facial hair. Lesson learned? Know thy face. I was reminded of this when I experimented with different looks in college and in my twenties. My conclusion: much as I'd love to cover it up, my face looks best naked.

PREPARE, PREPARE, PREPARE.

In August of 1996, I realized a lifelong dream when I got to meet Vin Scully for my first and only time. I was working at E! Entertainment Television as a producer on a hosted weekly magazine show called *FYE!* Ironically, the lead story was the release of *The Fan*, the baseball movie I referred to earlier as the worst of all time. I convinced my boss that we should shoot our host at Dodger Stadium so we could have a baseball tie-in. After securing a media credential through Derrick Hall in the Dodger publicity department, I was able to roam the field with my host and camera crew during batting practice. I recall interviews with Mike Piazza and Dave Hansen (who was game enough to participate in a lame sketch with our host in the dugout), but what I remember most was getting to poke my head in the radio booth to meet Vin Scully.

When I first spied him from behind, I could see only a shock of reddish-gray hair bobbing up and down as he voiced what I presumed was a pre-recorded piece. The Dodger representative who was with me waited until Vinny was finished, then introduced us. I got an immediate case of cotton mouth as Vin bellowed a friendly hello, all sparkly eyes and crooked smile. Imagine the animatronic Abe Lincoln coming to life to speak to you in the "Great Moments with Mr. Lincoln" attraction at Disneyland. That's how I felt.

As we were leaving to head over and interview organist Nancy Bea Hefley, I asked my contact, "So was that a radio ad he was voicing?"

He rubbed his chin. "Mmmmm . . . I think he was practicing."

"For the ad?"

"For the game."

The game wasn't going to start for at least an hour and a half. But even after almost fifty years, there was Vin, getting his game on, still living by the credo passed down to *him* by mentor Red Barber from their Brooklyn days: be there early, and be prepared.

I got to watch the game from the press box that night. It was "a very pleasant good evening." And I was exactly where I wanted to be.

APPENDIX
11 Greatest Franchise Moments 1977-1981

So many great moments, so little space left to get them all in. I couldn't narrow this list down to 10. So, like *This Is Spinal Tap*, this one goes to 11.

11. Ron Cey's diving catch of Mercer's bunt attempt, and subsequent doubling off of runner (October 23, 1981—Game 3 of World Series)

The only defensive play on this list, but given the stakes and the circumstances, there was no way I couldn't include it. The Dodgers were *this* close to going down 3–0 in the series.

10. Dusty Baker's 30th home run, making L.A. the first MLB team to have four players with 30 homers (October 2, 1977)

The fact that he hit it late in the last game of the season—against J.R. Richard, no less—makes it that much more impressive.

9. Manny Mota's last major league hit (October 5, 1980)

Everyone remembers Cey's home run—the

APPENDIX 321

eventual game-winner that led to the one-game play-off with Houston. But 42-year-old Mota delivered a key RBI single the inning before that, capping off an incredible career as a pinch hitter deluxe. For that reason, it's even more memorable than his Game 2 hit in the '77 NLCS.

8. Jerry Reuss's no-hitter against the Giants (June 27, 1980)

And there, but for the (lack of) grace of Bill Russell, goes a perfect game.

7. Joe Ferguson's walk-off homer in the 10th inning against the Astros (October 3, 1980)

Fergie and his helmet-tossing merriment made believers out of the Dodgers and us fans, leading to two more implausible wins against the Astros before the magic wore off in the tiebreaker.

6. Bill Russell's game-winning single in the 10th inning against the Phillies (October 7, 1978—Game 4 of NLCS)

Russell was clutch in the postseason, and proved it on this series-clinching RBI hit against Tug McGraw that catapulted the Dodgers into the World Series.

5. Ron Cey's game-winning home run against the Astros (October 5, 1980)

The Penguin's eighth-inning at-bat was a Gibson-esque mini-drama that climaxed with the Dodgers' biggest hit of the year. Again, it led to the one-game playoff.

4. Welch's strikeout of Reggie Jackson (October 11, 1978—Game 2 of World Series)

It was *Casey at the Bat* come to life, with New York

as Mudville.

3. **Rick Monday's game-winning home run in Montreal (October 19, 1981—Game 5 of NLCS)**

   After Kirk Gibson's '88 blast, the most storied home run in L.A. Dodger history, and really, more important since it vaulted the team into the World Series. And I'm still pissed at my high school geometry teacher.

2. **Fernando Valenzuela's 8–0 start in 1981**

   Fernando's miraculous rookie year—especially his first month and a half—was baseball's equivalent of a 100-year flood.

1. **1981 World Championship**

   The fact that the Dodgers did it while turning the tables on their former tormentors—right down to the humiliating way the Yanks lost (led by Reggie Jackson's momentum-shifting error in Game 4)—was a big, fat maraschino cherry on top.

REFERENCES

Print & Online

Alejo, Annie S. 2011. "Kenny Loggins returns to Manila in May." Manila Bulletin Publishing Corporation, February 8.

Amazon. 2011. "1978 Topps #145—Rick Monday." Baseball card. http://www.amazon.com.

"Another One for Valenzuela." 1981. *Los Angeles Times,* April 23.

Ariama. 2011. "Georges Bizet." http://www.ariama.com/georges-bizet?search_redirect=georges%20bizet.

"A-Rod breaks Vizquel's Streak; AL West earns eight of nine." 2002. *Sports Illustrated*, November 13.

"Astros force Lasorda to juggle." 1981. *The Leader-Post,* October 9, 1981.

"Attorney Says Guerrero Has IQ of Only 70." 2000. *Los Angeles Times*, June 1.

"Baker injured in Big O fight." 1981. *Montreal Gazette*, October 26.

Ballparks of Baseball. 2011. "Dodger Stadium." http://www.ballparksofbaseball.com/nl/DodgerStadium.htm.

———. 2011. "RFK Stadium." http://www.ballparksofbaseball.com/past/RFKStadium.htm.

Bartruff, Jim, and Toby Zwikel. 1982. *The Los Angeles Dodgers: The Championship Year*. Los Angeles: Rosebud Books.

Baseball Almanac. http://www.baseball-almanac.com.

The Baseball Cube. http://www.thebaseballcube.com.

Baseball Library. 2006. "Pedro Guerrero." http://www.baseballlibrary.com/ ballplayers/player.php?name=Pedro_Guerrero_1956.

The Baseball Page. http://www.thebaseballpage.com.

Baseball Parks. 2011. "Astrodome." http://baseballparks.com.

Baseball Reference. http://www.baseball-reference.com.

"BASEBALL: ROUNDUP." 2003. *New York Times*, March 31.

"Billboard Top 10." 1978. *Lawrence Journal-World*, June 10.

Biderman, David. 2010. "The Anatomy of a Baseball Broadcast." *Wall Street Journal*, October 6.

"Bob Watson carves spot in the books." 1981. *Lewiston Morning Tribune*, October 27.

Bock, Hal. 1981. "Yanks dedicated to free agents." *St. Joseph Gazette*, December 22.

Boxall, Bettina, Jason Song, and Matt Lait. 2007. "Malibu's worst fire in years." *Los Angeles Times*, November 25.

Brigham, Bob. 1995. "The Man Who Invented the High Five." Outsports. http://www.outsports.com/baseball/2003/0617glennburke.htm.

Burgin, Sandy. 2002. "Where've you gone, Kurt Bevacqua?" MLB, August 15. http://www.mlb.com/content/printer_friendly/sd/y2002/m08/ d15/c104641.jsp.

Calcaterra, Craig. 2010. "Steve Garvey would like to buy the Dodgers." *Hardball Talk*, December 9. http://hardballtalk.nbcsports. com/2010/12/09/steve-garvey-would-like-to-buy-the-dodgers.

Canadian Broadcasting Corporation Sports. 2004. "Key Dates in Expos history." September 29. http://www.cbc.ca/sports/indepth/expos/ timeline.html.

Chafets, Zev. 2009. "Let Steroids Into the Hall of Fame." *New York Times*, June 19.

Chass, Murray. 1980. "Yankees Sign Winfield for Up to $25 Million." *New York Times,* December 16.

"Champs happy—for now." 1981. *Rock Hill Herald*, October 27.

"City, team influenced John." 1978. *Spokesman-Review*, November 23.

Clash, James. 2001. "Because it's there." *Forbes,* October 29.

The Classic TV Archive. "US TV Nielsen Ratings 1978–1979." http://
www.ctva.biz/US/TV-Ratings/CTVA_NielsenRatings_1978-1979.htm

Click, Paul. 2001. "20 Years Ago, Fernando Valenzuela Was King of the
Hill." *Baseball Digest*, July.

Crasnick, Jerry. 2009. "Time for Miller's call from the Hall."
ESPN, December 1. http://sports.espn.go.com/mlb/columns/
story?columnist=crasnick_jerry&id=4700428.

Creamer, Robert. 1964. "The Transistor Kid." *Sports Illustrated,* May 4.

Crowe, Jerry. 2009. "Olden can still hear the answer to one question."
Los Angeles Times, July 20.

Delsohn, Steve. 2002. *True Blue: The Dramatic History of the Los Angeles
Dodgers, Told by the Men Who Lived It*. New York: Harper Perennial.

DeMarco, Tony. 1998. "The greatest stars in All-Star Game history."
Denver Post, July 4.

Dilbeck, Steve. 2010. "An 'embarrassed' Vin Scully recounts fall, hospital
visit." *Los Angeles Times,* March 21.

Dodgers.com. "25th Anniversary – '81 World Champs." http://losangeles.
dodgers.mlb.com/la/fan_forum/81_celebration.jsp?gcid=C12289x590.

"Dodgers Clinch Title By Trimming Padres." 1978. *Merced Sun-Star*,
September 25.

"Dodgers dump Clark, name Hendrick interim hitting coach." 2003.
Sports Illustrated, August 4.

"Dodgers' Gate Past 3 Million." 1978. *Youngstown Vindicator*,
September 16.

"Dodgers sign Don Stanhouse to 5-year pact." 1979. *Baltimore Sun*,
November 18.

"Dodgers still alive." 1980. *The Evening News*, October 4.

"Don Sutton makes apology." 1978. *Spokesman-Review*, August 25.

Downey, Mike. 1986. "Better to Wait Until Pedro Is Up to Speed." *Los Angeles Times,* August 6.

Durso, Joseph. 1981. "Cey Apprehensive, Unsure of Playing." *New York Times,* October 28.

ESPN. "Cabrera hits intentional ball in 10th as Marlins trip O's." 2006. June 22. http://scores.espn.go.com/mlb/recap?gameId=260622101.

———. 2006. "Dodger Dog creator Arthur dies at 84." June 27. http://sports.espn.go.com/mlb/news/story?id=2502061.

———. 2007. "Holliday's blast pumps Rockies to World Series after sweeping D-backs." October 15. http://scores.espn.go.com/mlb/recap?gameId=271015127.

———. "MLB Draft History—Los Angeles Dodgers." http://espn.go.com/mlb/history/draft/_/team/lad.

———. 2010. "New York 500 Club: Reggie Jackson." June 2. http://sports.espn.go.com/new-york/mlb/news/story?id=5188280.

———. 2010. "Pat Gillick elected to Hall of Fame." December 6. http://sports.espn.go.com/mlb/hof11/news/story?id=5890610.

ESPN SportsNation. 2003. "Major meltdowns." May 1. http://sports.espn.go.com/sportsnation/news/story?id=1546342.

"Expos' Charlie Lea Pitches 4–0 No-hitter." 1981. *New York Times,* May 11.

"The Fans Speak Out." 1986. *Baseball Digest,* April.

"Farrah, Lee Majors Are Granted Divorce." 1982. *Palm Beach Post,* February 17.

"Feeney released." 1979. *Ellensburg Daily Record,* June 28.

"'Fernando Fever' Rampant in L.A." 1981. *Observer-Reporter* (Washington, PA), May 14.

Fimrite, Ron. 1978. "His Old Self Is On The Shelf." *Sports Illustrated,* October 2.

Fitzgerald, Ray. 1981. "The Beanball: Baseball's Scariest Moment." *Boston Globe,* October 26.

Florence, Mal. 1990. "John Ramsey, Voice of L.A. Sports, Dies." *Los Angeles Times,* January 26.

"For the Yanks, it's just another day at the office." 1981. *Calgary Herald,* October 29.

"Free agent player salaries." 1979. *Bangor Daily News,* February 13.

Gallagher, Mark. 2003. *The Yankee Encyclopedia.* Champaign, IL: Sports Publishing LLC.

"George Steinbrenner: In His Own Words." 2010. *Sports Illustrated/CNN Online,* July 13. http://sportsillustrated.cnn.com.

"Goltz Finally Good As Gold." 1980. *Evening Independent,* April 24.

Greenberg, Alan. 1981. "Expos, Phils Open Series and It's a Certain Chiller." *Los Angeles Times,* October 7.

Grimsley, Will. 1980. "Don Newcombe Crusading Against Booze." *The Dispatch,* March 18.

Guerrero, Mark. 2005. "Lalo Guerrero: The Father of Chicano Music." *LaPrensa San Diego,* March 25.

"Hall of Fame Case: Steve Garvey." 2007. *JC Baseball Analysis Blog.* http://www.jc_baseball_analysis.mlblogs.com.

Heisler, Mark. 1980. "Giants Win, 6-3, in the 11th Inning." *Los Angeles Times,* October 1.

Henniger, Paul. 1980. "No Ifs for the Rams Faithful." *Los Angeles Times,* October 4.

Hoffarth, Tom. 2010. "Who does Garvey have to sleep with to get into the Hall of Fame?" *Daily News,* December 6. http://insidesocal.com/tomhoffarth/archives/2010/12/who-does-garvey.html.

Hollywood Sign. 2011. "Fast Facts About the Hollywood Sign." http://www.hollywoodsign.org/fastfacts.html.

Holtzman, Jerome. 1981. "Rain scrambles NL playoff, perils Series start." *Chicago Tribune,* October 19.

"Home Unsafe, Expos Move." *New York Times,* September 14, 1991.

Internet Movie Database. http://www.imdb.com.

"It's A's Vs. Yankees, Expos Vs. Dodgers In Pennant Matchups." 1981.
Times-Union, October 12.

Jackson, Tony. 2010. "Davey Lopes named to Dodgers staff." ESPN,
November 22. http://sports.espn.go.com/los-angeles/mlb/news/
story?id=5839060.

Jaffe, Chris. 2010. "When a team wins the first two World Series games . . .
" *Hardball Times,* October 28. http://www.hardballtimes.com/main/
blog_article/when-a-team-wins-the-first-two-world-series-games-.-.-/.

"John Kibler, Umpire for Bill Buckner's Error, Dies at 81." 2006.
New York Times, February 19.

Johnnie Speedie. 2004. "Memories from fellow Jim Healy Fans." http://
www.johnspeedie.com/healy/healymemories.html.

Johnson, Andrew. 2011. "Roberto Alomar, Bert Blyleven Elected to
Baseball Hall of Fame." *AOL News*, January 5. http://www.aolnews.
com/2011/01/05/roberto-alomar-bert-blyleven-elected-to-baseball-
hall-of-fame.

Kaplan, Jim. 1981. "Epidemic Of Fernando Fever." *Sports Illustrated,*
May 4.

Keenan, Sandy. 1985. "The Ballad of Davey Rocket." *Sports Illustrated,*
September 9.

Knight, Graham. 2007. "Dodger Stadium." BaseballPilgrimages.com, July
9. http://www.baseballpilgrimages.com/national/losangeles.html.

Kovacevic, Dejan. 2009. "On the Pirates: Stennett reflects on sweet seven."
Pittsburgh Post-Gazette, May 31.

Krasovic, Tom. 2010. "Reds Lose Thriller to Padres in Shadows." *AOL
News*, September 25. http://www.aolnews.com/2010/09/25/reds-lose-
thriller-to-padres-in-shadows.

Kuenster, John. 1980. "Rookie Rudy Law Adds New Dimension to the
Dodgers' Offense." *Baseball Digest*, August.

"Labor Pains." *Sports Illustrated/CNN Online.* http://sportsillustrated.cnn.
com/baseball/news/2002/05/25/work_stopppages.

Langill, Mark. 2004. *Dodger Stadium.* Charleston: Arcadia Publishing.

Lee, Ken. 2010. "Mel Gibson and Oksana Grigorieva: Why Their Custody Battle Went Nuclear." *People,* July 16. http://www.people.com/people/article/0,,20402847,00.html.

Lenburg, Jeff. 1986. *Baseball's All-Star Game: A Game-By-Game Guide.* Lincoln, NE: iUniverse.com.

Lincoln, Melissa Ludtke. 1978. "Making Another Kind of Pitch." *Sports Illustrated,* September 18.

Littwin, Mike. 1979. "Rau Is Out for the Season, Messersmith for 21 Days." *Los Angeles Times,* June 5.

Los Angeles Dodgers. http://www.losangelesdodgersonline.com.

Lowitt, Bruce. 1979. "Three losses don't worry Ozark." *The Day*, May 21.

"Man tells his side of fight with Steinbrenner." 1981. *Montreal Gazette.* October 28.

McNeil, William F. 2003. *The Dodgers Encyclopedia.* Champaign, IL: Sports Publishing LLC.

"Meet The Rolls-Reuss Of Pitchers." 1980. *Sports Illustrated,* August 25.

Merida, Kevin. 1998. "NBA Wives' Tale." *Washington Post,* October 27.

Merron, Jeff. 2003. "Olympic Stadium disaster timeline." ESPN, April 22. http://assets.espn.go.com/mlb/s/2003/0422/1542317.html.

Merron, Jeff. 2004. "The List: Player vs. Fan." ESPN, November 22. http://sports.espn.go.com/espn/page2/story?page=list/alltimebrawls.

MLB. "1963 World Series." http://mlb.mlb.com/mlb/history/postseason/mlb_ws_recaps.jsp?feature=1963.

———. 2006. "1981 title happy memory for Hooton." August. http://losangeles.dodgers.mlb.com/news/article.jsp?ymd=20060818&content_id=1616525&vkey=news_la&fext=.jsp&c_id=la.

———. "All-Star Results—1971." http://mlb.mlb.com/mlb/history/mlb_asgrecaps_story_headline.jsp?story_page=recap_1971.

———. 2004. "Dodgers to reconfigure broadcast format for 2005 season." October 22. http://losangeles.dodgers.mlb.com/news/press_releases/press_release.jsp?ymd=20041022&content_id=903318&vkey=pr_la&fext=.jsp&c_id=la.

———. "First Year Player Draft." http://mlb.mlb.com/mlb/history/draft/index.jsp?feature=decade1960s.

———. "Official Rules: 8.00 The Pitcher." http://mlb.mlb.com/mlb/official_info/official_rules/pitcher_8.jsp.

———. "Uniforms and Logos" (Pittsburgh Pirates). http://pittsburgh.pirates.mlb.com/pit/history/uniforms_logos.jsp.

Monday, Rick, and Ken Gurnick. 2006. *Rick Monday's Tales from the Dodgers Dugout.* Champaign, IL: Sports Publishing LLC.

Morong, Cyril. 2009. "Why Isn't Steve Garvey In The Hall Of Fame?" *Cybermetrics Blog,* May 25. http://cybermetric.blogspot.com/2009/05/why-isnt-steve-garvey-in-hall-of-fame.html.

Museum Stuff. "Terry Forster." http://www.museumstuff.com/learn/topics/Terry_Forster.

National Baseball Hall of Fame and Museum. "O'Malley, Walter." http://baseballhall.org/hof/omalley-walter.

National League Green Book. 1979–81. Los Angeles: M. G. BookGraphics.

Nelson, John. 1981. "John, Goose Puts Yanks 2 Up." *Daytona Beach Morning Journal,* October 22.

Nelson, Travis. 2007. "Book Review: The Stark Truth, by Jayson Stark." *Boy of Summer Blog,* July 2. http://www.boyofsummer.net.

Newhan, Ross. 1988. "Campanis Now Says It Was All for the Best." *Los Angeles Times,* April 6.

Neyer, Rob. 2010. "Tommy John leads Vets Committee ballot." ESPN, November 12. http://espn.go.com/blog/sweetspot/post/_/id/6281/tommy-john-leads-vets-committee-ballot.

Nissenson, Herschel. 1981. "N.L. West: Astros, Dodgers, Reds all have question marks." *Boca Raton News,* April 1.

Noe, Denise. "Out of the Twilight Zone." *truTV Online,* November 18. http://www.trutv.com/library/crime/notorious_murders/not_guilty/twilight_zone/2.html.

"Nolan Ryan: Fastest (and Richest?) Gun in Alvin." 1980. *Los Angeles Times,* April 17. Lowitt, Bruce. 1979. "Three losses don't worry Ozark." *The Day,* May 21.

The Notable Names Database. http://www.nndb.com.

O'Connor, John J. 1981. "Lee Majors Plays a Stunt Man." *New York Times,* October 28.

"OJ Says Girlfriend Not On Juice." 1999. *CBS News*, October 12. http://www.cbsnews.com/stories/1999/10/12/national/main66029.shtml.

Oliver, Myrna. 1997. "Richard Slattery; 'Murph' in Union Oil Commercials." *Los Angeles Times,* January 29.

Olney, Buster. 2006. "Election angst." *Buster Olney Blog,* January 10. http://insider.espn.go.com/mlb/blog?name=olney_buster&id=2286620&action=login&appRedirect=http%3a%2f%2finsider.espn.go.com%2fmlb%2fblog%3fname%3dolney_buster%26id%3d2286620.

Padres Nation. http://www.padresnation.com.

"Perfect Malibu firestorm ahead?" 2007. *Malibu Times,* May 23.

Perry, Dayn. 2010. "Reggie's greatest hits." *FOX Sports on MSN,* May 11. http://msn.foxsports.com/mlb/story/reggie-jacksons-greatest-hits-051110.

"Phils Use Patience to Beat Valenzuela." 1981. *Reading Eagle*, May 19.

Pinto, David. 2008. "Willie Randolph's firing parallels Billy Martin's 1978 departure." *Sporting News,* June 18.

"Playoff game on TV." 1980. *Lakeland Ledger*, October 6.

Plummer, William. 1995. "The Mouth That Roared." *People*, May 8.

Real Sports Heroes with Ross Porter. 2011. "Biography." http://realsportsheroes.com/about/biography.

Reilly, Rick. 1989. "America's Sweetheart." *Sports Illustrated*, November 27.

Retrosheet. http://www.retrosheet.org.

Ritter, Lawrence, and Donald Honig. 1988. *The 100 Greatest Baseball Players of All Time*. Westminster, MD: Random House Value Publishing.

Rivera, Eddie. 1981. "Only in America, Land of Opportunity . . . " *Inside Sports,* June 30.

Rose, Adam. 2009. "All Things Trojan." *Los Angeles Times,* January 14.

Schad, Jerry. 1991. *Afoot & Afield in Los Angeles County*. Berkeley, CA: Wilderness Press.

Schoenfield, David. 2010. "George Steinbrenner for Hall of Fame." ESPN, November 10. http://m.espn.go.com/nfl/ story?storyId=5787300&wjb=.

Shepard, Eric. 1996. "Friends Say Goodbye to Allan Malamud." *Los Angeles Times,* September 20.

Shubailat, Nadine. 2009. "McG Defends Christian Bale's 'Terminator' Rant." *ABC News Online*, May 21. http://abcnews.go.com/ Entertainment/Movies/story?id=7634132&page=1.

Smith, Billy. 2009. "Don Stanhouse: Earl's Bane of Existence." OriolesHangout.com, February 12.

"Sports Notes." 1981. *Madison Courier.* October 13.

Stark, Jayson. 2007. *The Stark Truth: The Most Overrated and Underrated Players in Baseball History*. Chicago: Triumph Books.

———. 2007. "Why I didn't vote for . . . " ESPN, January 10. http:// insider.espn.go.com/mlb/blog?name=stark_jayson&id=2727032&acti on=login&appRedirect=http%3a%2f%2finsider.espn.go.com%2fmlb %2fblog%3fname%3dstark_jayson%26id%3d2727032.

Steve Garvey Official Website. http://www.stevegarvey.com.

"Steve Garvey Is Hit With Paternity Suit." 1991. *Los Angeles Times.* November 28.

Stewart, Larry. 1997. "Doggett Dies of Natural Causes." *Los Angeles Times,* July 9.

Stone, Larry. 2004. "Man about Cooperstown: Molitor takes his place with game's best." *Seattle Times,* July 25.

———. 2011. "A closer look at Hall of Fame voting trends." *Seattle Times,* January 6.

Tucker, David. 1981. "The final game for Dodgers vs. Expos gets rained out; is rescheduled for today." *Daily News,* October 19.

"Two players cited." 1979. *Park City Daily News*, September 5.

Union Oil Auto Script advertisement. 1973. *Los Angeles Times,* October 28.

The Unofficial Addams Family World Wide Web Site. 2011. http://www. addamsfamily.com.

Vass, George. 2003. "Flops, Failures and Disappointments." *Baseball Digest*, October.

Vecsey, George. 1980. "Astros Lose to Reds; Still Ahead by 2." *New York Times,* September 29.

Vecsey, George. 1980. "Dodgers Beat Astros and Force Playoff Today; Dodgers Win, 4 to 3." *New York Times,* October 6.

Weiner, Larry and Jacob. 2009. Letter to the editor. *Los Angeles Times,* November 14.

Weisman, Jon. 2008. "The Gibson Signing at 20." *Dodger Thoughts Blog,* January 26. http://espn.go.com/blog/los-angeles/dodger-thoughts/post/_/id/1693/the-gibson-signing-at-20.

———. 2011. "Thirty years later, Fernando Valenzuela's legacy is his tenacity." *Dodger Thoughts Blog,* April 9. http://espn.go.com/blog/los-angeles/dodger-thoughts/post/_/id/12420/thirty-years-later-fernando-valenzuelas-legacy-is-his-tenacity.

———. 2011. "Episode 3: 'Nirvana: A state of bliss obtained through the extinction of the self.'" *Dodger Thoughts Blog,* May 16. http://espn.go.com/blog/los-angeles/dodger-thoughts/post/_/id/13390/nirvana.

Whiteside, Larry. 1981. "Cey Casts Himself in a Starring Role." *Boston Globe.* October 25.

———. 1981. "Dodgers Close In On Title." *Boston Globe.* October 26.

Wilker, Josh. 2011. "Terry Forster." CardboardGods.net, April 20. http://cardboardgods.net/category/teams/los-angeles-dodgers/terry-forster.

Woo, Elaine. 2006. "Thomas G. Arthur, 84; Made Dodger Dogs a Staple of L.A. Stadium Experience." *Los Angeles Times*, June 27.

Radio

All-Star Game. 1980. *CBS Radio*.

The Herd with Colin Cowherd. 2011. ESPN Radio.

Los Angeles Dodgers radio broadcasts. 1978–1981. KABC-AM 790.

Ross Porter's Viewpoints. 1980–1981. KABC-AM 790.

Sports Talk with Steve Somers. 1981. KMPC-AM 710.

Television

KNBC Sports Report. KNBC-TV.

Los Angeles Dodgers television broadcasts. KTTV-11.

The Tonight Show Starring Johnny Carson. TV show. NBC/Carson
    Productions. Produced by Fred DeCordova. Excerpts from June 1981.

World Series. 1978. NBC-TV

World Series. 1981. ABC-TV.

Film

The Bad News Bears. Feature movie. Directed by Michael Ritchie.
    Paramount Pictures. 1976.

Baseball Boogie, featuring the 1986 Dodgers. 1986. www.youtube.com/
    watch?v=uvEujW_KVnI

Jack LaLanne's Health Spa 1981. 1981. www.youtube.com/
    watch?v=AO2Okpx3LlA

Rabbit Fire. Animated Short. Directed by Chuck Jones. Warner Bros.
    Cartoons, Inc., 1951.

ACKNOWLEDGMENTS

I think I speak for countless readers when I say I cannot imagine a greater job than being paid to play baseball for a living (except maybe being an astronaut, although years of mechanical engineering courses would take some the fun out of it for me).

On a smaller scale, being able to write a book about the Dodgers and have it published is as close to a dream job as I'm ever going to get. I am indebted to several individuals who contributed to the cause, starting with Jeffrey Goldman from Santa Monica Press for believing in the project. My gratitude extends to the Los Angeles Dodgers, in particular Josh Rawitch, former vice president of communications, for taking the time to meet with me and offer his support amidst far more pressing concerns, as well as Mark Langill for his generosity in answering my random research queries along the way. Big thanks to the producers of ESPN's *30 for 30: Fernando Nation* and Chris Erskine of the *Los Angeles Times*, the former for giving me a platform to share my enthusiasm for Fernandomania, the latter for caring enough to write about it as part of his "Fan of the House" column.

An extra tip of the cap to friends Mark Turner and Rob Show, who offered their time and honest advice in reading these pages before they were ready for public consumption. And, of course, special thanks to my family, especially my parents, for providing me with the tools to feed my Dodger fix. Mom, I'm sorry again for ruining Mother's Day in 1978. I blame Dave Kingman.